CNN互动英语系列

STEP BY STEP 听懂 CNN 社会广角

CNN Society Watch

LiveABC 编著

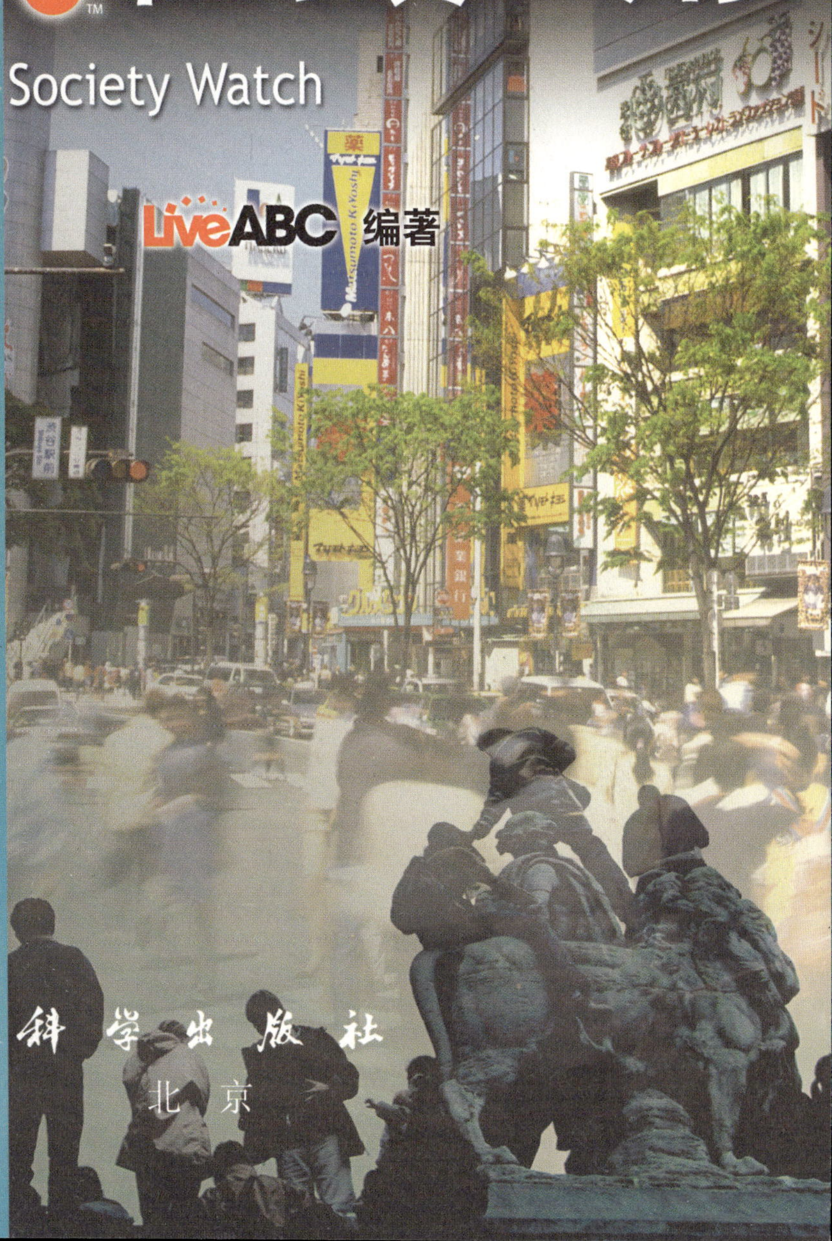

科学出版社
北京

图书在版编目（CIP）数据

Step by Step听懂CNN社会广角 / LiveABC编著. —北京：科学出版社，2013.1

（CNN互动英语系列）

ISBN 978-7-03-035751-9

Ⅰ. ①S… Ⅱ. ①L… Ⅲ. ①英语－听说教学－自学参考资料 Ⅳ. ①H319.9

中国版本图书馆CIP数据核字（2012）第239567号

责任编辑：阎 莉 / 责任校对：刘亚琦
责任印制：赵德静 / 封面设计：无极书装

联系电话：010-64030529 / 电子邮箱：yanli@mail.sciencep.com

科学出版社 出版
北京东黄城根北街16号
邮政编码：100717
http://www.sciencep.com

北京佳信达欣艺术印刷有限公司 印刷
科学出版社发行 各地新华书店经销

*

2013年1月第 一 版 开本：B5（720×1000）
2013年1月第一次印刷 印张：16 1/2
字数：480 000

定价：68.00元

（含DVD互动光盘1张）

（如有印装质量问题，我社负责调换）

前　　言

听懂英语新闻、与国际接轨的最佳选择!

学了这么多年英语，想看个英语新闻却觉得很吃力？看着新闻画面似乎不难猜出主要事件，但对于新闻细节却像是“鸭子听雷——听了也不动（懂）”？其实主要原因在于大多数人“听”英语的能力比阅读能力差，再加上不了解相关背景或专有名词、跟不上新闻播报速度等，就对收听英语新闻产生了却步情绪。

收听国际英语新闻是与国际接轨、掌握时事脉动的最佳方式，而 CNN 是最具国际知名度的新闻媒体之一。本书内容均取材自 CNN 电视新闻网，对于想提高英语能力及职场竞争力，并多方接触各领域焦点人物、拓宽视野、吸收新知的读者来说，本书是您最佳的选择。

本书精选 30 篇报道，依主题分为以下四大部分：

- ◈ 名流轶事
- ◈ 非常体验
- ◈ 生活咀嚼
- ◈ 天地之间

全书的新闻报道中英文对照，而且给出了单词与重要词组解析，并补充了相关词汇及延伸用法，同时针对主题内容补充了各种相关知识。随书附有电脑互动光盘。读者可以利用多媒体技术将文字（text）、影像（image）、声音（sound）结合在一起加深学习印象、增进学习效率。针对苦于跟不上英语新闻速度的读者们，互动光盘还在正常速度的原音报道 MP3 之外附有慢速的朗读 MP3。慢速语音由专业外教录制，清晰的发音让您循序渐进，由慢至快地理解新闻内容。

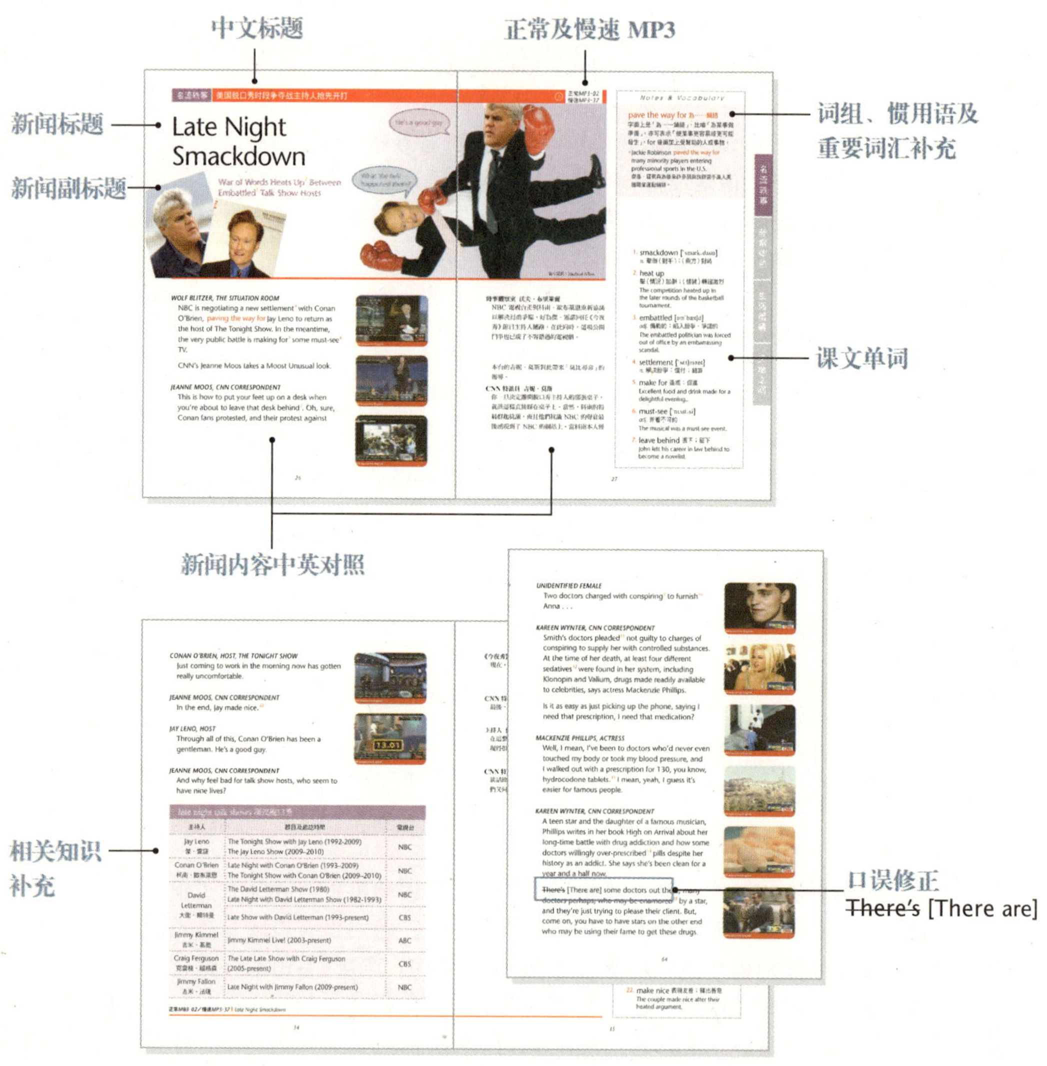

希望读者能通过本书专业的新闻报道学到老外最常用的英语单词、词组用法及口语表达，并循序渐进地锻炼听力、培养语感。相信这会是您精通英文的最佳途径！

目　录

生活咀嚼 125

光盘使用方法

★ 系统建议需求

[硬件]

* Pentium 4 以上处理器（或同等 AMD、Celeron 处理器）
* 512 MB 内存
* 屏幕分辨率 1024 * 768 像素以上
* 硬盘需求空间 200 MB
* 16 倍速以上光驱
* 声卡、扬声器及麦克风（内置或外接）

[软件]

* Microsoft Windows XP 、VISTA 、Windows7 简体中文版系统
* Microsoft Windows Media Player 9 以上
* Adobe Flash Player 10 以上

★ 请注意！

◎ 出于对版权的保护，本光盘只能在电脑上带盘运行，无法将光盘内容复制到电脑硬盘上再进行安装。

◎ 如果您的电脑装有 360 软件，请在安装光盘之前先关闭所有与 360 相关的软件，包括 360 杀毒软件、360 安全卫士、360 浏览器等。

◎ 在 Vista 系统中，安装互动光盘如遇到以下问题：

* 出现“安装字体错误”的信息。
* 出现“无法安装语音识别”的信息。

请运行以下步骤：

步骤一：删除该产品；

步骤二：进入控制面板；

步骤三：点击“用户账户”选项；

步骤四：点击“开启或关闭用户账户控制”；

步骤五：将“使用（用户账户控制）UAC 来协助保护您的电脑”选项取消勾选；

步骤六：再次运行安装光盘。

◎ 在 Windows7 系统中，安装互动光盘如遇到以下问题：

* 出现“安装字体错误”的信息。
* 出现“无法安装语音识别”的信息。

请运行以下步骤：

步骤一：进入控制面板，打开“程序”，进入“程序和功能”，卸载该产品；

步骤二：进入控制面板，点击“用户账户和家庭安全”选项；

步骤三：再点击“用户账户”；

步骤四：点击“更改用户账户控制设置”；

步骤五：将滑动条拖至最底端（“从不通知”的位置）；

步骤六：点击“确定”后，需重新启动电脑；

步骤七：再次运行安装光盘。

★ 光盘安装程序介绍

步骤一：进入中文操作系统。

步骤二：将光盘放进光驱。

步骤三：本产品具备 Auto Run 自动运行功能，如果您的电脑支持此功能，则将自动出现“CNN 互动英语系列——Step by Step 听懂 CNN 社会广角”的安装界面。

1. 如果您的电脑已安装过本系列任意产品，您可以直接点击“快速安装”图标，进行快速安装；否则请点击“安装”图标，进行完整安装。

2. 如果您的电脑不支持 Auto Run 光盘自动播放功能，请打开 Windows “我的电脑”，点击光驱，并运行光盘根目录下的 autorun.exe 程序。

3. 如果运行 autorun.exe 仍然无法安装，请进入本光盘的 setup 文件夹，运行 setup.exe 程序，即可进行安装。

4. 如果您要删除“CNN 互动英语系列——Step by Step 听懂 CNN 社会广角”，请点击“开始”，选择“设置”，选择“控制面板”，选择“添加或删除程序”，在菜单中点击“CNN 互动英语系列——Step by Step 听懂 CNN 社会广角”，并运行“更改 / 删除”即可。

5. 当语音识别系统或录音功能无法使用时，请检查声卡驱动程序是否正常，并确认硬盘空间足够且 Windows 录音程序可以使用。

★ 光盘操作说明

光盘安装后点击“运行”，即进入本光盘的学习内容。按顺序说明如下：

◎主画面

主画面说明：

1. 主画面共有 9 个图标，分别为：名流轶事、非常体验、生活咀嚼、天地之间、听力大考验、索引、说明、科学出版社及退出。

2. 点击“名流轶事”、“非常体验”、“生活咀嚼”、“天地之间”课程图标，将于屏幕中出现其中的单元名称，点击后即可进入该单元课程。

◎ 影片学习

影片学习工具栏说明：

1. 画面右侧由上至下依次为：自动播放、播放 / 暂停、播下一句、播上一句、反复播放本句、全屏幕播放及设置。

2. 画面左侧由上至下依次为：目录、上一篇、下一篇、单词解释、文字学习、主画面、退出。

3. 画面下方是英文及中文字幕，通过点击字幕前的图标，可以选择出现或隐藏字幕，便于做听力练习。

4. 点击“自动播放”图标，则自动由第一个影片开始播放。

5. 字幕上方有一个影片播放点控制栏，可决定影片播放的起点。

6. 点击“Setting”图标可调整反复播放、音量大小的设置。

◎ 文字学习

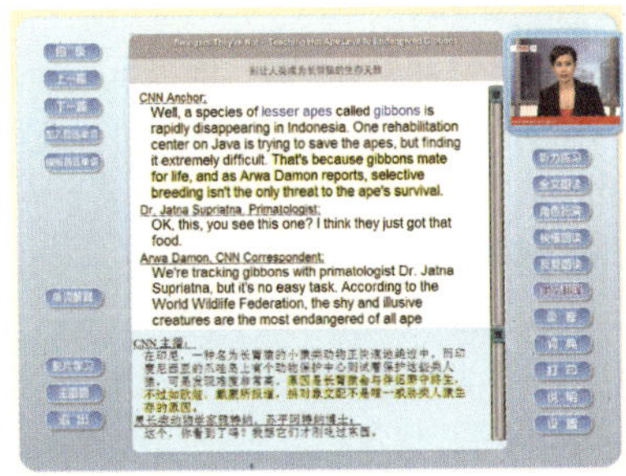

在影片学习中，点击“文字学习”图标，即可进入本画面。

文字学习工具栏说明：

听力练习

点击“听力练习”图标，电脑会自动朗读本段的内容，但不会显示出中、英文。

全文朗读

点击“全文朗读”图标，电脑会自动朗读本段新闻的内容。

角色扮演

点击“角色扮演”图标，则会在图标左侧出现人名。此时，您可选择要扮演的角色，程序将关闭该角色的声音，由您和电脑进行对话练习，当您的发音不正确时，则会出现一个对话框，您可以选择“再读一次”、“略过”或“读给我听”来完成或跳过该句对话；也可以调整语音识别的灵敏度。若您的发音正确，则对话会一直进行下去。

快慢朗读

当您觉得对话速度太快时，可以点击“快慢朗读”图标，再点击“全文朗读”图标或任意句子，朗读速度将变慢，让您听得更清楚。若您开始觉得速度太慢，想恢复一般速度，只要再次点击“快慢朗读”图标，即可恢复成一般速度。

反复朗读

点击“反复朗读”图标后，再点击任意句子，即反复播放该句。

中文翻译

点击“中文翻译”图标后，画面下方将出现中文翻译框，您可在中文翻译框内看到课文的中文翻译。若您点击中文翻译框中的某句中文，则会朗读相对应的英文句子；同样，点击正文中的任意英文句子，也会朗读该句英文，并标示出其中文翻译。

（当反蓝字无法使用重复或慢速朗读功能时，请开启中文翻译功能后，再次点击即可。）

录　音

1. 点击“录音”图标后，开启录音功能控制栏，截图如下。

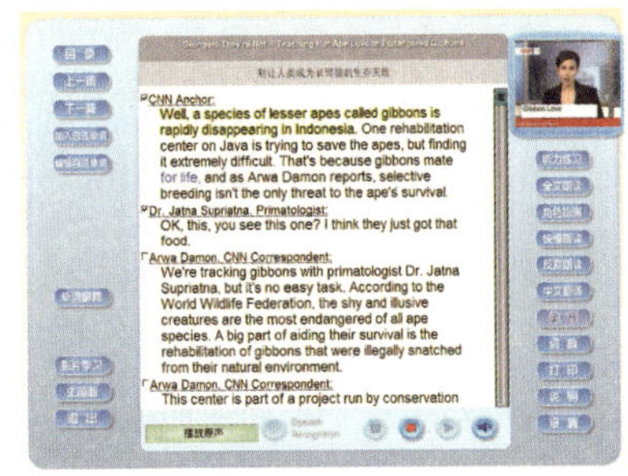

2. 按键功能由左至右为：全选、录音／停止、播放／暂停以及播放影片声音。点击最左方的“全选”图标，会出现全部句子录音；若您只想选择某段正文，只要在该段前方的方框（□）点击一下即可。若您点击最右方的“播放影片声音”图标，则在您进行录音或播放录音前，都将播放该段的影片原声。

3. 录音步骤如下：

(1) 先点击您要进行录音的句子，并选择是否要在录音前播放原声。

(2) 点击“录音”键。

(3) 请在电脑播放完原声后，对着麦克风读出您所点击的句子。

(4) 当您完成该句录音后，请按键盘上的“空格键”，结束录音。

(5) 点击“播放”键，即可听到您所录的声音。

4. 点击左方的“Speech Recognition”图标，将启动“语音识别”功能，请依照以下步骤进行语音识别：

(1) 先选择要进行语音识别的句子，并选择是否要在语音识别前播放原声。

(2) 点击“Speech Recognition”图标。

(3) 画面出现“请录音”时，请对着麦克风读出您点击的句子，如果您的发音正确，则将继续进行下一句；如果发音不正确，则会出现一个对话框，您可选择“再读一次”、“略过”或“读给我听”来完成或跳过该句对话；也可在此调整语音识别的灵敏度。

5. 当您要在中途结束录音或语音识别时，请在任意处点击一下即可结束该功能。

词 典

当您点击“词典”图标后，在画面下方将出现词典框，此时点击课文中的任意单词，词典框内会出现该单词的音标及中文翻译，并读出该词发音。

打 印

当您点击“打印”图标后，在画面下方将出现打印控制键。您可选择“全部打印”或“部分打印”；打印内容可选择是否包括中文翻译。此外，本光盘还提供存盘功能，您可以选择全部储存或部分储存；并选择是否储存中文翻译。

说 明

当您点击“说明”图标时，即会进入辅助说明页。您可借此了解本光盘内容的各项操作说明及用法。

设 置

若您想多次收听朗读，选取“设置”图标，将出现一个控制视窗，您可在此设置反复的间隔秒数及句子的反复次数，也可在此调整播放音量大小。

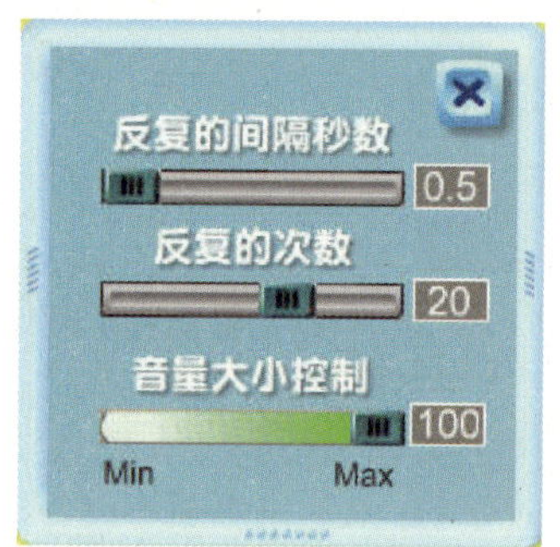

点击“加入自选单词”图标后，您可以点击您要记录的单词。

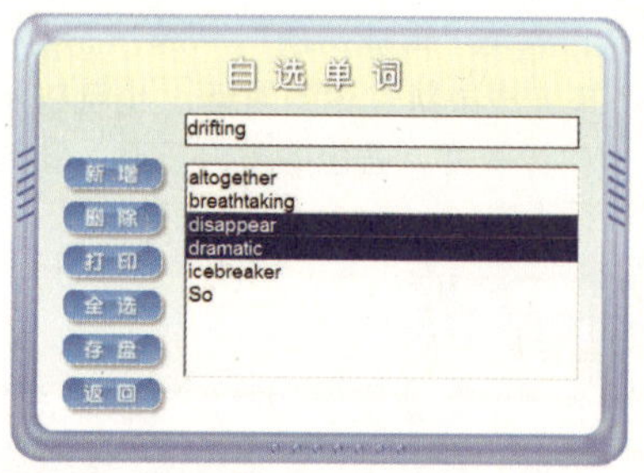

在此，您可以进行单词学习也可以删除或打印任意单词。

单词解释

列出本场景的重点单词（词性、音标、中文解释），点击该单词会发声。

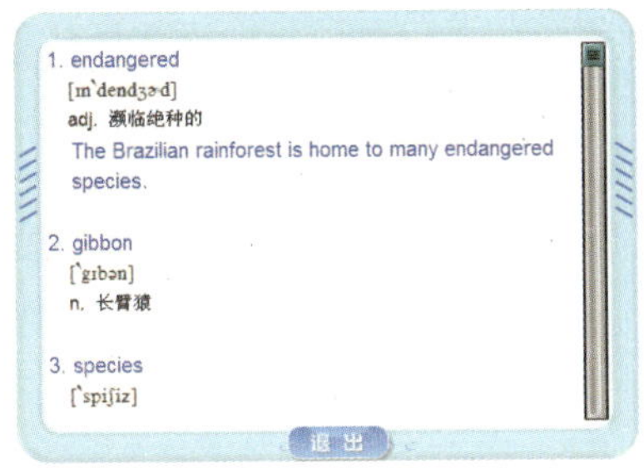

学习重点

如：Northwest Passage.

当您在点击文中蓝色字体的学习重点时，画面下方会出现说明框，并有发音；若在开启“中文翻译”功能时点击，则朗读您点击的句子。

段落朗读

如：Bear Grylls, Adventurer:

当您点击文中的人名时，程序将自动朗读此人的该段会话。

◎ 索引

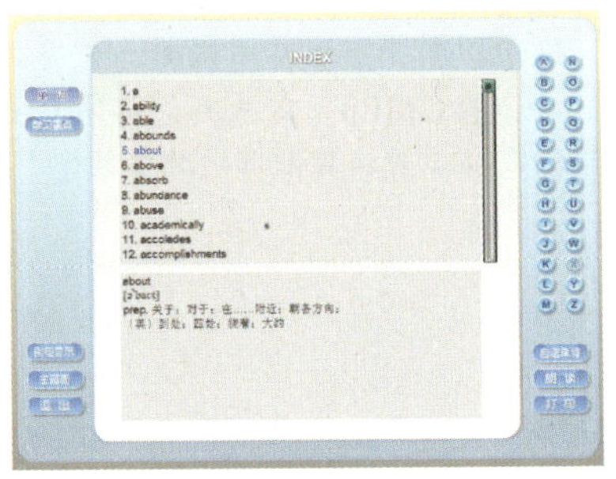

索引说明：

1. 在主画面点击“索引”图标，进入索引画面，其中包括单词及学习重点索引。

2. 单词：

   (1) 在此将所有的单词按字母分类，点击单词会出现该单词的音标、中文翻译及发音。

   (2) 连续点击单词两次或点击“例句显示”图标，即会出现该单词的课文例句。

   (3) 连续点击例句两次或点击“连接课文”图标，即跳至该例句的“文字学习”画面。

   (4) 点击“自选单词”图标，您可以在此看到您在学习过程中加入的自选单词。

   (5) 点击“朗读”图标，则会将所选字母的单词从头到尾读一次；点击“打印”图标，则将以该字母开头的所有单词打印出来。

   (6) 点击任意单词后，再点击“打印”图标，可打印该单词的内容。

3. 学习重点：

   (1) 在此列出本光盘所有课程的学习重点。用鼠标点击任意学习重点，会自动朗读。

   (2) 连续点击两次或点击“连接课文”图标，即跳至该学习重点的“文字学习”画面。

   (3) 点击“返回”图标，则回到单词检索画面。

   (4) 点击“朗读”图标，则会将所有的词语从头到尾读一次；点击“打印”图标，则将所有的学习重点打印出来。

◎ 听力大考验

1. 听力填空：

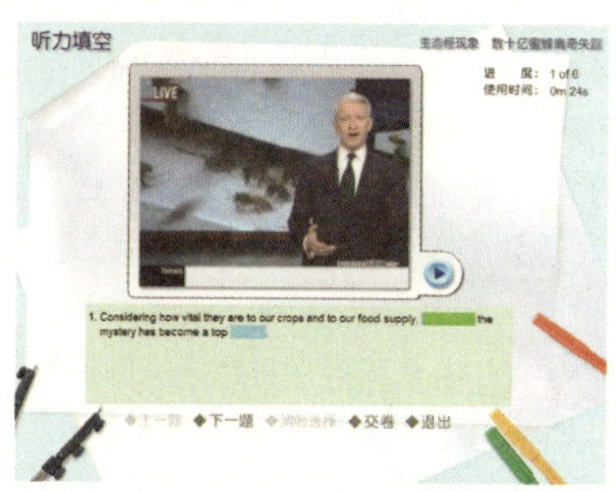

(1) 点击画面右方的“播放键”即可听到该题的声音，请逐一填入正确答案。

(2) 上方的进度将提示您目前正进行到第几题，完成题目后请点击“下一题”图标，继续进行测验。

(3) 完成所有的题组后，请点击“交卷”图标，进行评估，点击“查看内容”图标即可查阅该次测验的答题过程；也可点击“再试一次”重新进行评估。

(4) 点击“放弃作答”图标，将退出测验画面并不记录答题过程。

2. 听力理解：

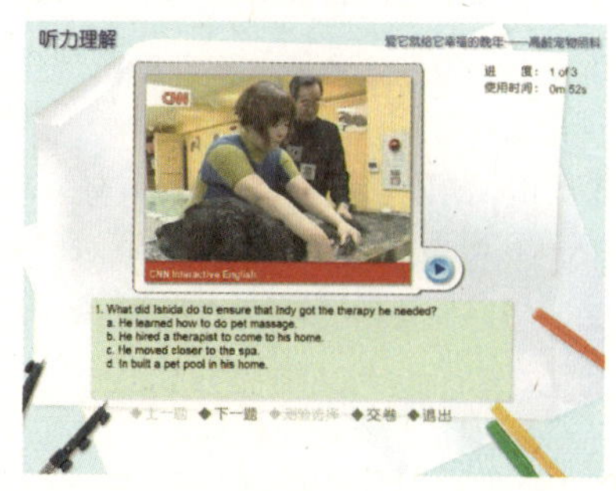

(1) 点击画面右方的播放键即可听到该段影片的声音，请选择正确答案。

(2) 上方的进度将提示您目前正进行到第几题，完成题目后请点击“下一题”图标，继续进行测验。

(3) 完成所有的题组后，请点击“交卷”图标，进行评估，点击“查看内容”图标即可查阅该次测验的答题过程；也可点击“再试一次”重新进行评估。

(4) 点击“放弃作答”图标，将退出测验画面并不记录答题过程。

◎ 说明

1. 在主画面点击“说明”图标，在此提供“操作说明”及“语音识别设置说明”。
2. 您可了解本光盘内容的各项操作说明、用法及语音识别设置上的安装说明。

◎ 科学出版社

点击本图标，将连接到科学出版社官方网站。

★ 原文朗读 MP3

互动光盘中含有新闻原声及慢速朗读 MP3 内容，您可以将光盘放在电脑中，打开本光盘，从中选择“MP3”文件夹，将里面的内容复制到电脑中或者其他播放器中收听。

CNN Society Watch

名流轶事

名流轶事 ❶ 名模走秀的足下梦魇——伸展台连环摔

Falling for[1] Fashion

Stumbling[2] and Tumbling[3] Models Strut[4] Their Way through Fashion Week

WOLF BLITZER, THE SITUATION ROOM

It's a runway[5] model's biggest nightmare—taking a topple. CNN's Jeanne Moos has this Moost Unusual look at Fashion Week.

JEANNE MOOS, CNN CORRESPONDENT

If there's one thing that can bring a model to her knees, it's falling to her knees. It's how New York kicked off[6] Fashion Week.

JAY ALEXANDER, MODELLING CONSULTANT

Not once, but twice.

JEANNE MOOS, CNN CORRESPONDENT

Less than five seconds after Agnes Dean arose to applause at the Fashion for Haiti Relief show,

01-F.MP3
01-S.MP3

图片提供：Reuters 达志

《时事观察室》沃尔夫·布利策
这是伸展台上模特儿最大的梦魇——跌一跤。CNN 的吉妮·莫斯在时装周中带来“莫比寻常”的报道。

CNN 特派员　吉妮·莫斯
如果有件事能够使模特儿崩溃的话，那便是跌倒。而这正是揭开纽约时装周序幕的情况。

时装模特儿顾问　杰·亚历山大
不是一次，而是两次。

CNN 特派员　吉妮·莫斯
艾格妮丝·迪恩在“援助海地时装秀”中爬起接受掌声，不到五秒钟，她又再度跌倒

Notes & Vocabulary

take a topple
跌一跤
topple 是“跌倒”的意思，较常见的说法是 take a fall/tumble/spill，文中的 take a topple 较少见，但非错误用法。

- Josie took a fall when she slipped on a patch of ice.
  裘西在一块冰上失足跌倒了。

bring sb. to sb.'s knees
迫使某人屈服
bring sb. to sb.'s knees 原指“使某人屈膝下跪”，引申指“迫使某人屈服、顺从、投降”，或是“击败、阻止某人”。

- The scandal brought the government to its knees.
  这则丑闻大大打击了政府。

1. fall for 爱上；受害
   Tim fell for his iPhone from the moment he first turned it on.
2. stumble [ˋstʌmbl̩]
   v. 跌跌撞撞地走；说话结巴
   The inexperienced speaker stumbled his way through his speech.
3. tumble [ˋtʌmbl̩] v. 跌倒；滚落
   Jack tumbled down the stairs to his apartment.
4. strut [strʌt]
   v. 趾高气扬地走；大步迈进
   The model strutted across the stage in the fashion show.
5. runway [ˋrʌnˏwe] n. 走秀伸展台
6. kick off（活动）开始
   The conference kicked off with an address by its founder.

名流轶事
非常体验
生活咀嚼
天地之间

down she went again—a perfect excuse to recall[7] our favorite falls, to recall our favorite sprawls,[8] from catching[9] a heel in the pants to falling through the runway. Apparently unaware the center was only paper, someone ran to her rescue.[10]

No one helped the time the great Naomi Campbell went down.[11]

DAVID LETTERMAN, HOST, THE LATE SHOW

Get a photo. Let's get a photo.

NAOMI CAMPBELL, MODEL

Yeah, let me get a photo.

DAVID LETTERMAN, HOST, THE LATE SHOW

Idiots! What is wrong with people?

JEANNE MOOS, CNN CORRESPONDENT

Naomi made her fall into an insurance commercial.

JAY ALEXANDER, MODELING CONSULTANT

Because Naomi Campbell is smart.

JEANNE MOOS, CNN CORRESPONDENT

Jay Alexander teaches models how to walk and how not to. Carmen Electra demonstrated how not to, and then the lady running to her rescue followed in her footfalls.

Most of the time, you can blame the high heels.

What we have here is a potential shoe emergency.

了——这成了回顾我们最爱的跌倒或四脚朝天画面的最佳理由，从鞋跟卡到裤子到踏破伸展台掉进洞里。很显然，她没注意到伸展台中央是纸做的，有人跑过来解救她了。

但是当知名的内奥米•坎贝尔跌倒时，却没有人来帮她。

《午夜脱口秀》主持人　大卫•赖特曼
拍照。快点拍张照。

模特儿　内奥米•坎贝尔
对啊，帮我拍张照吧。

《午夜脱口秀》主持人　大卫•赖特曼
笨蛋！大家到底怎么了？

CNN 特派员　吉妮•莫斯
内奥米把她的失足变成了保险广告。

时装模特儿顾问　杰•亚历山大
因为内奥米•坎贝尔很聪明。

CNN 特派员　吉妮•莫斯
杰•亚历山大教导模特儿走台步该注意的事。卡门•伊莱特拉示范了应该避免的走法，跑来解救她的模特儿则步上了她的后尘。

多半情况下你可以把跌倒的原因归咎于高跟鞋。

现在我们面临的情况是可能发生的鞋子突发事件。

Notes & Vocabulary

7. recall [rɪˋkɔl] *v.* 使想起
Ted recalled many fond memories when flipping through his high school yearbook.

8. sprawl [sprɔl]
n. 伸开四肢坐或躺

9. catch [kætʃ]
v. 使陷于；使纠缠；勾到
Jackie caught her new sweater on a nail.

10. run to sb.'s rescue
援救某人
When Trish was too sick to take care of herself, her mother ran to her rescue.

11. go down 倒在地上
The boxer went down with one punch.

A beaded[12] spat[13] come undone[14] could undo a model here at the Pamela Rollins show. But the shoes here are tame[15] compared to the late Alexander McQueen's.

UNIDENTIFIED MODEL

Did you see the shoes from the show last year?

JEANNE MOOS, CNN CORRESPONDENT

Armadillo shoes, they were dubbed.[16]

UNIDENTIFIED MODEL

And there were a couple of girls that wouldn't do the show 'cause it's just so dangerous.

JEANNE MOOS, CNN CORRESPONDENT

After falling twice in seven-inch heels at the show for Haiti Relief, what a relief. Take those heels off. We've seen Miss USAs fall twice in recent years.

RACHEL SMITH, MISS USA

Oops.

JEANNE MOOS, CNN CORRESPONDENT

We've seen models conk[17] their heads. We've seen a martial arts[18] performer make a hole in the runway then watched the model who followed his act fall in.

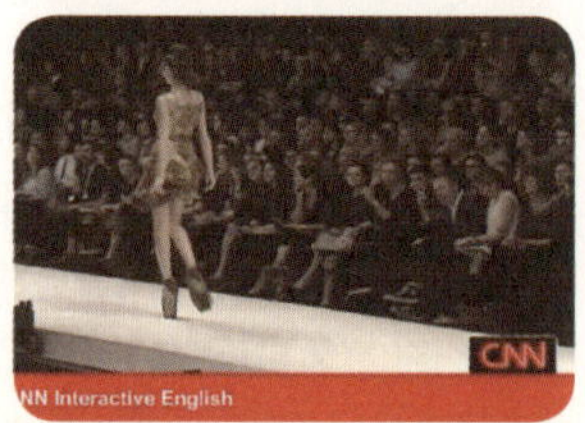

But there's one classic . . .

缀有珠饰的鞋罩松脱可能会让帕梅拉·罗林斯时装秀上的模特儿举手投降。但是这里的鞋子和上次亚历山大·麦克奎恩（注）时装秀中的鞋子比起来可就不算什么了。

不知名模特儿
你看过去年时装秀上的鞋子吗？

CNN 特派员　吉妮·莫斯
这种鞋被称为“犰狳”鞋。

不知名模特儿
有些女孩不愿意走这场秀，因为那实在是太危险了。

CNN 特派员　吉妮·莫斯
在“援助海地时装秀”中穿着七寸高的高跟鞋跌倒两次之后，能脱掉它们实在是种解脱。我们近年来也两度看到美国小姐跌倒。

美国小姐　瑞秋·史密斯
哇。

CNN 特派员　吉妮·莫斯
我们看到模特儿狠狠地撞到了头。我们看到武术表演者在伸展台上弄了个洞，然后看到他之后跟着走出的模特儿踩空掉了进去。

但是还有个经典画面……

注：亚历山大·麦克奎恩在时尚圈向来以大胆、天马行空的创意闻名，演艺圈名人如 Lady Gaga 就是支持者之一。2009 年年底巴黎时尚周爆出模特儿因麦克奎恩的走秀高跟鞋太高而拒穿的新闻，2010 年在纽约时尚周前他疑因丧母而自杀身亡。

Notes & Vocabulary

12. beaded [ˋbidɪd] *adj.* 以珠子装饰的
Donna wore a beaded dress to the dinner.

13. spat [spæt] *n.* 鞋罩

14. undone [ʌnˋdʌn] *adj.* 松脱的
The rope tethering the boat to the dock came undone.

15. tame [tem] *adj.* 平淡无奇的
Sharon found the movie's content to be quite tame.

16. dub [dʌb] *v.* 戏称为；起绰号
Fans dubbed the singer the "king of cool."

17. conk [kɔŋk] *v.* 重击（某人）的头部
The bicyclist conked his head on a tree branch.

18. martial art [ˋmɑrʃəl] [ɑrt] 武术

UNIDENTIFIED MODEL

I love watching that.

UNIDENTIFIED MODEL

Oh my god.

JEANNE MOOS, CNN CORRESPONDENT

. . . that leaves even the models chortling.[19] Maybe it's the Washington, D.C. anchors . . .

UNIDENTIFIED MALE NEWS ANCHOR

She never quite recovered after that. There she goes again.

JEANNE MOOS, CNN CORRESPONDENT

. . . preserved forever on YouTube, replaying and laughing.

UNIDENTIFIED FEMALE NEWS ANCHOR

You try walking in those shoes.

JEANNE MOOS, CNN CORRESPONDENT

Laughing and replaying.

UNIDENTIFIED MALE NEWS ANCHOR

We want to apologize.

UNIDENTIFIED MALE NEWS ANCHOR

Hold on![20] Hold on!

JEANNE MOOS, CNN CORRESPONDENT

Fashion can stagger[21] more than just the imagination.

01-F.MP3 / 01-S.MP3 | *Falling for Fashion*

不知名模特儿
我喜欢看那画面。

不知名模特儿
噢，我的天哪。

CNN 特派员　吉妮·莫斯
……甚至让模特儿笑翻了。而这则可能是华盛顿那边的主播……

不知名男性新闻主播
她还没完全走好呢，结果又跌倒了。

CNN 特派员　吉妮·莫斯
……永远被保留在 YouTube 网站上，人们一再重播然后大笑。

不知名女性新闻主播
你试着穿着那些鞋子走走看。

CNN 特派员　吉妮·莫斯
大笑之后再重播。

不知名男性新闻主播
我们想说声抱歉。

不知名男性新闻主播
等一下！等一下！

CNN 特派员　吉妮·莫斯
时尚之路可能比你所想的更难走。

Notes & Vocabulary

19. chortle [ˋtʃɔrtl̩]
v. 哈哈大笑；高兴地咯咯笑
Megan chortled when she heard a silly joke.

20. hold on【口】等一等
Hold on. I'm not finished eating that.

21. stagger [ˋstægɚ]
v.（使）摇晃；（使）跌跌撞撞；（使）动摇
The economic crisis staggered many people's faith in banks.

名流轶事 ② 美国脱口秀时段争夺战　主持人抢先开打

Late Night Smackdown[1]

War of Words Heats Up[2] Between Embattled[3] Talk Show Hosts

WOLF BLITZER, THE SITUATION ROOM

NBC is negotiating a new settlement[4] with Conan O'Brien, paving the way for Jay Leno to return as the host of The Tonight Show. In the meantime, the very public battle is making for[5] some must-see[6] TV.

CNN's Jeanne Moos takes a Moost Unusual look.

JEANNE MOOS, CNN CORRESPONDENT

This is how to put your feet up on a desk when you're about to leave that desk behind[7]. Oh, sure, Conan fans protested, and their protest against

02-F.MP3
02-S.MP3

图片提供：Michael Albov

《时事观察室》　沃夫·布里策尔

NBC 电视台正与科南·欧布莱恩重新协议以解决目前争端，好为杰·雷诺回任《今夜秀》节目主持人铺路。与此同时，这场公开斗争也已成为不容错过的电视剧。

本台的吉妮·莫斯对此带来"莫比寻常"的报道。

CNN 特派员　吉妮·莫斯

你一旦决定离开脱口秀主持人的那张桌子，就该这样直接踩在桌子上。当然，科南的粉丝群起抗议，而且他们抗议 NBC 的声音最后涌现到了 NBC 的网站上。当科南本人慢

Notes & Vocabulary

pave the way for 为……铺路

字面上意为"为……铺路"，比喻"为某事做准备"，也可表示"使某事更容易或更可能发生"，for 后接受帮助的人或事物。

· Jackie Robinson **paved the way for** many minority players entering professional sports in the U.S.

杰基·罗宾森为后来许多弱势族群选手进入美国职业运动铺了路。

1. smackdown [ˋsmækˏdaun]
   n. 击倒（对手）；（两方）对峙
2. heat up
   （情况）加剧；（情绪）转趋激烈
   The competition heated up in the later rounds of the basketball tournament.
3. embattled [ɪmˋbætl̩d]
   adj. 备战的；陷入纷争、争议的
   The embattled politician was forced out of office by an embarrassing scandal.
4. settlement [ˋsɛtl̩mənt]
   n.（解决纷争的）协议；欠款的偿付；结算
5. make for 造成；促进
   Excellent food and drink made for a delightful evening.
6. must-see [ˋmʌstˏsi]
   adj. 非看不可的
   The musical was a must-see event.
7. leave behind 丢下；留下
   John left his career in law behind to become a novelist.

NBC ended up[8] on NBC's Web site. Fans went nuts[9] when Conan himself jogged by. All they were saying …

CONAN O'BRIEN FANS

… is give Conan a chance!

JEANNE MOOS, CNN CORRESPONDENT

But at least it gave us the chance to savor[10] a late night smackdown.

CONAN O'BRIEN, HOST, THE TONIGHT SHOW

What the hell happened there?

JEANNE MOOS, CNN CORRESPONDENT

With other comedians imitating Leno …

DAVID LETTERMAN, HOST, THE LATE SHOW

Yeah, OK, well, that sounds pretty good.

JEANNE MOOS, CNN CORRESPONDENT

Jimmy Kimmel did his whole show impersonating[11] Leno and dissed[12] him on Jay's own show.

JAY LENO, HOST

Have you ever ordered anything off the TV?

JIMMY KIMMEL, HOST, JIMMY KIMMEL LIVE

Like NBC ordered your show off the TV?

JAY LENO, HOST

Yeah. Yeah. No, no. No, no.

跑经过的时候，粉丝都为之疯狂。他们说的只是……

科南·欧布莱恩的粉丝
……给科南一个机会！

CNN 特派员　吉妮·莫斯
不过，至少这次事件让我们有机会欣赏一场深夜大战。

《今夜秀》主持人　科南·欧布莱恩
这里到底发生了什么鸟事？

CNN 特派员　吉妮·莫斯
其他喜剧演员都纷纷模仿雷诺……

《午夜脱口秀》主持人　大卫·赖特曼
哦，好吧，听起来不错。

CNN 特派员　吉妮·莫斯
吉米·金默尔以一整集节目模仿雷诺，而且还在杰·雷诺的节目上羞辱他。

主持人　杰·雷诺
你有没有命令过电视台把这节目砍了？

《吉米·金默尔实时秀》主持人　吉米·金默尔
就像 NBC 砍掉你的节目那样吗？

主持人　杰·雷诺
对，对。不对，不对，不对。

Notes & Vocabulary

8. end up 最终抵达某处；结果
The lost hikers ended up on a deserted beach.

9. go nuts 失去理智；陷入疯狂
The fans went nuts when the singer stepped out of his hotel.

10. savor [`sevɚ] v. 欣赏；细细品味
Jeff savored his tennis victory over his brother.

11. impersonate [ɪm`pɝsə͵net] v. 扮演；模仿
The actor has impersonated several historical figures.

12. diss [dɪs] v. 轻视侮辱（尤指言辞上，也可写作 dis，为 disrespect 的衍生词）
Brenda dissed Alice's fashion sense.

JEANNE MOOS, CNN CORRESPONDENT

Letterman took some of the sharpest jabs. He even showed Leno taking over a dead talk show host's show.

TV ANNOUNCER

And takes over Merv Griffin's grave.

JAY LENO, HOST

Your local news starts right now.

UNIDENTIFIED MALE

In the television industry, there are two types of talk show hosts—Jay Leno and those who have been victimized[13] by Jay Leno.

JAY LENO, HOST

Even Dave Letterman [is] taking shots at me, which is a surprise. Usually he's just taking shots at interns.[14] I couldn't believe ...

JEANNE MOOS, CNN CORRESPONDENT

The deadliest shots were aimed at NBC Universal's president, Jeff Zucker.

JON STEWART, HOST

Yeah, he's like the Cheney of television. He's just shooting shows in the face.

JEANNE MOOS, CNN CORRESPONDENT

Zucker was taken aback by the blowback.[15]

CNN 特派员　吉妮·莫斯
赖特曼的嘲讽则是最尖酸刻薄的。他甚至还让雷诺接手一名已故脱口秀主持人的节目。

电视播报员
他还接手了莫弗·葛瑞芬的坟墓。

主持人　杰·雷诺
现在为您带来地方新闻。

不知名男子
电视圈里只有两种脱口秀主持人——杰·雷诺和被杰·雷诺欺负过的人。

主持人　杰·雷诺
连大卫·赖特曼都趁机修理我，真是意外。他通常只会修理菜鸟。我实在不敢相信……

CNN 特派员　吉妮·莫斯
最狠的攻击则是以 NBC 环球集团总裁杰夫·札克为对象。

主持人　强·史都华
没错，他就像是电视圈的切尼（注）。他根本是直接羞辱这些脱口秀节目。

CNN 特派员　吉妮·莫斯
札克对于他预料之外的反应深感诧异。

注：布什时期的副总统切尼（Richard Bruce Cheney）自卸任后，便屡屡对奥巴马政府的各项施政提出严厉批评。

Notes & Vocabulary

take a jab 攻击；侮辱

jab 有“戳、刺、用拳快速猛击”之意，所以 take a jab 便可指“击打；攻击；戳刺”，后面用 at 加上攻击的对象，也可比喻抽象的“侮辱；讥讽”等，类似 take a dig。

· The comedian took a jab at the president during his routine.
这名喜剧演员老是讥讽总统。

take a (pot) shot at 随意批评

pot shot 原是指“近距离射击；胡乱扫射”，所以 take a pot shot at 便可指“未经深思熟虑，随便找个对象就做出让人意想不到且不公平的批评”。但如今人们使用此词组常省略 pot，仅以 take a shot at 表示相同的意思。

· Bob took a shot at his sister by saying her cooking wasn't as good as their mother's.
鲍勃随意批评姐姐说她的厨艺不如妈妈。

taken aback 震惊；吓一跳

taken aback 原指“帆船航行时风向突然逆转，让船行方向难以控制”，后来便从“船行方向突然变得难以控制，掌控”衍生出“震惊；吓一跳”之意。

· The teacher was taken aback by the student's rude behavior.
这名老师被学生粗鲁的举动吓一大跳。

13. victimize [ˋvɪktə͵maɪz]
v. 使受害；使受苦
Unscrupulous officials victimized the immigrants.

14. intern [ˋɪntɜn] *n.* 实习生

15. blowback [ˋblo͵bæk]
n.（未预料到且不受欢迎的）效应;结果

JEFF ZUCKER, PRESIDENT, NBC UNIVERSAL

People delivering death threats over a program moving back a half hour.

JEANNE MOOS, CNN CORRESPONDENT

As if the late night drama wasn't animated[16] enough …

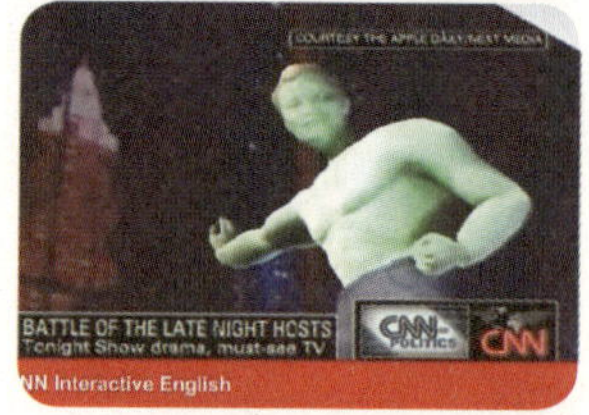

UNIDENTIFIED APPLE DAILY ANNOUNCER

Zucker tried to get O'Brien to fall in line[17] by threatening to keep him off the air.

JEANNE MOOS, CNN CORRESPONDENT

A Taiwanese tabloid's[18] Web site turned it into an animation—with Leno as a tubby[19] Superman and Conan as The Hulk.

UNIDENTIFIED APPLE DAILY ANNOUNCER

He pretty much said, "Hell no, I won't go." NBC management was getting insulted night after night on their own network.

JEANNE MOOS, CNN CORRESPONDENT

Five years ago, Conan was thrilled[20] to get The Tonight Show.

CONAN O'BRIEN, HOST, THE TONIGHT SHOW

I give my heartfelt[21] thanks to everybody at NBC, particularly to Jay Leno.

JEANNE MOOS, CNN CORRESPONDENT

But that was then, this is now.

NBC 环球集团总裁　杰夫·札克
只不过是把节目时间延后半个小时，就有人发出死亡威胁了。

CNN 特派员　吉妮·莫斯
仿佛这场深夜好戏火药味还不够浓……

不知名的《苹果日报》播报员
为了让欧布莱恩听话，札克不惜威胁让他上不了节目。

CNN 特派员　吉妮·莫斯
中国台湾一家八卦报纸的网站把这起事件做成了动画——把雷诺画成矮胖的超人，科南则是绿巨人浩克。

不知名的《苹果日报》播报员
他基本上就是在说："休想，我才不会走。" NBC 的管理高层每晚都在自己的电视台上遭到羞辱。

CNN 特派员　吉妮·莫斯
五年前，科南对于自己能够接下《今夜秀》节目深感兴奋。

《今夜秀》主持人　科南·欧布莱恩
我衷心感谢 NBC 电视台所有的人，特别是杰·雷诺。

CNN 特派员　吉妮·莫斯
但那是过去的事，现在则是这样。

Notes & Vocabulary

16. **animated** [ˋænəˏmetɪd]
adj. 充满能量或活力的
Though she is always calm, Bonnie becomes quite animated on stage.

17. **fall in line** 顺从；服从（规则）
The coach warned his players to fall in line or they would be kicked off the team.

18. **tabloid** [ˋtæˏblɔɪd]
n.（八卦）小报

19. **tubby** [ˋtʌbɪ]
adj. 矮胖的
The tubby police officer was told he would have to lose weight.

20. **thrilled** [θrɪld]
adj. 非常兴奋、激动
Joyce was thrilled to win a small lottery prize.

21. **heartfelt** [ˋhɑrtˏfɛlt]
adj. 衷心的；真诚的
The flood victim gave heartfelt thanks to her rescuers.

CONAN O'BRIEN, HOST, THE TONIGHT SHOW

Just coming to work in the morning now has gotten really uncomfortable.

JEANNE MOOS, CNN CORRESPONDENT

In the end, Jay made nice.[22]

JAY LENO, HOST

Through all of this, Conan O'Brien has been a gentleman. He's a good guy.

JEANNE MOOS, CNN CORRESPONDENT

And why feel bad for talk show hosts, who seem to have nine lives?

late night talk shows 深夜脱口秀

主持人	节目及起止时间	电视台
Jay Leno 杰・雷诺	The Tonight Show with Jay Leno (1992-2009) The Jay Leno Show (2009-2010)	NBC
Conan O'Brien 柯南・欧布莱恩	Late Night with Conan O'Brien (1993-2009) The Tonight Show with Conan O'Brien (2009-2010)	NBC
David Letterman 戴维・赖特曼	The David Letterman Show (1980) Late Night with David Letterman Show (1982-1993)	NBC
	Late Show with David Letterman (1993-present)	CBS
Jimmy Kimmel 吉米・金默尔	Jimmy Kimmel Live! (2003-present)	ABC
Craig Ferguson 克雷格・福格森	The Late Late Show with Craig Ferguson (2005-present)	CBS
Jimmy Fallon 吉米・法隆	Late Night with Jimmy Fallon (2009-present)	NBC

《今夜秀》主持人　科南·欧布莱恩

现在，光是早上出门去工作都让我很难受。

CNN 特派员　吉妮·莫斯

最后，杰·雷诺表示了友善。

主持人　杰·雷诺

在这整个事件当中，科南·欧布莱恩一直表现得很绅士。他是个好人。

CNN 特派员　吉妮·莫斯

谈话节目主持人显然都是打不死的蟑螂，我们又何必为他们感到难过呢？

Notes & Vocabulary

22. make nice 表现友善；释出善意
The couple made nice after their heated argument.

名流轶事 ③ 当副总统满嘴脏话

The Curse[1] of Joe Biden

Vice President Drops F-Bomb During Health Bill Signing

ZAIN VERJEE, CNN ANCHOR

Mr. Obama's second in command,[2] U.S. Vice President Joe Biden, is well-known for his verbal[3] slipups,[4] but he may have even outdone[5] himself at that signing ceremony. CNN's Jeanne Moos was there.

JEANNE MOOS, CNN CORRESPONDENT

Amid the big hugs and the big smiles, the thrill[6] of health care victory[7] had everyone fired up.[8]

Joe Biden was fired up all right[9]— lavishing[10] praise on the president.

03-F.MP3
03-S.MP3

图片提供：Reuters 达志

CNN 主播 洁茵·维尔吉
奥巴马的副手，也就是副总统乔·拜登，素以说错话著称，但他在医保法案的签署仪式上的表现可能较以往更夸张了。本台特派员吉妮·莫斯当时人就在现场。

CNN 特派员 吉妮·莫斯
大伙儿热情拥抱、笑容满面，医保案顺利通过所带来的兴奋感让大家都情绪高涨。

Notes & Vocabulary

标题扫描

F-bomb F 开头的脏字

F-bomb 是 F 开头脏话的代称，即 F-word 。F-bomb 来自 A-bomb “原子弹”或是 B-bomb “氢弹”，以炸弹的破坏力比喻该字之不当与惊人的程度。

1. curse [kɜs]
   n. 脏话；诅咒 v. 讲脏话；诅咒
2. second in command
   副司令；第二高位者
   Phil is second in command on a fishing boat.
3. verbal [ˋvɜbəl]
   adj. 口头上的；口语的
   After a brief negotiation, both parties reached a verbal agreement.
4. slipup [ˋslɪp͵ʌp] *n.* 疏漏；差错
5. outdo [͵autˋdu] *v.* 胜过
   Yvonne outdid herself preparing for the dinner party.
6. thrill [θrɪl] *n.* 兴奋感；激动
7. victory [ˋvɪktərɪ] *n.* 胜利
8. fire up
   使充满激情；激起……热情
   The speaker fired up the audience.
9. all right 无疑地
   Out of money and miles from home, we are in a difficult situation all right.
10. lavish [ˋlævɪʃ] *v.* 过分给予；滥施
    The hosts lavished gifts on their guests.

名流轶事
非常体验
生活咀嚼
天地之间

JOE BIDEN, VICE PRESIDENT OF THE UNITED STATES

I've gotten to know you well enough. You want me to stop, because I'm embarrassing[11] you.

UNIDENTIFIED MALE

T minus 10.

JEANNE MOOS, CNN CORRESPONDENT

Actually, he's about to embarrass him by dropping a bomb.

UNIDENTIFIED MALE

Three, two, one.

JOE BIDEN, VICE PRESIDENT OF THE UNITED STATES

This is a big (expletive language) deal.

JEANNE MOOS, CNN CORRESPONDENT

Pardon me?

JOE BIDEN, VICE PRESIDENT OF THE UNITED STATES

This is a big (expletive language) deal.

JEANNE MOOS, CNN CORRESPONDENT

From Joe Biden's lips to the media's ears.

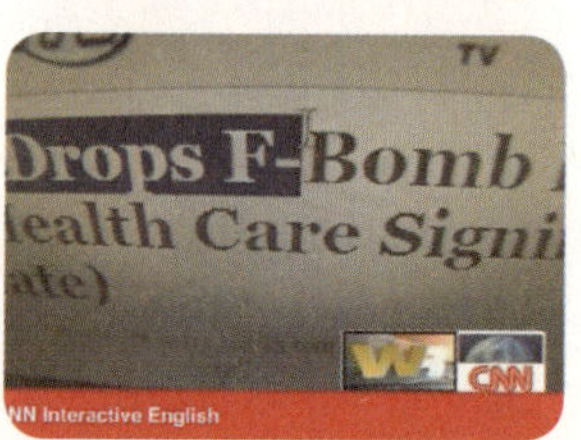

BRIT HUME, FOX NEWS ANCHOR

He has always had difficulty puttin' a sock in it.

JEANNE MOOS, CNN CORRESPONDENT

Another excuse for us to trot out[12] the V.P.'s previous bloopers,[13] like the time he urged the guy in the wheelchair. . .

乔·拜登真的很兴奋——拼命称赞总统。

美国副总统　乔·拜登
我已经很了解你这个人了。你要我别再这么做，因为我会让你觉得难堪。

不知名男性
倒数 10 秒。

CNN 特派员　吉妮·莫斯
事实上，他就快因为丢出一颗炸弹而让自己难堪了。

不知名男性
3、2、1。

美国副总统　乔·拜登
这件事真他 X 的了不起。

CNN 特派员　吉妮·莫斯
你说什么？

美国副总统　乔·拜登
这件事真他 X 的了不起。

CNN 特派员　吉妮·莫斯
从乔·拜登嘴里说出的话进到了媒体的耳朵里。

福克斯新闻主播　布利特·休姆
少说几句对来他说总是很难。

CNN 特派员　吉妮·莫斯
这又让我们找到借口来给大家看看这位副总统之前出洋相的镜头，像是那次他要求坐轮椅的那位仁兄……

Notes & Vocabulary

put a sock in it
让某人闭嘴
字面上是“把袜子塞到（嘴）里”的意思，口语中用来表示“要某人闭嘴、别讲话”的意思。

- When Billy kept complaining, Wilson told him to put a sock in it.
  当比利一直抱怨时，威尔森请他安静。

其他常用表示“闭嘴”的惯用语

button one's lip
闭嘴；忍住不说

- Irene buttoned her lip and didn't mention her sister's awful haircut.
  艾琳忍住不提她姐姐那个剪得很糟的发型。

hold one's tongue
闭嘴；忍不住说

- Jack held his tongue rather than criticize his wife's cooking.
  杰克闭嘴不去批评他太太的厨艺。

11. embarrass [ɪm`bærəs]
v. 使……尴尬
Don always embarrasses his teenage children in front of their friends.

12. trot out 拿出；掏出
Steven trotted out his usual excuses for being late to the meeting.

13. blooper [`blupɚ]
n. 当众出洋相；出丑

JOE BIDEN, VICE PRESIDENT OF THE UNITED STATES
Stand up, Chuck. Let 'em see you.

JEANNE MOOS, CNN CORRESPONDENT
The other day, when he referred to the Irish prime minister's mother. . .

JOE BIDEN, VICE PRESIDENT OF THE UNITED STATES
God rest her soul and although she's . . . wait, your mom's still, your mom's still alive. It is your dad [who's] passed. God bless her soul!

JEANNE MOOS, CNN CORRESPONDENT
Bless his soul for providing us with fodder.[14]

UNIDENTIFIED REPORTER
Every 10 minutes, there's a shift in sort of what the strategy is. Again, I. . .

JOE BIDEN, VICE PRESIDENT OF THE UNITED STATES
Who gives a (expletive language)?

JEANNE MOOS, CNN CORRESPONDENT
This isn't the first time a mic has picked up the V.P. dropping the F-bomb.

JOE BIDEN, VICE PRESIDENT OF THE UNITED STATES
An hour late? Give me a (expletive language) . . .

美国副总统　乔·拜登
站起来，查克，让他们看看你。

CNN 特派员　吉妮·莫斯
还有某一天，他提到爱尔兰总理的母亲……

美国副总统　乔·拜登
愿上帝让她的灵魂安息，虽然她……等等，你妈妈还活着，死掉的人是你爸。愿上帝祝福她的灵魂！

CNN 特派员　吉妮·莫斯
愿上帝因为他提供给我们新闻素材而祝福他的灵魂。

不知名特派员
每隔 10 分钟，策略就会有所改变，我……

美国副总统　乔·拜登
谁 X 在乎呢？

CNN 特派员　吉妮·莫斯
这并非这位副总统首次通过麦克风口出秽言。

美国副总统　乔·拜登
晚一小时？他 X 的拜托。

Notes & Vocabulary

14. fodder [ˋfadɚ] *n.* 现成材料

JEANNE MOOS, CNN CORRESPONDENT

But, hey, the previous V.P., Dick Cheney, used it in anger, telling Senator Patrick Leahy to you-know-what[15] himself.

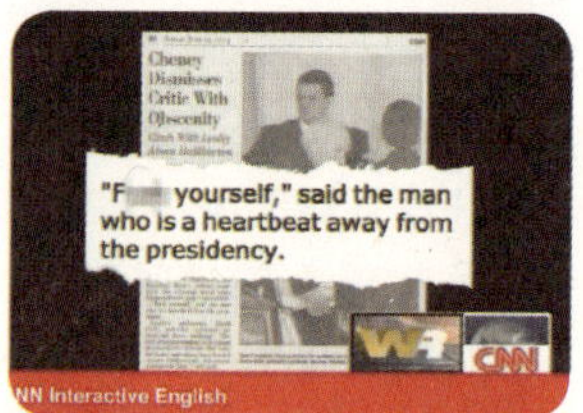

NEIL CAVUTO, FOX NEWS ANCHOR

Do you have any regrets?

DICK CHENEY, FORMER U.S. VICE PRESIDENT

No, I said it.

JEANNE MOOS, CNN CORRESPONDENT

If the White House regretted Vice President Biden's remark[16] about health care. . .

JOE BIDEN, VICE PRESIDENT OF THE UNITED STATES

This is a big (expletive language) deal.

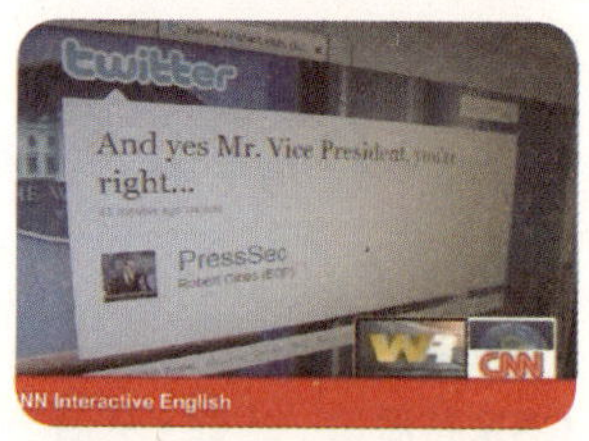

JEANNE MOOS, CNN CORRESPONDENT

. . . they weren't letting on[17]. Press Secretary Gibbs tweeted,[18] "And yes, Mr. V.P., you're right."

The vice president's faux pas[19] was such a big friggin'[20] deal that within two hours of his utterance,[21] it was already emblazoned[22] on T-shirts. The guy really known for salty[23] language is Chief of Staff Rahm Emanuel, who wouldn't tell on the president when he talked to 60 Minutes.

RAHM EMANUEL, WHITE HOUSE CHIEF OF STAFF

But I do not curse in the Oval Office.

CNN 特派员　吉妮•莫斯

不过，嘿，前副总统迪克•切尼在火冒三丈时也曾叫参议员帕特里克•莱希“X 自己”。

福克斯新闻主播　尼尔•卡伍托

你会感到后悔吗？

前副总统　迪克•切尼

不会，我说了就是说了。

CNN 特派员　吉妮•莫斯

如果白宫对于副总统拜登在医保方面的发言感到遗憾的话……

美国副总统　乔•拜登

这件事真他 X 的了不起。

CNN 特派员　吉妮•莫斯

他们就是装作不知情。白宫新闻秘书吉布斯就曾在推特页面中写道：“是的，副总统，您说得对。”

副总统的失态实在是要命的一件大事，在他此话脱口而出后的两小时内，他的话立刻被印在 T 恤上。真正以辛辣语言著称的人是白宫幕僚长拉姆•伊曼纽尔，他在接受《六十分钟》访问时拒绝谈论总统的事。

白宫幕僚长　拉姆•伊曼纽尔

但是我在白宫总统办公室里不会飙脏话。

Notes & Vocabulary

15. you-know-what [ˋjuˋnoˋwɑt]
n. 那个；那样（代替不便明说的字眼，人、物或动作）

16. remark [rɪˋmɑrk]
n. 评论

17. let on
表露出来；表现出来自己知道某事
Stanley let on that he may be looking for a new job.

18. tweet [twit]
v. 发送推特信息；（小鸟）吱啾叫
Ben tweeted that he had just seen a famous actor on the street.

19. faux pas 失态；失言
The diplomat caused a faux pas when he didn't bow to the Japanese prime minister.

20. frigging [ˋfrɪgɪŋ]
adj. 该死的；非常的（强调语气，口语多作 friggin'）

21. utterance [ˋʌtərəns]
n. 说话

22. emblazon [ɪmˋblezn̩]
v.（用图案或文字醒目地）装饰
The monument is emblazoned with the names of several national heroes.

23. salty [ˋsɔltɪ]
adj. 有趣而略嫌粗俗的
Richard is known for using salty language around his peers.

KATIE COURIC, 60 MINUTES HOST

Does he curse?

JEANNE MOOS, CNN CORRESPONDENT

On a day of triumph, once again, the curse of Biden strikes,[24] in the form of[25] an actual curse.

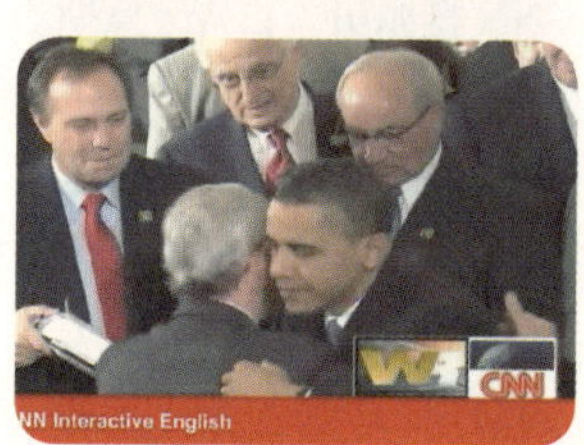

JOE BIDEN, VICE PRESIDENT OF THE UNITED STATES

This is a big (expletive language) deal.

BARACK OBAMA, PRESIDENT OF THE UNITED STATES

Thank you, Joe.

03-F.MP3 / 03-S.MP3 | *The Curse of Joe Biden*

《六十分钟》主持人　凯蒂·库瑞克

他会飙脏话吗？

CNN 特派员　吉妮·莫斯

在赢得胜利的一天中，拜登的辛辣脏话又来了。

美国副总统　乔·拜登

这件事真他 X 的了不起。

美国总统　巴拉克·奥巴马

谢谢你，乔。

Notes & Vocabulary

24. strike [straɪk] *v.* 开始
The thieves struck again last night when they broke into a jewelry shop.

25. in the form of 以……的形式
The transaction was carried out in the form of a trade.

美国全民医保概况

过去美国并没有全民医保机制，官商并存的医疗保险制度成本（costs）相当高，导致投保人数覆盖率（coverage）偏低，资金也严重不足。民众一旦生病，医疗费用往往成为沉重的经济负担，而病人若无力支付医疗费，医院会将部分欠款转嫁到政府身上，又增加美国财政赤字（deficit）。为减少个人和政府的医疗支出，奥巴马推动的医保改革案目标包括（1）提供医疗保险给未投保者，不足者提高投保层级；（2）要求民间保险机构减少限制；（3）强迫企业主为员工投保。但如今美国背负着庞大的财政压力，外界对政府如何执行医保改革方案持怀疑态度。不过，对中下阶层的民众来说，他们的医疗资源与品质将更有保障。

名流轶事 ④ 怀念小布什总统的胡言乱语

Goodbye to Bushisms

图片提供：Reuters 达志

Linguists[1] Bid Farewell to the Former President's Unique Turns of Phrase

CNN ANCHOR

Well, don't underestimate[2] U.S. president George W. Bush. He will be remembered for many things, including his rather unique grasp[3] of English grammar and pronunciation—or misunderestimate, as he might say. A group that monitors[4] language has compiled[5] a list of some quotable quotes,[6] which they call "Bushisms," and Josh Levs helps us take a look at that.

GEORGE W. BUSH, FORMER U.S. PRESIDENT

I hear the voices.

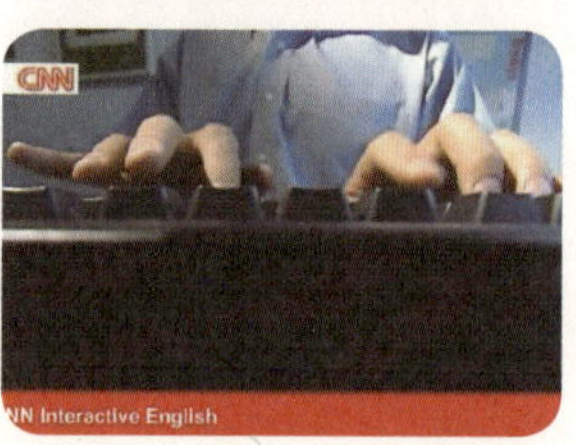

04-F.MP3
04-S.MP3

CNN 主播
可别低估了美国总统小布什。他有许多言行必然会长存在后人的记忆里，包括他对英语语法及发音的独特掌握方式——或者就像他说的，别错误低估了他。一个观察语言的团体汇整了若干名言，称之为“布什语录”。乔许•列弗斯带我们来看一看。

前美国总统　小布什
我听到了那些声音。

Notes & Vocabulary

标题扫描

a turn of phrase 说话方式

turn 有“性情；素质”、“行为；举止”等意思，这里指语言的“特色；措词”。a turn of phrase 可指一个人“说话的方式”或“良好的表达能力”。

- The poet was known for his clever turns of phrase.
那位诗人以其慧黠的措词著称。

misunderestimate

小布什最有名的自创词之一，起源不可考，一般认为是 misunderstand “误解；不了解”加上 underestimate “低估”，指“误解且低估；严重低估”。例如他在得克萨斯州竞选时说过“They misunderestimated me.”。在告别记者会上，小布什又对记者们说了“Sometimes you misunderestimated me.”，以此幽自己一默。

1. linguist [ˋlɪŋgwɪst] *n.* 语言学家
2. underestimate [ˏʌndɚˋɛstəmet] *v.* 低估；估计太少
Dan underestimated his sister's strength.
3. grasp [græsp] *n.* 理解；领会；掌控
4. monitor [ˋmɑnətɚ] *v.* 监测；监控
U.N. observers monitored the election.
5. compile [kəmˋpaɪl] *v.* 汇编；汇整
Randall compiled a list of his strengths and weaknesses.
6. quote [kwot] *n.* 引用；引述

名流轶事
非常体验
生活咀嚼
天地之间

JOSH LEVS, CNN CORRESPONDENT

There are plenty to choose from, whether on his job description . . .

GEORGE W. BUSH, FORMER U.S. PRESIDENT

I'm the decider.

JOSH LEVS, CNN CORRESPONDENT

. . . or his computer-savvy[7] . . .

GEORGE W. BUSH, FORMER U.S. PRESIDENT

I hear there's rumors on the Internets.

One of the things I used on the Google is to pull up[8] maps.

JOSH LEVS, CNN CORRESPONDENT

. . . or his thoughts on education.

GEORGE W. BUSH, FORMER U.S. PRESIDENT

Rarely is the question asked: Is our children learning?

JOSH LEVS, CNN CORRESPONDENT

That was President Bush making fun of one of his own unique turns of phrase. Of all the so-called Bushisms, which is number one? The Global Language Monitor, which studies trends in the English language, tracked how often some different quotes showed up in the media and on blogs.

At number three, a remark[9] about a man widely blamed for part of the government's failure during Hurricane Katrina.

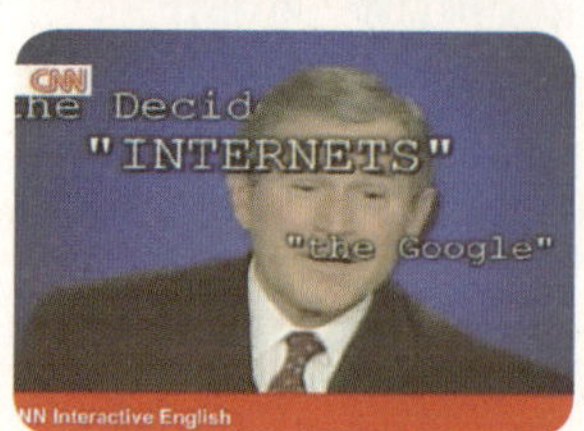

CNN 特派员　乔许•列弗斯
有许多名言任你挑选，像是他说明自己工作状况的描述……

美国前总统　小布什
我是决定人。

CNN 特派员　乔许•列弗斯
……或是他对计算机的理解。

美国前总统　小布什
我听说网络上有各种谣言。

我在谷歌上用过的一个功能是提取地图。

CNN 特派员　乔许•列弗斯
……或是他对教育的看法。

美国前总统　小布什
很少有人提这个问题：我们的孩子在学习吗?

CNN 特派员　乔许•列弗斯
这是布什总统要着自己独特的词句排列方式。在这些所谓的布什语录里，哪一句排名第一呢？研究英语演变趋势的全球语言观察组织，追踪了各项语录在媒体与博客里出现的情形。

名列第三的语录，是他针对一个人所说的话。一般认为这个人必须为政府在卡特里娜飓风期间的拙劣表现负起部分责任。

Notes & Vocabulary

更正

decider
正确的用词应是 decision maker “决策者”。decider 在语法上并没有错，但现在是指“定输赢的事物”，如运动赛事中的“决胜球；决胜局”。

there's rumors on the Internets
rumors是复数，there's 应该改成 there're。Internet “网络” 没有复数形式。

the Google
专有名词一般来说前面不需加（定）冠词 a 或 the，Google 就是 Google，没有这个、那个之分吧！

Is our children learning
children 是复数，Is 应该改成 Are。讽刺的是，小布什当时正在谈教育问题，而他身为总统却会犯这么基本的语法错误，显示美国教育真的需要检讨。

7. **-savvy** [ˋsævɪ] *sufx.* 有……知识的
Julia is the most media-savvy associate at the law firm.
8. **pull up** [pul] [ʌp] 提取出资料
The police officer pulled up Dave's driving record.
9. **remark** [rɪˋmɑrk]
n. 评论；言论

GEORGE W. BUSH, FORMER U.S. PRESIDENT

And, Brownie, you're doin' a heck of a job.

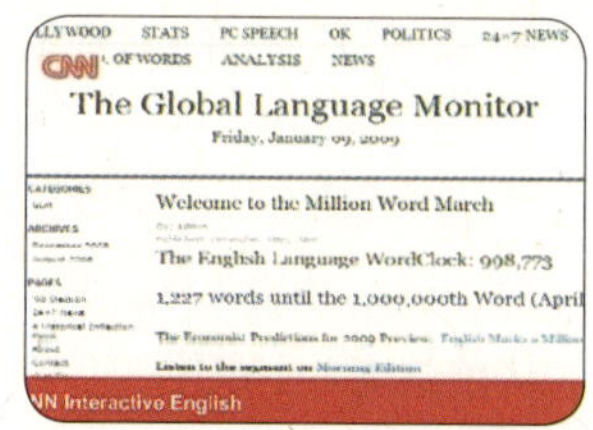

JOSH LEVS, CNN CORRESPONDENT

Number two is something the president didn't actually say—the "mission accomplished" banner that flew behind him when he was declaring[10] the end of major combat in Iraq. The president recently told CNN he regrets it.

GEORGE W. BUSH, FORMER U.S. PRESIDENT

To some it said, well, Bush thinks the war in Iraq is over, when I didn't think that.

JOSH LEVS, CNN CORRESPONDENT

The most quoted Bushism of all time? Misunderestimate, which the president tried to stop saying.

GEORGE W. BUSH, FORMER U.S. PRESIDENT

Those who think that they can say we're only going to have a stimulus[11] package,[12] but let's forget tax relief, misunderestimate . . . or, excuse me, underestimate.

JOSH LEVS, CNN CORRESPONDENT

Not everything made the Global Language Monitor's list. There are other gems,[13] including peeance freeance, a cult[14] favorite online.

美国前总统　小布什

还有，布朗尼，你真是干得好呀。

CNN 特派员　乔许·列弗斯

第二名其实不是总统嘴巴里说出来的话，而是他宣布伊拉克主要战事已经结束的时候，在他背后飘扬着的“任务完成”布条。布什总统近来向 CNN 表示他对此颇感后悔。

美国前总统　小布什

有些人认为那幅布条表示布什认为伊拉克战争已经结束了，可是我其实没有那样想。

CNN 特派员　乔许·列弗斯

至于人们引用最多的布什语录，究竟是哪一句呢？就是“错误低估”这句话，但当时总统其实改口了。

美国前总统　小布什

认为我们只打算提出刺激经济方案的那些人，大家把减轻赋税忘了，错误低估了……呃，抱歉，是低估。

CNN 特派员　乔许·列弗斯

不是每一句奇言都收进了全球语言观察组织的语录里。还有些遗珠，包括“和之平、自之由”这句网友的最爱。

Notes & Vocabulary

a heck of

非常；极；很

heck 在口语中用来作为 hell 的委婉语，在表示惊吓、咒骂、恼怒、厌烦等感叹句中加强语气。a heck of 也是口语用法，是“非常；实在很”的意思。

- What the heck are you doing?
  你到底在干什么啊！
- It took a heck of a long time for Nadia to locate a person to talk to after calling the customer service line.
  娜迪亚打电话到客服专线，搞了很久很久才有人接听。

10. declare [dɪ`klɛr] *v.* 宣布；宣告
    Holly declared her love for donuts.
11. stimulus [`stɪmjələs]
    n. 刺激；刺激物
12. package [`pækɪdʒ]
    n. 套组；配套措施
13. gem [dʒɛm] *n.* 珍品；宝物
14. cult [kʌlt] *n.* 狂热；崇拜

GEORGE W. BUSH, FORMER U.S. PRESIDENT

A free and secure and peaceful Iraq. A peeance, freeance, secure Iraq.

JOSH LEVS, CNN CORRESPONDENT

While he's taken ribbing[15] and criticism for his linguistic gaffes,[16] the president has joked about them, like comparing himself to California governor Arnold Schwarzenegger.

GEORGE W. BUSH, FORMER U.S. PRESIDENT

We both have trouble with the English language.

JOSH LEVS, CNN CORRESPONDENT

Mr. Bush will remain one of the most prominent[17] figures in America, but with the end of his presidency, the Global Language Monitor says it's time to declare an end to the era of Bushisms.

美国前总统　小布什
一个自由、安全、和平的伊拉克。一个和之平、自之由、又安全的伊拉克。

CNN 特派员　乔许 • 列弗斯
布什总统虽然因为自己在言语上屡出洋相而备受嘲讽批评，他却也会自我解嘲，例如把自己比拟为加利福尼亚州州长阿诺 • 史瓦辛格。

美国前总统　小布什
我们两人的英语都不太好。

CNN 特派员　乔许 • 列弗斯
布什先生仍将会是美国最引人注目的人物之一。不过，全球语言观察组织表示，随着他的总统任期结束，布什语录的时代也该告一段落了。

Notes & Vocabulary

peeance, freeance

peeance 和 freeance 应该就是指前一句中的 peaceful 和 free 。小布什原本可能是想讲 peaceful and free and secure ，把“和平的、自由的”移到前面做强调，结果却把各音节混在一起了。

15. ribbing [ˋrɪbɪŋ]
n.【俚】戏弄

16. gaffe [gæf]
n.（社交、外交场合）失态；失礼

17. prominent [ˋprɑmənənt]
adj. 著名的；显著的
Ralph is a prominent figure in the local theater community.

名流轶事 ⑤ 是天生？是故意？奥巴马签名怪姿成话题

Obama's Most Unusual Signature

Left-Handed President Puts Pen to Paper from a Different Angle

图片提供：Reuters

WOLF BLITZER, THE SITUATION ROOM

If you watched that bill signing ceremony yesterday, you may have noticed that President Obama has a most unusual signature. Jeanne Moos tells us why.

JEANNE MOOS, CNN CORRESPONDENT

It's not just what he signs, but how he signs it.

UNIDENTIFIED MALE

That contorted[1] . . . whatever.

UNIDENTIFIED MALE

He's got the curve,[2] the hand over.

JEANNE MOOS, CNN CORRESPONDENT

He goes like this.

05-F.MP3
05-S.MP3

《现场直播室》 沃夫·布利兹
如果您看了昨天的法案签署仪式，您可能已经注意到奥巴马总统的签名相当不寻常。吉妮·莫斯要告诉我们原因。

CNN 特派员 吉妮·莫斯
不只是他签署的内容，而是他签署的方式。

不具名男子
算是……扭曲吧。

不具名女子
他弯着手腕，手是绕过来的。

CNN 特派员 吉妮·莫斯
他像这个样子签名。

Notes & Vocabulary

标题扫描

put pen to paper

写下

字面上是“把笔放到纸上”，也就是“用笔写下；记下来”，有中文中强调的“以白纸黑字记下来”的意思。标题说奥巴马 puts pen to paper from a different angle，一方面指他签名的手势角度特别，一方面指他制订振兴经济法案思考的角度。

- The two parties put pen to paper and signed the contract.
  双方白纸黑字签订了合约。

1. contort [kən`tɔrt] *v.* 扭曲
   The stomachache left Tina contorted with pain.
2. curve [kɜv] *n.* 弧线；弯曲部分

UNIDENTIFIED MALE

And he really curls.[3]

JEANNE MOOS, CNN CORRESPONDENT

And if it curls your toes, well, you're obviously not a lefty.[4] Lefties for Obama love having one of their own in the White House, but President Obama's signature style is a bit more hooked than that of most lefties.

UNIDENTIFIED FEMALE

He never learned how to hold his pen and he looks like Joe Cocker.

JEANNE MOOS, CNN CORRESPONDENT

But lefties have an explanation.

UNIDENTIFIED MALE

I think it's because he doesn't want to smudge[5] the ink, because when . . . if you go like that, then you're not gonna run over your signature.

DR. SAMUAL WANG, NEUROSCIENCE PROFESSOR, PRINCETON UNIVERSITY

It would be kind of embarrassing to sign a nearly $800 billion stimulus[6] bill and then smear[7] the ink.

JEANNE MOOS, CNN CORRESPONDENT

Neuroscience[8] professor and author Sam Wang say[s] righties[9] only use one side of their brain to process language. But lefties . . .

不具名女子
他的手弯得很厉害。

CNN 特派员　吉妮·莫斯
如果这对你来说很困难，那你显然不是个左撇子。支持奥巴马的左撇子喜欢有左撇子入主白宫，但奥巴马总统的签名姿势比大多数左撇子的签名姿势还要扭曲。

不具名女子
他没学过怎么握笔，他看起来好像乔·库克弹吉他的时候。

CNN 特派员　吉妮·莫斯
但是左撇子对此提出了解释。

不具名女子
我想是因为他不想抹到墨水，因为当你……如果你这样签的话，手就不会碰到你的签名。

普林斯顿大学神经学教授　王山姆医师
如果签署一份价值近 8000 亿美元的经济振兴法案，还把墨水弄糊，就真有点让人觉得难为情。

CNN 特派员　吉妮·莫斯
神经学教授兼作家王山姆表示，惯用右手的人只会用一边的大脑来处理语言。但是惯用左手的人……

Notes & Vocabulary

curl one's toes

使尴尬；使为难

字面上是“使某人的脚趾卷起”的意思，比喻某事物“让人感到尴尬；使人为难；令人生怯”，也可写成 make one's toes curl 。

- The scent of stinky tofu curls Wendy's toes.
  臭豆腐的味道让温迪退避三舍。

3. curl [kɜl] *v.* 卷曲；卷起
   The kitty curled into a ball on the pillow.
4. lefty [ˋlɛftɪ] *n.* 左撇子
5. smudge [smʌdʒ]
   v. 弄脏；涂污
   Jenny accidentally smudged the ink on her drawing.
6. stimulus [ˋstɪmjələs]
   n. 刺激；刺激物
7. smear [smɪr] *v.* 擦抹
   The rain smeared Claire's makeup.
8. neuroscience [ˏnuroəˋsaɪəns]
   n.【医】神经科学
9. righty [ˋraɪtɪ] *n.* 右撇子

DR. SAMUAL WANG, NEUROSCIENCE PROFESSOR, PRINCETON UNIVERSITY

One in seven lefties showed activity in both sides of the brain.

JEANNE MOOS, CNN CORRESPONDENT

Six of the past 12 presidents have been lefties, including presidents Clinton and George Bush, Sr.

But before you lefties start gloating[10] about having higher SAT scores . . .

DR. SAMUAL WANG, NEUROSCIENCE PROFESSOR, PRINCETON UNIVERSITY

They are also overrepresented[11] among criminals and among the mentally retarded.[12]

JEANNE MOOS, CNN CORRESPONDENT

His FBI profile[13] says Osama bin Laden is a lefty.

Maybe you're left wondering, "How many pens does it take to sign a bill?"

BARACK H. OBAMA, PRESIDENT OF THE UNITED STATES

I've got to use 10 pens.

JEANNE MOOS, CNN CORRESPONDENT

The president often signs his signature in bits so he can use more pens, which he then hands out as souvenirs.[14]

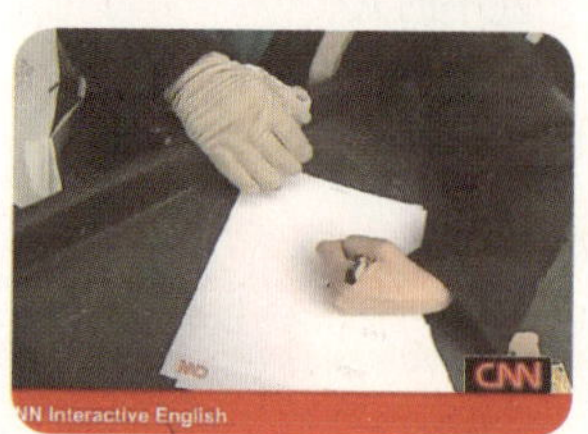

UNIDENTIFIED MALE

I want the guy to be a success. I don't care if he writes with his foot.

普林斯顿大学神经学教授　王山姆医师
每七个左撇子中就有一人两边的脑子会同时活动。

CNN 特派员　吉妮 • 莫斯
过去十二任美国总统中，就有六人是左撇子，包括克林顿和老布什。

但是你们这些左撇子先别为自己较高的 SAT 分数洋洋得意……

普林斯顿大学神经学教授　王山姆医师
罪犯和弱智的人里也明显绝大多数是左撇子。

CNN 特派员　吉妮 • 莫斯
王教授的联邦调查局档案资料中显示，本 • 拉登就是个左撇子。

也许您会想知道：签署一份法案需要用几支笔？

美国总统　巴拉克 • 奥巴马
我得用 10 支笔。

CNN 特派员　吉妮 • 莫斯
总统经常分段式地签名，以便能用上更多支笔，接着他会将笔交出作为纪念品。

不具名男子
我希望他是个成功的总统。就算他用脚写字我也不在乎。

Notes & Vocabulary

10. **gloat** [ˋglot] *v.* 洋洋得意；心满意足
The child gloated when he won the game.

11. **overrepresented**
[ˏovɚˋrɛprɪzɛntəd]
adj.【统】过度表现的；明显超过的
Women were overrepresented at the first meeting of the cooking club.

12. **retarded** [ˋrɪtɑrdəd]
adj. 弱智的
Most people prefer the term "developmentally disabled" for what was once classified as a retarded individual.

13. **profile** [ˋprofaɪl]
n. 简介；个人档案

14. **souvenir** [ˋsuvəˏnɪr] *n.* 纪念品

JEANNE MOOS, CNN CORRESPONDENT

But lefties worried about a twist in the president's wrist have some advice for him.

UNIDENTIFIED FEMALE

Turn the paper. Turn the paper, not your wrist.

JEANNE MOOS, CNN CORRESPONDENT

These days . . .

Which hand do you use?

OK. Now let's see . . .

JEANNE MOOS, CNN CORRESPONDENT

Lefties like Eve don't get much flak from teachers, but 40 or 50 years ago?

UNIDENTIFIED MALE

They had me bring in a tie of my father's, and I used to have to sit in school with my left hand tied to my leg.

JEANNE MOOS, CNN CORRESPONDENT

Now that sounds like the kind of torture[15] a lefty president should outlaw[16] by signing a bill.

BARACK H. OBAMA, PRESIDENT OF THE UNITED STATES

There you go.

CNN 特派员　吉妮·莫斯
但是那些担心总统的手腕会扭到的左撇子想给总统一些忠告。

不具名女子
把纸转个方向，转纸，不是转手腕。

CNN 特派员　吉妮·莫斯
如今……

你惯用哪只手？

好，咱们来瞧瞧……

CNN 特派员　吉妮·莫斯
和伊娃一样的左撇子不会挨老师太多的骂，但四五十年前呢？

不具名男子
老师要我带一条我父亲的领带到学校，以前我在学校坐着的时候，左手都是和我的脚绑在一起。

CNN 特派员　吉妮·莫斯
这听起来像是一个左撇子总统应该通过签署法案将其列为非法的酷刑。

美国总统　巴拉克·奥巴马
签好了。

Notes & Vocabulary

get flak

被责骂；被炮轰

flak 原本是"高射炮；高射炮弹"的意思，引申为"抨击；责骂"，口语用 get flak 表示"被责骂；被猛烈抨击"，类似中文说的"被炮轰"，也可写为 take flak 。

- Kevin got flak for forgetting his girlfriend's birthday.
  凯文因为忘记他女友的生日而遭骂。

15. torture [ˋtɔrtʃɚ]
n. 折磨；酷刑

16. outlaw [ˋaut͵lɔ]
v. 宣布为非法
The government outlawed unlicensed preschools.

名流轶事 ⑥ 揭开好莱坞名人浮滥用药的秘密

High in Hollywood

Celebrity Addicts[1] Face Unique Temptations[2] and Challenges

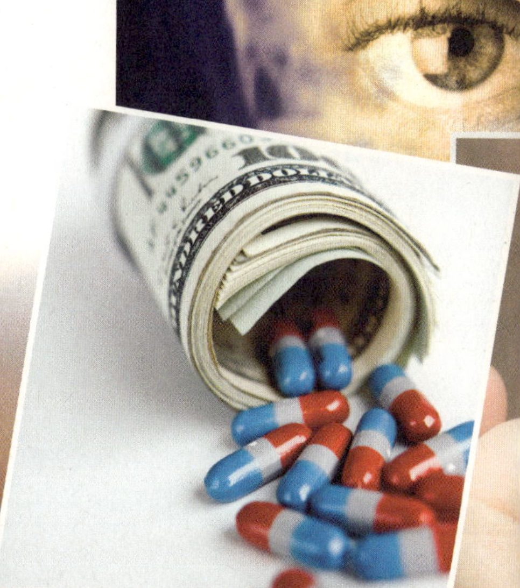

图片提供：Rob & Jules、Howie Berlin、Georges Biard

ANNA COREN, CNN ANCHOR

Well, we've heard over the last few weeks about celebrities who've died as a result of taking prescription[3] medication in an overdose[4] amount. And the ugly truth is celebrity culture and the kind of power celebrities have means that stars can get their hands on[5] any substance[6] they desire. And usually it seems perfectly legal until some of them end up dead. Kareen Wynter has that story.

KAREEN WYNTER, CNN CORRESPONDENT

Heath Ledger, Michael Jackson, Corey Haim, Anna Nicole Smith—their deaths raised questions about one of Hollywood's dirty little secrets: prescription drug abuse[7] that in recent months has dominated[8] the headlines.

06-F.MP3
06-S.MP3

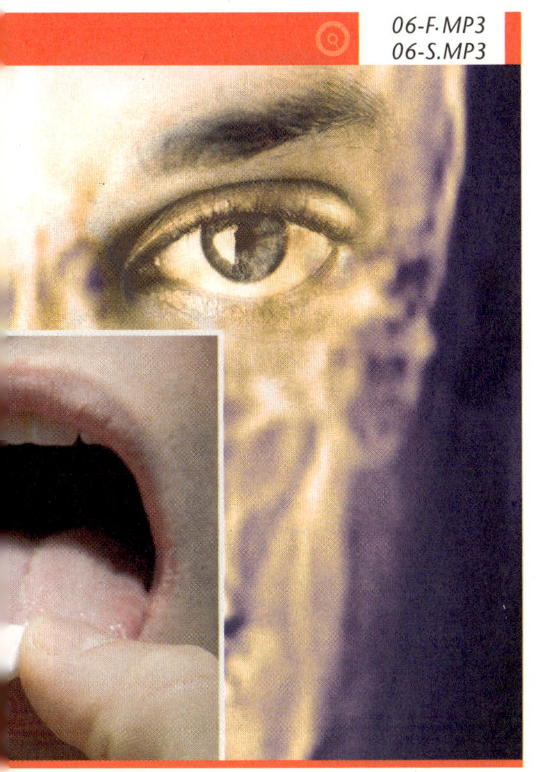

CNN 主播　安娜・可伦

过去几周来，我们听到许多名人因使用处方药物过量而死亡的消息。丑陋的真相是，由于名人文化及名人的权势，明星不论想要什么药品都能够获得。而且通常表面上他们获得的方式看起来完全合法，一直到有人送命，问题才会爆发出来。请看凯琳・温特的报道。

CNN 特派员　凯琳・温特

希斯・莱杰、迈克尔・杰克逊、科里・汉姆、安娜・妮可・史密斯——这些人的死亡引起众人质疑好莱坞不足为外人道的秘密：也就是近几个月来，一再登上新闻头条的处方药物滥用现象。

Notes & Vocabulary

1. addict [ˋædɪkt]
   n. 上瘾者；入迷的人
2. temptation [tɛmpˋteʃən]
   n. 引诱；诱惑
3. prescription [prɪsˋkrɪpʃən]
   n. 处方签；药方
4. overdose [ˋovɚˏdos]
   n. 用药过量；剂量过重
5. get one's hands on
   得到；取得
   Randy got his hands on a rare baseball card at the estate auction.
6. substance [ˋsʌbstəns]
   n. 物质；药物
7. abuse [əˋbjus]
   n. 滥用；不当使用（药物、权力等）
8. dominate [ˋdɑməˏnet]
   v. 支配；控制；主宰
   Celebrity scandals seem to dominate the news.

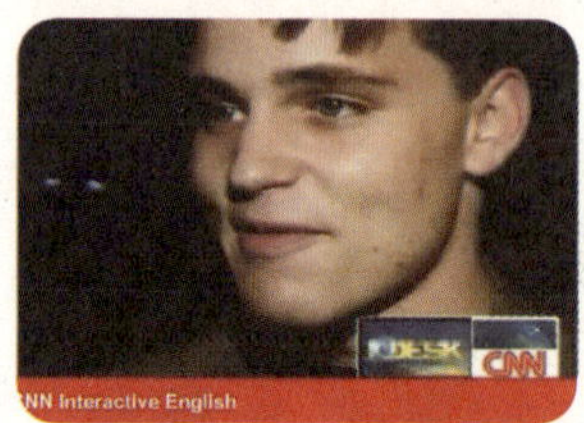

UNIDENTIFIED FEMALE

Two doctors charged with conspiring[9] to furnish[10] Anna . . .

KAREEN WYNTER, CNN CORRESPONDENT

Smith's doctors pleaded[11] not guilty to charges of conspiring to supply her with controlled substances. At the time of her death, at least four different sedatives[12] were found in her system, including Klonopin and Valium, drugs made readily available to celebrities, says actress Mackenzie Phillips.

Is it as easy as just picking up the phone, saying I need that prescription, I need that medication?

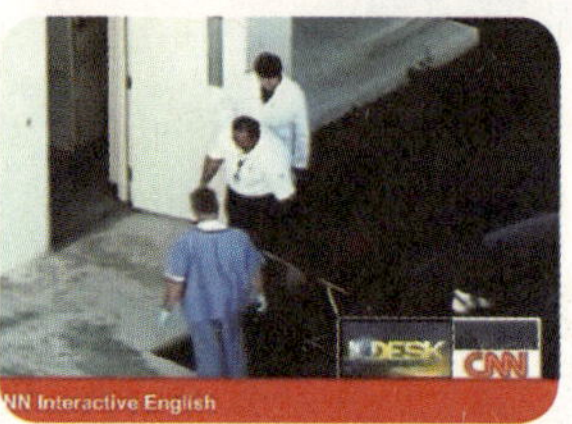

MACKENZIE PHILLIPS, ACTRESS

Well, I mean, I've been to doctors who'd never even touched my body or took my blood pressure, and I walked out with a prescription for 130, you know, hydrocodone tablets.[13] I mean, yeah, I guess it's easier for famous people.

KAREEN WYNTER, CNN CORRESPONDENT

A teen star and the daughter of a famous musician, Phillips writes in her book *High on Arrival* about her long-time battle with drug addiction and how some doctors willingly over-prescribed[14] pills despite her history as an addict. She says she's been clean for a year and a half now.

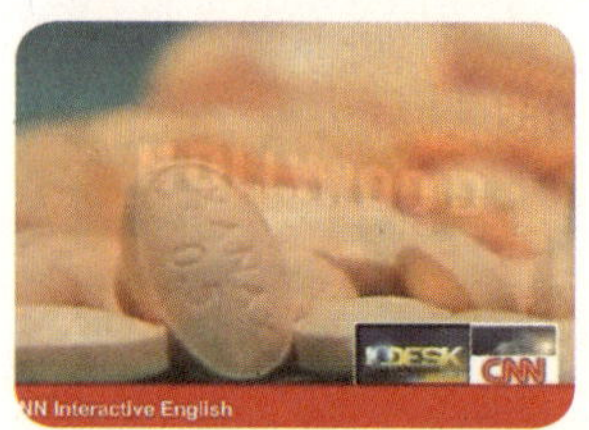

~~There's~~ [There are] some doctors out there, many doctors perhaps, who may be enamored[15] by a star, and they're just trying to please their client. But, come on, you have to have stars on the other end who may be using their fame to get these drugs.

匿名女子
两名医生被控共谋为安娜……

CNN 特派员　凯琳·温特
针对预谋为史密斯提供管制药品的罪名，她的医生提出不认罪的抗辩。她死亡时体内至少有四种不同的镇静剂，包括氯硝西泮与安定等。女演员麦坎西·菲立普斯说，名人可轻易获得这类药物。

有这么简单吗？只要拿起电话，说我需要这份处方笺，我需要这种药物就可以了？

女演员　麦坎西·菲立普斯
我是说……我找过一些医生，他们根本连碰都不必碰我的身体，或帮我量血压，我就能取得 130 颗氢可酮药片的处方笺了。没错，我猜名人会比较容易获得吧。

CNN 特派员　凯琳·温特
菲立普斯在少女时期曾是明星，父亲是著名音乐人，她在《期待到来》这本书里讲述了自己长期对抗毒瘾的经验，也提到自己虽有毒瘾记录，有些医生却还是愿意开立过多药物给她。她说她已有一年半没碰过毒品了。

有些医生，可能为数还不少，他们可能会受到明星的光芒迷惑，他们会只想着讨好客户。但是，拜托，这还得看另一头的明星们，他们可能会利用自己的名气获得这些药物。

Notes & Vocabulary

9. conspire [kən`spaɪr]
v. 密谋；策划；合力促成
The diplomat conspired to sell state secrets.

10. furnish [`fɜnɪʃ] v. 提供；供应
Ted's company furnishes him with a car and driver.

11. plead [plid]
v. 辩护；答辩（过去式 pleaded 或 pled）
The suspect pled guilty to stealing the money.

12. sedative [`sɛdətɪv] n. 镇静剂

13. tablet [`tæblət] n. 药片

14. prescribe [prɪ`skraɪb]
v. 开药；规定；指定医嘱
The doctor prescribed medicine for Tracy's severe headaches.

15. enamor [ɪ`næmɚ]
v. 使迷惑；使倾倒
Kelly is enamored with the attention she gets when singing.

MACKENZIE PHILLIPS, ACTRESS

Well, I'm sure that that is definitely something that helps them to get the doctor to give them whatever they want. And I know I've been in that position myself.

KAREEN WYNTER, CNN CORRESPONDENT

Addiction specialist[16] Dr. Drew Pinsky has worked with stars like Phillips and says the power of celebrity addicts can present unique challenges for doctors.

DR. DREW PINSKY, ADDICTION SPECIALIST

I tell my peers[17] that are trying to take care of celebrities, do not go there alone. You must have a team. It's too seductive.[18] Addiction is too powerful. You will get sucked right into it.

KAREEN WYNTER, CNN CORRESPONDENT

How does it work? You have a celebrity with so much power, and they want to get their hands on this drug. They're addicts.

DR. DREW PINSKY, ADDICTION SPECIALIST

They may not be consciously thinking that way. It's not like, "I've got to get my Vicodin." They're thinking, "I hear Dr. Smith is pretty good." Translated—"gives lots of good medication." So they go see Dr. Smith, and they offer Dr. Smith a lot of money, and they tell Dr. Smith, "You are the best doctor. You made me feel so great. I'm gonna tell . . . I have lots of important friends. I'm gonna tell them all how great you are, and I'm gonna pay you a lot of money." That patient starts getting out of control with their medicine.

女演员　麦坎西·菲立普斯

我敢说名气确实有助于他们说服医生开立他们想要的药物。我知道，我自己也曾是那样的人。

CNN 特派员　凯琳·温特

成瘾问题专家德鲁·平斯基医师曾治疗过像菲立普斯这样的明星，他说名人成瘾患者对医生可能会是一种独特的挑战。

成瘾问题专家　德鲁·平斯基医师

我会对想治疗名人的同事们说，不要单独去会诊，一定要有一整组人，不然诱惑力太大了。成瘾的力量非常强大，你会被吸进去的。

CNN 特派员　凯琳·温特

这是怎么回事呢？名人有权有势，而且想得到这种药物，因为他们是成瘾患者。

成瘾问题专家　德鲁·平斯基医师

他们也许不是刻意要这么做。他们并不是想着："我一定要拿到维柯丁。"而是想着："听说史密斯医生很好。"意思就是，"他会开很多好药给病患。"于是他们会去找史密斯医生，给史密斯医生很多钱，跟史密斯医生说："你是最好的医生，你让我觉得好多了。我要告诉……我有很多显赫的朋友，我要告诉他们你有多棒，而且我会付你很多钱。"然后该病患在药物方面就这么失控了。

Notes & Vocabulary

16. specialist [ˋspɛʃəlɪst]
n. 专家；专业人士

17. peer [pɪr] *n.* 同僚；同事；同辈

18. seductive [sɪˋdʌktɪv]
adj. 诱惑人的；有吸引力的
The chance at brief fame can be seductive to many would-be reality television stars.

名流轶事

非常体验

生活咀嚼

天地之间

JERRY BROWN, CALIFORNIA ATTORNEY GENERAL

When you get the high anxiety[19] that celebrity. . . temporary as it is, that then feeds the addictive[20] propensity,[21] and then on top of that,[22] if someone is a celebrity, then these obscure[23] doctors get a bit of a contact high, if I can call it that, by prescribing and being in part of the mix.

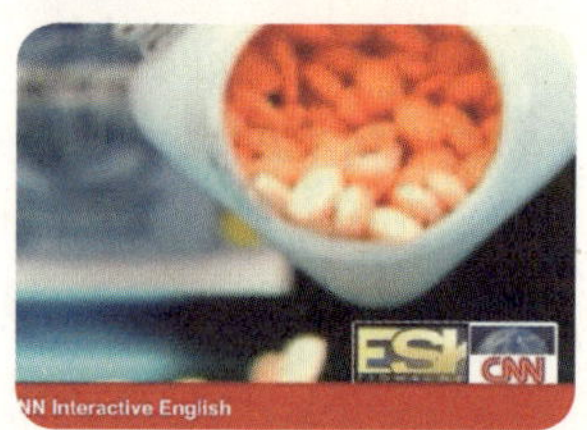

KAREEN WYNTER, CNN CORRESPONDENT

California's attorney general,[24] Jerry Brown, says it's a problem that goes beyond Tinseltown. His office has launched investigations into more than 200 prescription drug cases involving addict patients and physicians[25] who help them cross the line—an underground drug world Mackenzie Phillips says she's glad she's left behind and cautions[26]. . .

MACKENZIE PHILLIPS, ACTRESS

We've become this society that just take . . . I'm sad, take a pill. I'm in pain, take a pill. Take a pill, take a pill. And really, it's just so . . . it's just so dangerous. People are dying.

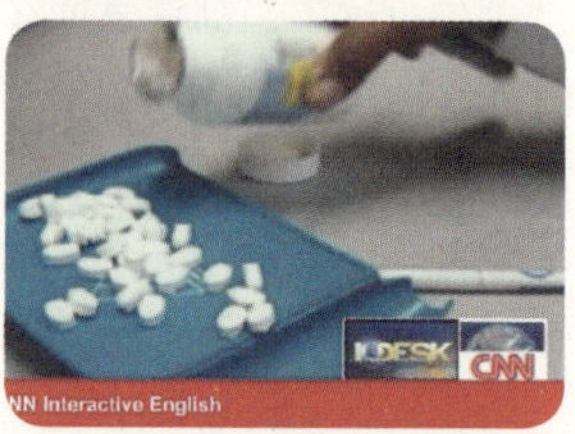

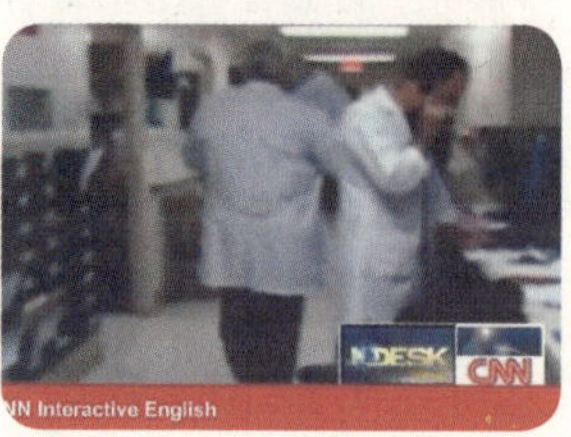

加利福尼亚州首席检察官　杰瑞・布朗

如果你高度焦虑，像名人那样……虽然是暂时性的，还是会把上瘾的倾向愈养愈大。此外，一旦遇到名人，有些默默无闻的医生因为接触到名人而冲昏了头，我会说那是接触性的快感，因为能替他们开药、成为事件的一部分。

CNN 特派员　凯琳・温特

加利福尼亚州检察总长杰瑞・布朗表示，这个问题不仅见于绚丽浮华的好莱坞。他的办公室已针对两百多起案件展开调查，都是医生帮成瘾病患开立处方药物，协助他们跨越了地下药瘾世界的界线。麦坎西・菲立普斯说，她很高兴自己已远离了那个世界，也要告诫社会大众……

女演员　麦坎西・菲立普斯

我们的社会已经变成就去吃……我心情难过，吃颗药吧；我哪里痛，吃颗药吧；吃颗药吧，吃颗药吧。这种行为实在……实在很危险。已经有很多人因此丧命了。

Notes & Vocabulary

contact high 接触性的快感

原本是指因接近嗑药的人，间接吸入、接触到药物而产生和嗑药者相似的兴奋反应。另外也可表示虽然没有用药，但因为心理因素而不自觉被影响，产生如用药般的快感。文中是指医生被名人的名气、光环诱惑而乐于为他们开药，但却可能疏于监督用药安全。

Tinseltown 好莱坞／浮华城

tinsel [`tɪnsl̩] 指“金丝；金箔”，常引申指“华而不实的东西”。加利福尼亚州好莱坞有许多明星聚集于此，因此有了 Tinseltown“浮华城”这个别称，表示这里是个光鲜绚丽、五光十色的“花花世界”。

19. anxiety [æŋ`zaɪətɪ] *n.* 焦虑；渴望

20. addictive [ə`dɪktɪv]
adj. 使成瘾的；上瘾的
Many prescription drugs can be addictive.

21. propensity [prə`pɛnsətɪ]
n. 癖好；倾向；偏爱

22. on top of sth. 除……之外
On top of losing his house, James lost his car and cash in the fire.

23. obscure [əb`skjʊr]
adj. 没名气的；不出色的
Carl is a fan of an obscure Japanese pop group.

24. attorney general
[ə`tɜnɪ] [`dʒɛnərəl] *n.* 首席检察官

25. physician [fɪ`zɪʃən]
n. 医师；治疗者

26. caution [`kɔʃən] *v.* 告诫；警告
The government cautions against traveling in some remote areas because of safety issues.

近年来用药不当致死的好莱坞明星

安娜·妮可·史密斯 Anna Nicole Smith ／演员

2007 年 2 月 8 日过量使用安眠药，混用过敏药、抗癫痫头痛药、镇静剂导致药物中毒。

汉姆·柯里 Corey Haim ／演员

2010 年 3 月 10 日疑因感冒混用过量止痛剂、镇静剂、肌肉松弛剂，解剖后判定死因为肺炎（pneumonia）。

希斯·莱杰 Heath Ledger ／演员

2008 年 1 月 22 日过量混用多种麻醉止痛剂、镇静剂、安眠药、抗组织胺剂等导致药物中毒。

布兰妮·墨菲 Brittany Murphy ／演员

2009 年 12 月 20 日混用兴奋剂、麻醉止痛剂、镇静剂导致心脏衰竭。

麦可·杰克森 Michael Jackson ／歌手

2009 年 1 月 25 日注射 Propofol“异丙酚”及服用其他镇静剂，加上长期使用止痛剂、安眠药，导致心脏衰竭。

图片提供：Howie Berlin 、Rob & Jules 、Georges Biard

药物小辞典

Klonopin 氯硝西泮

药品名称：美国罗氏制药（Roche）的产品名，即 Clonazepam“氯硝西泮”。

类　　型：镇静剂（depressant）

适 应 症：癫痫（seizure），缓解（relieve）紧张、焦虑，帮助睡眠。

副 作 用：眩晕（dizziness）、注意力不集中、嗜睡（somnolence）。

Valium 安定

药品名称：罗氏制药的产品名，即 Diazepam“安定”。

类　　型：镇静剂（depressant）

适 应 症：失眠（insomnia）、癫痫、肌肉痉挛（muscle spasms）、强迫症（obsessive compulsive disorder）、酒精戒断综合征（Alcohol Withdrawal Syndrome）。

副 作 用：走路不稳（unsteadiness）、眩晕、嗜睡、沮丧、口齿不清、食欲改变。

Vicodin 维柯丁

药品名称：美国雅培制药（Abbott）的产品名，结合鸦片衍生物 hydrocodone“氢可酮”和 acetaminophen“对乙酰氨基酚”（或 paracetamol、APAP）。另一个较知名的类似成分产品为华生制药（Watson）的 Norco“诺科”。

类　　型：麻醉止痛剂（narcotic）

适 应 症：中度及强度疼痛。

副 作 用：胃部不适、呕吐（nausea）、头昏（light-headedness），少数有过敏反应、幻觉（hallucinations）、四肢无力等。

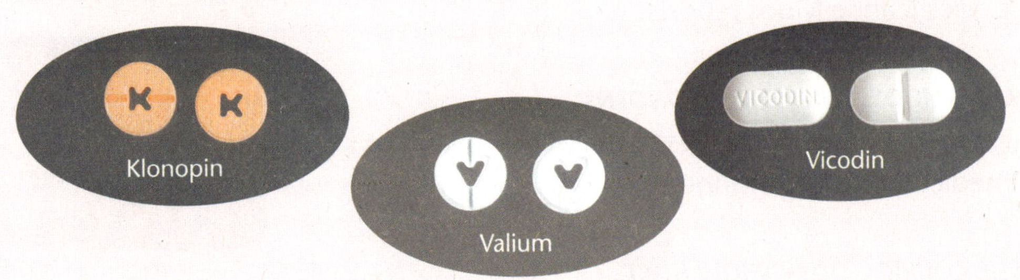

图片提供：U.S. Drug Enforcement Administration

名流轶事 ⑦ 世足赛最受瞩目的巨星——章鱼哥保罗

Eight-Legged Oracle[1]

Paul the Octopus Prognosticates[2] the World Cup Winners

图片提供：Reuters 达志

ANNA COREN, CNN ANCHOR

Well, what has eight arms and a penchant[3] for picking football games? Paul the Oracle Octopus is celebrated by some for his soccer-predicting skills, but some just want to serve him up[4] for dinner. CNN's Jeanne Moos reports.

JEANNE MOOS, CNN CORRESPONDENT

He's an octopus who doesn't realize his goal is to predict World Cup winners.

KATIE COURIC, TODAY SHOW HOST

Paul, the oracle octopus.

MATT TREZZA, RT.COM CORRESPONDENT

Psychic[5] sea creature.

07-F.MP3
07-S.MP3

CNN 主播　安娜 • 科伦
什么东西有八只手臂和挑选足球比赛的特殊嗜好？神算章鱼哥保罗因为其预测足球比赛的技能受到一些人称颂，但有些人只想把他送上餐桌当晚餐。本台吉妮 • 莫斯带来以下报道。

CNN 特派员　吉妮 • 莫斯
他是只章鱼，并不知道自己的目的是用来预测世界杯足球赛的胜利队伍。

《今日秀》主持人　凯蒂 • 克瑞可
神算章鱼哥保罗。

RT.com 特派员　麦特 • 特蕾扎
有特异功能的海洋生物。

Notes & Vocabulary

1. oracle [ˋɔrəkəl]
   n. 神谕；能提供宝贵信息的人或书
2. prognosticate [prɑgˋnɔstəˏket]
   v. 预知；预言
   Dan successfully prognosticated the downturn in the stock market.
3. penchant [ˋpɛntʃənt]
   n. 强烈倾向；嗜好
4. serve sth. up 端上（食物）
   The chef served up the ribs with a spicy barbecue sauce.
5. psychic [ˋsaɪkɪk]
   n. 有特异功能的人；有通灵术的人

名流轶事
非常体验
生活咀嚼
天地之间

UNIDENTIFIED MALE TELEGRAPH CORRESPONDENT

The tentacled[6] oracle.

MATT TREZZA, RT.COM CORRESPONDENT

The psychic cephalopod.[7]

UNIDENTIFIED FEMALE NPR CORRESPONDENT

The mystic[8] mollusk[9] has gotten famous.

JEANNE MOOS, CNN CORRESPONDENT

Paul lives at the Sea Life Aquarium in Germany, where they lower two boxes labeled with the flags of competing teams. Each box contains mussels,[10] one of Paul's favorite foods.

He picked the winner, like, six times in a row.[11]

UNIDENTIFIED MALE

They're very sensitive, ~~octopus~~ [octopuses].

JEANNE MOOS, CNN CORRESPONDENT

Faced with a choice between Germany—his current home—and Spain, Paul loitered[12] atop[13] Germany then slinked[14] over to Spain and later straddled[15] the two before making his final pick by opening the box with the Spanish flag. Paul's less lucky relatives were on sale at New York's Fairway Market.

Octopus, $3.99 a pound: Paul's worth a heck[16] of a lot more than that.

Some who were buying octopus were skeptical.[17]

不知名 Telegraph 男性特派员

有触手的神算。

RT.com 特派员　麦特·特蕾扎

有特异功能的头足类动物。

不知名 NPR 女性特派员

这只不可思议的软体动物可出名了。

CNN 特派员　吉妮·莫斯

保罗住在德国的海洋生物水族馆，馆方会把两个盒子沉入水里，分别标了两队竞争队伍的国旗。盒子里都放了贻贝，那是保罗最喜爱的食物之一。

他已经连续六次选中胜利队伍了。

不知名男子

章鱼很敏感。

CNN 特派员　吉妮·莫斯

面临在他目前居住的德国和西班牙之间做抉择时，保罗在德国上面徘徊了一下，然后溜到西班牙那边，之后又横跨两边，才做出最后决定打开有西班牙国旗的盒子。保罗的亲戚就没那么幸运了，落到在纽约的华人市场特价拍卖。

章鱼，一磅 3.99 美元，保罗的价值比那大多了。

有些买章鱼的人则持怀疑态度。

Notes & Vocabulary

6. tentacled [ˋtɛntɪkəld]
   adj. 有触手的
   Tentacled animals like squids and octopuses scare Laura.
7. cephalopod [ˋsɛfələˏpɑd]
   n. 头足类动物
8. mystic [ˋmɪstɪk]
   adj. 神秘的；不可思议的
   Dawn has many mystic beliefs about the afterlife.
9. mollusk [ˋmɑləsk] *n.* 软体动物
10. mussel [ˋmʌsəl] *n.* 蚌类；贻贝
11. in a row 连续不断
    The team won eight games in a row to finish out the season.
12. loiter [ˋlɔɪtɚ] *v.* 走走停停；徘徊
    Fans loitered outside the locker room hoping to get the player's autograph.
13. atop [əˋtɑp] *prep.* 在……上方
    The man placed his fedora atop his head.
14. slink [slɪŋk] *v.* 偷偷摸摸地走；潜逃
    Alex slinked out the door while his wife was on the phone.
15. straddle [ˋstrædl̩]
    v. 骑；跨坐；横跨
    The child straddled the seesaw waiting for his friend to climb on the other end.
16. heck [hɛk]
    n. / interj.【口】【婉】多；大（加强语气）；表示懊恼或惊讶的感叹词
17. skeptical [ˋskɛptɪkəl]
    adj. 表示怀疑的；多疑的
    Some people are skeptical of the existence of global warming.

UNIDENTIFIED MALE

I'm saying it must be fixed. I don't believe that there's some genius octopus.

JEANNE MOOS, CNN CORRESPONDENT

Paul isn't the first animal prognosticator. Princess the camel picked winning football teams by selecting one of two graham crackers[18] from her owners' labeled palms, while Chippy the pundit[19] chimp was pitted[20] against human pundits deciding between Rudy and Hillary for U.S. Senate. But Chippy never made it big like Paul, who has his own Web site—"Don't tell any of my handlers[21] that I can type"—and his own Twitter account.

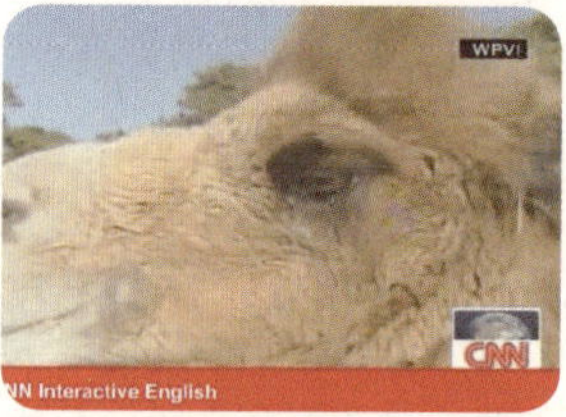

PETA has even gotten into the act demanding that Paul be set free. They're saying an octopus is not a prop[22] that should be used for entertainment.

After correctly predicting Germany's loss to Spain, the psychic octopus has even received death threats.

"Put that thing on the menu."

"I ate your mother."

OLIVER WALECIAK, SEA LIFE AQUARIUM

We take a little bit more care about our octopus than before, because there are quite a lot of visitors who want to kill and to eat him.

不知名男子

要我说，那一定是造的假。我不相信有什么天才章鱼。

CNN 特派员　吉妮·莫斯

保罗并不是第一只动物预言家。骆驼公主通过从她主人做了标记的手心上选择一片全麦饼干，来挑选胜利的足球队伍。而专家猩猩奇普则和人类评论员较量，选择鲁迪或希拉里当美国参议员。但是奇普从没像保罗这么有名，保罗拥有自己的网站“别跟任何一位训练员说我会打字”以及推特账号。

善待动物组织甚至采取行动要求还保罗自由。他们表示章鱼不应该是用来娱乐的道具。

在正确预测德国败给西班牙之后，这只具有特异功能的章鱼甚至收到死亡威胁。

“把他列在菜单上。”

“我吃了你妈。”

海洋生物水族馆　奥利弗·维谢克

我们对自家章鱼的照顾比以往要多，因为有不少参观民众想杀了他或吃了他。

Notes & Vocabulary

PETA

全名为 People for the Ethical Treatment of Animals，是美国的动物权利非营利机构，最著名的标语是“Animals are not ours to eat, wear, experiment on, or use for entertainment.”（“动物不是让我们食用、穿戴、实验或用来娱乐的。”）

18. graham cracker [ˋgreəm] [ˋkrækɚ] 全麦饼干
19. pundit [ˋpʌndət] *n.* 行家；权威；专家
20. pit [pɪt] *v.* 使竞争；使较量
    The boxing match pitted the aging champ against an unknown challenger.
21. handler [ˋhændl̩ɚ] *n.* 驯兽员
22. prop [prɑp] *n.* 道具

名流轶事

非常体验

生活咀嚼

天地之间

JEANNE MOOS, CNN CORRESPONDENT

Prime Minister of Spain joked about sending Paul a protective team, and after Spain beat Germany, Spanish celebrity chef Jose Andres took octopus off the menu. But a jokester[23] on YouTube made Paul the target of a Hitler assassination[24] plot.

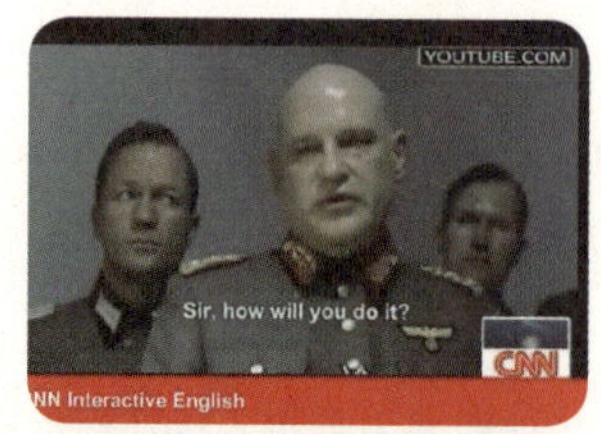

Posted one fan: "With eight tentacles, I'd love to see him do a penalty kick."

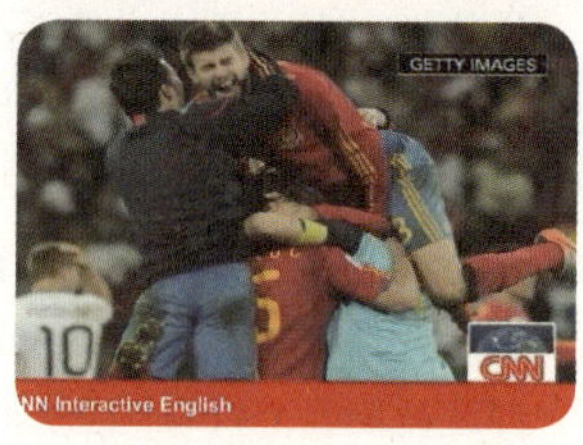

章鱼小档案

别称：石居、八爪鱼、坐蛸、石吸、望潮、死牛

分类：软体动物门（Mollusca）、头足纲（Cephalopoda）、八腕目（Octopoda）

习性：

- 章鱼有三颗心脏，寿命只有半年到五年。
- 章鱼是所有无脊椎动物（invertebrates ）中智商最高的，可通过训练学会辨认形状和图样。
- 当章鱼遇到敌人攻击时，会喷出墨汁（ink）逃走，或者以变色伪装（camouflage）。章鱼墨汁含有麻痹敌人的毒素，但对人类无害、可食用，储积"墨汁"需要半个多小时的时间。

食物：螃蟹、鱼类、贝类，大型的章鱼甚至捕食龙虾、大鱼及中小型的鲨鱼。

亲戚：鱿鱼（squid），同门同纲但属于管鱿目
乌贼（cuttle fish），同门同纲但属于乌贼目

CNN 特派员　吉妮·莫斯

西班牙首相笑称要派给保罗一个保护小组，而在西班牙打败德国后，西班牙名厨荷西·安德斯却把章鱼从菜单上撤掉了。但 YouTube 上有人开玩笑把保罗变成希特勒暗杀阴谋的目标。

一位球迷贴文说："有那八只脚，我很想见识它踢罚球看看。"

Notes & Vocabulary

23. jokester [ˋdʒokstɚ] *n.* 玩笑者

24. assassination [əˏsæsəˋneʃən] *n.* 暗杀；行刺

章鱼料理

世界杯足球赛期间，有球迷扬言要把章鱼哥煮了吃，各国有什么著名的章鱼料理呢？

Ⓐ takoyaki　日式章鱼烧

调味面糊中加入配菜及一块章鱼，以铁烤盘煎熟后成丸子状食用，也称章鱼小丸子。

Ⓑ polbo á feira　西班章鱼冷盘

氽烫章鱼后拌入粗盐、辣椒粉及橄榄油，常搭配马铃薯及面包食用，也可搭饮红酒。

Ⓒ sannakji　韩式章鱼生鱼片

可切小块或整只小章鱼生吃，常佐以麻油及芝麻。

非常体检

非常体验 ⑧ 日本男人拼经济　小孩形同没有爸爸

Where's Daddy?

Sagging[1] Economy Means Japanese Kids See Even Less of Their Parents

CNN ANCHOR

Staying in Japan, a phenomenon born of culture and difficult economic times, two-parent homes, but one parent works so many hours he or sometimes she becomes a stranger to the children. Our Kyung Lah reports on the emerging[2] trend.

KYUNG LAH, CNN CORRESPONDENT

It's five in the morning. The Takayamas are starting their day. Before Yoshinori Takayama leaves home, he says good-bye to his one-and-a-half-year-old daughter, Yuriya. She is still fast asleep.

08-F.MP3
08-S.MP3

CNN 主播

下面是日本新闻。这是一个因文化背景和经济不景气而产生的现象。双亲家庭，但是父母亲其中一人的工作时间太久，以至于有时候孩子对这位父亲或母亲感到十分陌生。本台特派员景兰要报道这个新兴的趋势。

CNN 特派员　景兰

时间是清晨 5 点。高山一家人正要开始他们的一天。高山义德在离家之前，向他一岁半的女儿由里叶说再见。她仍在熟睡中。

Notes & Vocabulary

1. sag [sæg] *v.* 下降；下跌；疲弱
Housing prices sagged, creating an opportunity for first-time home buyers.

2. emerging [ɪˋmɜdʒɪŋ] *adj.* 新兴的
Jim invests most of his money in emerging markets.

Then it's off to the office: a pre-dawn walk to the train station, then a 90-minute commute[3] into downtown Tokyo for the computer engineer who works 12 to 14 hours every day. He won't come home until 11:00 at night, working longer and harder as Japan dips[4] into recession.[5] It's what you do, says Takayama, to survive.[6]

"I have to support[7] my family," he says. "I'm afraid of what would happen if I got laid off."

At home, Yuriya plays with her mother, who doesn't work so she can raise her daughter full-time.[8]

"She's forgotten who her father is many times," says Tomomi Takayama. "She used to cry when she saw him."

The amount of time the fathers spend with their children has been shrinking[9] in Japan since the '70s. According to the latest report by the government, one third of all fathers get home after 9 p.m., and

接着就该出发去上班了：他在天亮前步行到火车站，然后乘坐 90 分钟的车到东京市区，他是个计算机工程师，每天要工作 12 到 14 个小时。他一直要到晚上 11 点才回家。随着日本经济陷入衰退，他的工作时间越来越长，工作也越来越努力。高山说，你必须如此才能生存。

高山义德说："我必须养家，我很担心万一我被解雇，这个家会怎么样。"

在家里，由里叶和母亲一起玩，她的母亲不工作，这样才能全天候带女儿。

高山朋美说："她有很多次都忘了自己的爸爸是谁，她以前看到他的时候还会哭。"

在日本，父亲和孩子相处的时间自 20 世纪 70 年代以来便逐渐减少。日本政府最新的报告显示，日本有三分之一的父亲是在晚上

Notes & Vocabulary

lay off 解雇；遣散；裁员

lay off 以人为宾语，表示暂时停止或永久解除某人的职务，即"解雇；遣散"的意思，尤其指遣散整批员工；若以事物为宾语，则表示"停止做某事"。

- The software company **laid off** half of its staff.
  那家软件公司遣散了一半的员工。
- Abby **laid off** teasing her little brother after being scolded by her mother.
  艾比被妈妈责备后就停止了嘲弄弟弟。

延伸学习

在英文中常用的 fire、dismiss 是指因个人过失而遭到公司直接"开除"的意思。

同义词

▶ terminate = disemploy
= except for
give notice = give the axe
= give the sack

3. commute [kə`mjut] *n.* 通勤
4. dip [dɪp] *v.* 下降；下沉
   The price of oil dipped after the holidays.
5. recession [rɪ`sɛʃən]
   n.（经济）衰退；衰退期
6. survive [sɚ`vaɪv] *v.* 存活下来
   Fred survived the latest round of layoffs in his office.
7. support [sə`port] *v.* 抚养；支撑
   Mindy supports her children by holding down two jobs.
8. full-time [`fʊl`taɪm]
   adv. 全天地；全职地
9. shrink [ʃrɪŋk] *v.* 缩水；缩减
   Ben's savings shrank considerably after his divorce settlement.

a quarter[10] of them never see their children awake during the week.

It's a problem notable even for a nation of workaholics.[11] Japan's government says parents spend less time with their children now than in the past 40 years. The recession is only expected to make it worse.

Just next door, Yuriya's neighbor, three-year-old Jinta, barely[12] sees his father either.

"I see in Hollywood movies that fathers come home early and they take vacations," says Misachi Mikazuki. "For me, that's like a dream."

But the nightmare in this economy, she says, would be getting fired.

At 10 p.m., Takayama has finished his day, a little early for him. Tonight, a rare[13] gift—Yuriya can't sleep. A few moments with his daughter, a brief reminder[14] of why he continues to work the long hours away from home.

9 点以后回到家，还有四分之一在整周工作日里从未在孩子醒着的时候见过他们。

即便在这个充满工作狂的国家里，这个问题也十分值得注意。日本政府表示，现在父母亲和孩子相处的时间与过去 40 年相比要少。预计经济衰退只会让情况更糟。

由里叶的隔壁邻居，三岁的甚太也几乎没见过他的父亲。

月出美纱纪说：“我在好莱坞电影里看到父亲很早下班，然后家人会去度假，对我而言，那简直像是一场梦。”

但是她说，在这样的经济情况下，被解雇才是真正的噩梦。

晚上 10 点，高山先生结束了一天的工作，对他而言还算早了点。今天晚上有个难能可贵的礼物——由里叶睡不着。和女儿相处的片刻时光，瞬间提醒了他继续长时间离家工作为的是什么。

Notes & Vocabulary

10. quarter [ˋkwɔrtɚ] *n.* 四分之一
11. workaholic [ˋwɚkəˏhɔlɪk] *n.* 工作狂；工作投入的人
12. barely [ˋbɛrlɪ] *adv.* 几乎没有；罕有地
13. rare [rɛr] *adj.* 稀有的；难得的
    Cindy saw the invitation to teach a summer session at the Italian university as a rare opportunity.
14. reminder [rɪˋmaɪndɚ] *n.* 提醒物

非常体验 ⑨ 世上最棒的工作——澳大利亚岛屿管理员

Island Hoping

Applicants[1] Vie[2] for the Job of a Lifetime

CNN ANCHOR

Applying for jobs is a hot topic these days, but some folks are just applying for a hot job. An Australian marketing campaign[3] had thousands applying for a fabulous[4] position on a tropical island, and now the public can help select a potential winner. CNN's Atika Shubert tells us all about the job and how you can participate.

MITCHELL, CANADA, APPLICANT

. . . if you told me that I could get out of here I go!

09-F.MP3
09-S.MP3

CNN 主播

应聘工作是这一阵子的热门话题，但有些人则是忙着应聘一份热门工作。澳大利亚一场营销活动，吸引了数千人应聘一座热带岛屿上的一个绝佳职位，民众还可以帮忙选出可能的赢家。本台的阿缇卡·舒伯特要为我们说明这份工作，也要告诉各位观众如何参与其中。

加拿大应聘者　米切尔

……如果你告诉我我可以离开这里，我立刻就走！

Notes & Vocabulary

标题扫描

island hoping

从 island hopping 取谐音转变而来。hop 意为“跳”，口语中有“短程旅行”的意思，island hopping 是指在航程中停靠数个岛屿，而非直接跨海航向目的地。标题把 hopping 改成 hoping “希望”，暗示应聘者希望能够到澳大利亚岛屿去。

1. applicant [ˋæplɪkənt]
   n. 申请者
2. vie [vi] *v.* 争；竞争
   Both Gina and Elaine vied for their handsome professor's attention.
3. campaign [ˏkæmˋpen]
   n.（广告、竞选等）活动
4. fabulous [ˋfæbjələs]
   adj. 极好的；惊人的
   The crowd applauded the dancer's fabulous performance.

名流轶事　非常体验　生活咀嚼　天地之间

ATIKA SHUBERT, CNN CORRESPONDENT

You can sing, don[5] your best bikini or your best flippers,[6] whatever it takes to clinch[7] that interview for the best job in the world.

VOICEOVER

. . . island caretaker!

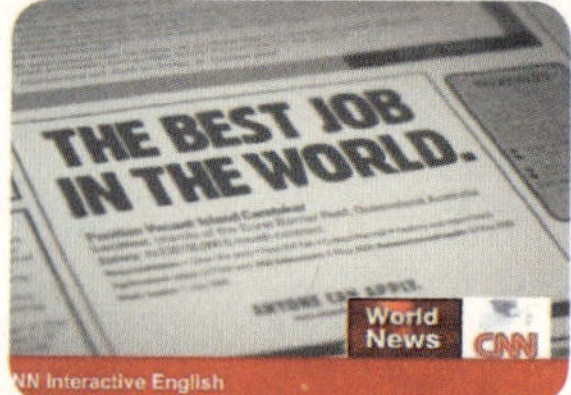

ATIKA SHUBERT, CNN CORRESPONDENT

That's what the Queensland Tourism Board of Australia is calling its six-month marketing ploy[8]—$100,000 for six months of being the caretaker of tropical Hamilton Island. Your only responsibility—blogging about your adventures on Australia's Great Barrier Reef, from diving to beach snoozing.[9]

More than 34,000 applied with slick[10] homemade videos tailored for the YouTube generation.[11]

GRORGE, IRELAND, APPLICANT

. . . I've got the double rock!

CNN 特派员　阿缇卡 • 舒伯特

你可以唱歌，或者穿上你最棒的比基尼或蛙鞋，全力争取世上最理想工作的面试机会。

配音

……岛屿管理员！

CNN 特派员　阿缇卡 • 舒伯特

这就是澳大利亚昆士兰旅游局为期 6 个月的营销工作——10 万美元，担任哈密尔顿岛的管理员 6 个月。这份工作唯一的职责是，在博客上书写自己在澳大利亚大堡礁的探险经历，包括潜水和在海滩上午睡。

34 000 多人投递了机智诙谐的自拍短片来应聘这份工作，这是为 YouTube 世代量身打造的项目。

爱尔兰应聘者　乔治

……我是个重口味摇滚客！

Notes & Vocabulary

tailor for

为……而制造或修改

tailor 原本当名词意为“(男装)裁缝师”，当动词意为“裁制；定做(衣服)”，引申为“修改；使适合”，tailor for 有“为某人或事物量身打造”的意思。

- The restaurant is tailored for families with small children.
  那家餐厅是为招待有幼儿的家庭来设计的。

5. don [dɑn] *v.* 穿上；披上；戴上
   Jack donned his new hat before hitting the town.
6. flipper [ˋflɪpɚ] *n.* 蛙鞋
7. clinch [klɪntʃ]
   v. 最终得胜；把握；钉牢
   The basketball team clinched a spot in the playoffs.
8. ploy [plɔɪ]
   n.【口】工作；活动；伎俩
9. snooze [snuz] *v.* 打盹；小睡
   The cat snoozed in the window.
10. slick [slɪk]
    adj. 机智的；圆滑的；滑溜的
    Jules slipped on a slick spot on the icy sidewalk.
11. generation [ˏdʒɛnəˋreʃən]
    n. 世代

ATIKA SHUBERT, CNN CORRESPONDENT

Ten have been short-listed for a final round of interviews in Australia, but the public has a chance to vote in one more wild card candidate.[12]

STEVEN, UNITED STATES, APPLICANT

. . . this is gonna be really cold.

ATIKA SHUBERT, CNN CORRESPONDENT

There are 50 to choose from at Islandreefjob.com. The candidate with the most votes wins an interview slot,[13] and the deadline[14] is March 18th.

JULIA, RUSSIA, APPLICANT

. . . enjoy the beauty of the Great Barrier Reef, to see it for real, not only in books.

ATIKA SHUBERT, CNN CORRESPONDENT

And don't let that bikini fool you. These are global professionals. Julia is a marine biologist[15] from Russia.

JULIA, RUSSIA, APPLICANT

I have a degree in marine biology.

ATIKA SHUBERT, CNN CORRESPONDENT

Anjaan is a radio DJ from India and Kiran is a chef from Kenya. It's a tough[16] choice, and they make applying look so much fun, it may make you wish you tried for that job yourself.

CNN 特派员　阿缇卡・舒伯特
目前已有 10 人入选赴澳大利亚接受面试的决选名单，但民众还有机会投票选出一名外卡候选人。

美国应聘者　斯蒂文
……这一定会冷死了。

CNN 特派员　阿缇卡・舒伯特
在 Islandreefjob.com 网站上有 50 人可以选，获得最多票数的应聘者将可获得面试机会。投票截止日为 3 月 18 日。

俄罗斯应聘者　朱莉娅
……享受大堡礁的美景。亲眼目睹，不只是看书里的照片而已。

CNN 特派员　阿缇卡・舒伯特
别让她身上那件比基尼骗了。这些应聘者都是来自世界各地的专业人士。朱莉娅是俄罗斯的海洋生物学家。

俄罗斯应聘者　朱莉娅
我有海洋生物学学位。

CNN 特派员　阿缇卡・舒伯特
安冉是印度的电台节目主持人，基兰是肯尼亚的厨师。这实在让人难以抉择，而且他们让人觉得应聘这份工作看起来非常有趣，让人不禁希望自己也尝试去应聘那份工作了。

Notes & Vocabulary

short-list 挑出决选的人选

名词 short-list 是指列出重要事物或人选的简短清单，尤其指“最后供挑选的候选人名单”，short-list 当动词用表示“把……列在决选名单上”，也就是“挑出决选的人选”。

- The selection committee short-listed several scientists for the Nobel Prize.
  评审委员会挑出最后几位入选诺贝尔奖的科学家。

wild card 外卡

wild card 原本是纸牌游戏中的“百搭牌”，可由玩家任意定义、代替其他纸牌的功能，引申为“不确定或不可测之因素”。在体育竞赛中，wild card 是指“非经正常预赛渠道加入决赛的参赛者”，大多是让正规赛落败的选手争取，中文译为“外卡”。

- The tennis player was a wild card choice for the tournament finals.
  那位网球选手是锦标赛决赛的外卡人选。

12. candidate [ˋkændəˏdet]
    n. 候选人；求职应聘者
13. slot [slɑt] *n.*【C】职位；位置
14. deadline [ˋdɛdˏlaɪn]
    n. 最后期限；截止期限
15. marine biologist
    [məˋrin] [baɪˋɑlədʒɪst]
    海洋生物学家
16. tough [tʌf]
    adj. 棘手的；困难的
    Max was stumped by a tough test question.

名流轶事　非常体验　生活咀嚼　天地之间

世上最理想的工作——哈密尔顿岛管理员

职责

- 探索和汇报——体验昆士兰旅游局安排的活动，如潜水、水疗 Spa、丛林徒步旅行（bushwalking）等，需拍照并在博客上发表心得。
- 喂饲鱼类——分担大堡礁 1500 种鱼类的喂饲工作。
- 清洁游泳池——有自动过滤器（automatic filter），但需清理水面的落叶等。
- 收集信件——协助航空邮递服务，是鸟瞰（get a bird's eye view）大堡礁风景的好机会。

福利

哈密尔顿岛蓝珍珠湾（Blue Pearl）度假中心免费住宿 6 个月，可接待亲友同住，免费使用所有设施，薪资 15 万澳元。

资格

爱冒险（adventurous）、热爱户外活动、具备良好沟通技巧（communication skills）、有各方面的经验，以及：

- 对工作饱含热情（enthusiasm）
- 拥有娱乐的价值〔个性和创造力〕
- 具备表现技巧〔对媒体友善〕（media-friendly）
- 至少一年以上相关经验（relevant experience）

甄选过程

- 2009/1/9~2009/2/22 接受申请，需填表及拍摄 60 秒英文自我推荐影片，共 34 684 人申请。
- 2009/2/23~2009/3/2 昆士兰旅游局及相关单位筛选出 50 人。
- 2009/3/2~2009/3/24 民众上网投票，得票最高者成为参加决选的外卡候选人，中国台湾的王秀毓以 151 676 票胜出。
- 2009/3/24~2009/4/2 选出 10 人入围最后面试决选，后来增额 5 人。

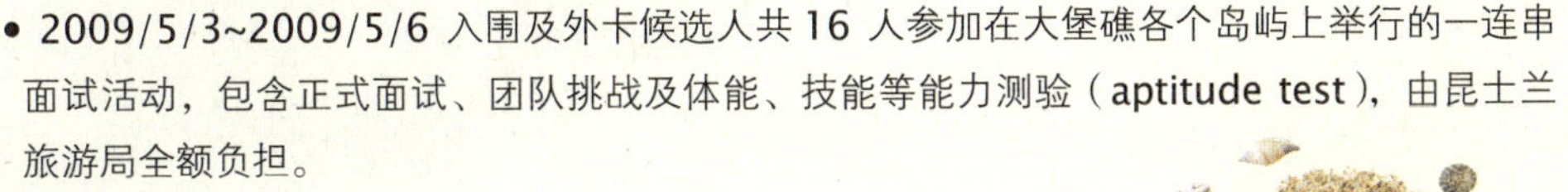

- 2009/5/3~2009/5/6 入围及外卡候选人共 16 人参加在大堡礁各个岛屿上举行的一连串面试活动，包含正式面试、团队挑战及体能、技能等能力测验（aptitude test），由昆士兰旅游局全额负担。
- 2009/5/6 于媒体接待晚会（media function ）上宣布当选人。
- 2009/7/1 合约正式生效。

岛屿管理员将驻守的Hamilton Island 哈密尔顿岛

位于昆士兰外海，为圣灵降临群岛（Whitsunday Islands）74 个岛屿中的第二大岛，面积约 5 平方千米，人口约 5000 人。该群岛为古代山脉潜海而成，位于大堡礁（Great Barrier Reef）中间，其中 8 座已开发为度假岛屿，目前哈密尔顿岛最完善，被誉为“大堡礁之星”。

非常体验 ⑩ 拯救珊瑚礁的海底英雄

Undersea Hero

Scuba Diver Hatches[1] a Plan to Save the World's Reefs

图片提供：AP

CNN ANCHOR

Well, now to another of our CNN Heroes, ordinary people making an extraordinary[2] impact on the world. And it's viewers like you who tell us about them on our Web site. This week we want to introduce you to Todd Barber. He's an avid[3] scuba diver trying to save dying coral reefs[4] around the world, and he's making a difference.

TODD BARBER, CNN HERO

Reefs are dying. Human activity around the world is impacting what's happening underwater. If we

10-F.MP3
10-S.MP3

CNN 主播

接着要向另一位“CNN 无名英雄”致敬，就是对世界产生重大影响的平凡人物。这是像您这样的观众在本台网站上告诉我们的。本周我们要向各位介绍托德·巴伯。他是一位热爱潜水的水肺潜水员，试图拯救世界各地垂危的珊瑚礁，而且已经有了重大成果。

CNN 无名英雄　托德·巴伯

珊瑚礁已命在旦夕。世界各地的人类活动对海底环境造成了冲击。我们如果不采取行动

Notes & Vocabulary

make a difference 造成影响；改善

make a difference 是指”在事情或情况上有很大的正面影响”。其反义词是 make no difference。

- Jennifer made a difference in her community by volunteering at a youth activity center.
  詹妮弗自愿在青年活动中心担任志愿者，对她的社区帮助很大。

其他与 difference 连用的词组

same difference 相同；一样

- Whether I get fired or quit, it's the same difference—I am out of a job.
  不论我是被炒鱿鱼还是辞职，结果都是一样的——我失业了。

split the difference

折中；各让一步

- Neither the buyer nor seller could agree on a price at first, so they decided to split the difference.
  买家与卖家起初无法在价钱上达成共识，所以他们决定各退一步。

1. hatch [hætʃ] *v.* 策划；孵育
   Hal hatched a scheme to get his old job back.
2. extraordinary [ɪk`strɔrdə͵nɛrɪ]
   adj. 非凡的；特别的
   Shelly is an extraordinary example of someone who gives back to her community.
3. avid [`ævəd]
   adj. 热心的；劲头十足的
   Wendy is an avid gardener.
4. reef [rif] *n.* 礁；礁脉；沙洲；暗礁

don't do something to save our coral reefs, we will lose them all and the impact will be devastating[5] for humanity.[6]

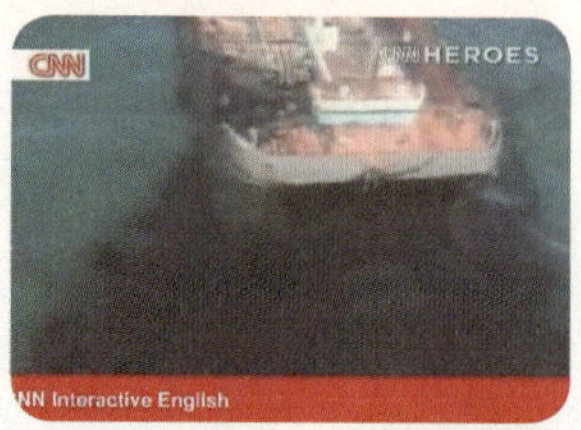

In 1988, I was on a trip with my father and we went to the Cayman Islands, and we're looking at a coral reef that I had been taking pictures of since I was a baby and the reef was gone. My heart sank,[7] and I had a strong passion to try to change that, and my father and I sat down one night and came up with the idea of how to fix it.

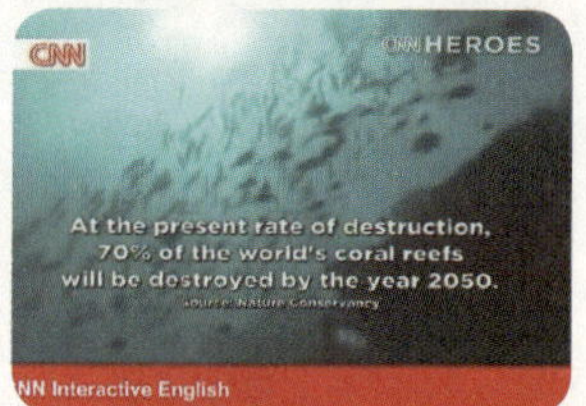

My name is Todd Barber and I make reef balls used to help restore[8] reefs around the world. Reef balls serve as the base habitat[9] for a natural reef to grow upon. They were designed so that you can plant corals on them. My goal was to mimic[10] nature, not dictate[11] nature.

拯救珊瑚礁，它们将会彻底消失，对人类造成灾难性的后果。

1988 年，我和我父亲前往开曼群岛。我们看着一座从我小时候就一直拍照的珊瑚礁，但是珊瑚都已经不见了。我的心情跌到了谷底，进而产生了一股想要改变这种情况的强烈热情。有一天晚上，父亲和我坐在一起聊天，我们想出了如何修复这种状况的主意。

我的名字叫托德·巴伯，我制作珊瑚礁球以协助恢复世界各地的珊瑚礁。珊瑚礁球可充当基础栖息地，供自然的珊瑚礁在上面生长。珊瑚礁球经过特殊设计，你可以在上面种植珊瑚。我的目标是要模仿自然，不是控制自然。

Notes & Vocabulary

come up with 想出（办法）

是指经过思考和发展而得到某种结果，常用来表示“想出方法；找出解答”。文中的 came up with the idea 意为“想出了这个主意”。

- Todd came up with a way to make money while enjoying his favorite hobby.
  托德找到了一个可以兼顾兴趣与赚钱的方法。

5. devastating [ˋdɛvəˏstetɪŋ]
   adj. 毁灭性的
   Brad's drug problem had devastating consequences on his life.
6. humanity [hjuˋmænətɪ]
   n.（总称）人；人类
7. sink [sɪŋk] *v.* 下沉
   Vanessa's heart sank when she learned that the trip was canceled.
8. restore [rɪˋstɔr] *v.* 恢复；修复
   Ralph restores historic homes in his town.
9. habitat [ˋhæbəˏtæt]
   n. 栖息地；产地
10. mimic [ˋmɪmɪk] *v.* 模仿；模拟
    The harmless snake mimics more dangerous species to scare away potential predators.
11. dictate [ˋdɪktet] *v.* 支配；命令
    Donald's job dictates his schedule.

Reef balls are made with a special cement[12] that lasts over 500 years. They're portable,[13] inexpensive and they're environmentally friendly.

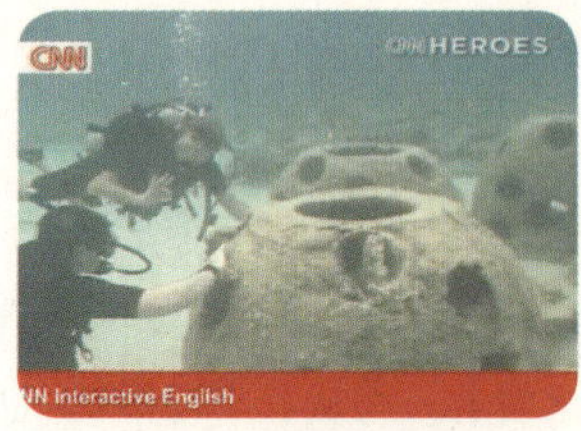

I call this hatching a reef ball.

For me personally, the satisfaction comes from diving on a reef ball and seeing that the environment has been rehabilitated[14] and that the reef is actually there and that our grandkids will be able to see the same thing.

The Reef Ball Foundation 珊瑚礁球基金会

托德·巴伯在 1993 年成立珊瑚礁球基金会，该基金会属于国际性的公益（non-profit）组织。主要的任务是修复地球的海洋生态系统（ecosystems），以及保护天然的岩礁环境。

目前基金会已将珊瑚礁球推广至 70 多个国家，此外还进行多项海洋环保计划，包括海口（estuary）重建、红树林（red mangrove）栽植、兴建牡蛎礁、珊瑚繁殖（propagation）等。

10-F.MP3 / 10-S.MP3 | *Undersea Hero*

珊瑚礁球由一种特殊的水泥制成，寿命长达500年以上。它们移动很方便，价格低廉，而且对环境无害。

我把这个过程称作孵化珊瑚礁球。

对我个人来说，只要潜入水下观察珊瑚礁球，看到环境复原，珊瑚真的在那里，知道我们的子子孙孙也能够看到同样的景象，我就感到非常满足了。

Reef Balls 珊瑚礁球

大小从直径0.3米/15千克到2.5米/3500千克都有，除了标准的钟罩型，还有千层糕型（layer cake）、钟乳石型（stalactite）、石笋型（stalagmite）等。

Notes & Vocabulary

friendly 有利于……的；对……方便的

形容词friendly一般解释为“友善的；友好的”，文中environmentally friendly是以副词来修饰形容词，意思是”对环境无害的”。另外，较常出现的是在前面加上名词，用连字符形成复合形容词，表示”有利于……的；对……方便的”。

- This new mobile device is very user-friendly.
  这个新的行动装置对使用者而言非常便利。

12. cement [sɪˋmɛnt] *n.* 水泥
13. portable [ˋpɔrtəbl̩] *adj.* 可携带的
    Louis brought a portable DVD player on the bus ride.
14. rehabilitate [ˏriəˋbɪlətet] *v.* 使复兴；使恢复原状
    An environmental group rehabilitated acres of forest damaged by logging.

名流轶事 非常体验 生活咀嚼 天地之间

非常体验 ⑪ 为什么现代男性没有“男人味”

Menaissance Men

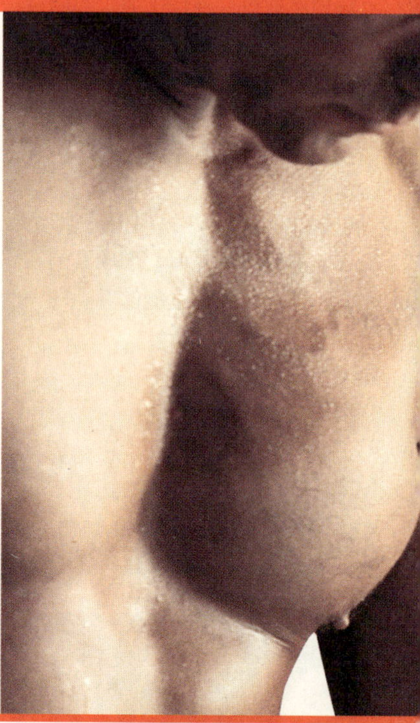

Retrosexuals Usher in[1] a Return to Masculinity[2]

KRISTIE LU STOUT, CNN ANCHOR

So, the first lady, she's out on her own. Hillary Clinton speaks for the U.S. across the globe. Many businesswomen now earn more than men. Has equality[3] gone too far? A weird question. Some people think it's time to get back to the days when men were men. Carol Costello tells us they have got a plan.

CAROL COSTELLO, CNN CORRESPONDENT

Mad Men, the TV show, is many a contemporary[4] man's fantasy. In 1960s America, men were men. Today . . .

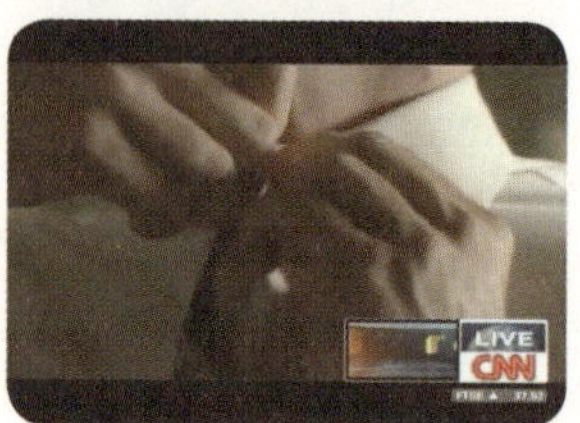

What would you say the state of men is right now?

11-F.MP3
11-S.MP3

CNN 主播　克莉丝蒂·陆·史道

第一夫人独自出击。希拉里·克林顿在全球各地为美国发言。现在许多职场女性的收入比男人还高，男女平等是不是发展得过头了？这个问题很奇怪。有些人认为我们应该回到过去那个男人就是男人的时代。卡萝·科斯特洛带来的报道显示，这些人已经有了一套计划。

CNN 特派员　卡萝·科斯特洛

电视节目《广告狂人》是许多现代男人的幻想。在 20 世纪 60 年代的美国，男人就是男人，但如今……

你认为现在男人的地位如何？

Notes & Vocabulary

标题扫描

menaissance

男性雄风复兴

menaissance [ˌmɛnəˋsɑns] 是新创的单词，结合 men “男人；男性” 和 renaissance [ˌrɛnəˋsɑns] “新生；重生；复兴”，可翻译作 “男性雄风复兴；男性气概再起”。

retrosexual

随性男

retrosexual [ˌrɛtroˋsɛkʃwəl] 是指不修边幅不重视外表的异性恋男性，可翻译成 “反型男；随性男”。1994 年英国记者 Mark Simpson 在《独立报》自创新词 metrosexuality，指讲究品味与装扮的都市（metropolitan）异性恋（heterosexual）男性的性感。之后他又衍生出 metrosexual [ˌmɛtroˋsɛkʃwəl] “型男；潮男”，隔年再提出相对的 retrosexual “反型男；随性男”。

1. usher in 开创（新局）；引领
   The election of U.S. President Barack Obama is thought to have ushered in a new era in race relations.

2. masculinity [ˌmæskjəˋlɪnətɪ]
   n. 男子气概

3. equality [iˋkwɑlətɪ]
   n. 平等；相等

4. contemporary [kənˋtɛmpəˌrɛrɪ]
   adj. 当代的；现代的
   Most contemporary music is not popular with the older generation.

LIONEL TIGER, RUTGERS UNIVERSITY

Males are at a point now where they're experiencing a considerable amount of dismay[5] and uncertainty, and [are] somewhat scorned[6] in principle[7] by females.

CAROL COSTELLO, CNN CORRESPONDENT

Lionel Tiger is one in a group of professors—all men—who support a new academic discipline,[8] male studies. It explores the biology[9] behind masculinity. It was born in part out of a concern our culture is feminizing[10] boys.

LIONEL TIGER, RUTGERS UNIVERSITY

Don't by any means[11] let them drug[12] your child to turn it into a girl, which is what effectively they do.

CAROL COSTELLO, CNN CORRESPONDENT

Do you think that's really true? That if you give a kid Ritalin and it's a boy that they want to transform him into a she?

LIONEL TIGER, RUTGERS UNIVERSITY

[He] becomes less active, more physically compliant,[13] less likely to bounce[14] around the room.

罗格斯大学　莱昂内尔·泰格
当今男性经历了相当程度的恐慌和不确定性，而且基本上有点受到女性鄙视。

CNN 特派员　卡萝·科斯特洛
莱昂内尔·泰格和一群清一色的男性教授们都支持一门新学科——男性研究，目的在于探究男子气概背后的生物学因素。这门学科之所以诞生，部分是源自于担忧我们的文化把男性变得女性化了。

罗格斯大学　莱昂内尔·泰格
千万别让他们毒害你的孩子，把他变成女孩，他们实际上就是这么做的。

CNN 特派员　卡萝·科斯特洛
你真的认为如此吗？若让男孩服用利他林（注），就是要把他变成女孩？

罗格斯大学　莱昂内尔·泰格
他会变得不太好动、比较温顺，不太会在房间里跑跑跳跳。

注：利他林为一种中枢神经兴奋药。

Notes & Vocabulary

5. dismay [dɪsˋme] *n.* 沮丧；气馁

6. scorn [skɔrn] *v.* 奚落；嘲笑；蔑视
The new advertising campaign was scorned at the company meeting for being a failure.

7. in principle 基本上；大体上
I like your ideas in principle, but let me tell you why I think they won't work.

8. discipline [ˋdɪsəplən]
n. 学科；知识领域

9. biology [baɪˋɑlədʒɪ] *n.* 生物学

10. feminize [ˋfɛmə͵naɪz]
v. 使女性化；使阴柔化
After moving into the apartment, the woman wanted to feminize it and make it more comfortable.

11. by any means
无论如何；总而言之
The government needs to get food to the starving people by any means.

12. drug [drʌg] *v.* 毒害；施以麻醉药剂
For the long plane ride, the animal was drugged so it wouldn't cause any problems.

13. compliant [kəmˋplaɪənt]
adj. 顺从的；服从的
The compliant student did the work as the teacher had asked.

14. bounce [baʊns]
v. 弹跳；弹起
Mary sat on a chair and bounced her baby boy on her knee.

CAROL COSTELLO, CNN CORRESPONDENT

While you may or may not agree with that one, the fear of feminization is out there. Other men are fighting it, too, not by studying the problem, but by going retro[15] à la[16] Mad Men.

They're dismissing[17] less-than-masculine[18] heroes like the guys in HBO's Entourage, and embracing[19] the macho[20] heroes of old, like Theodore Roosevelt and Steve McQueen.

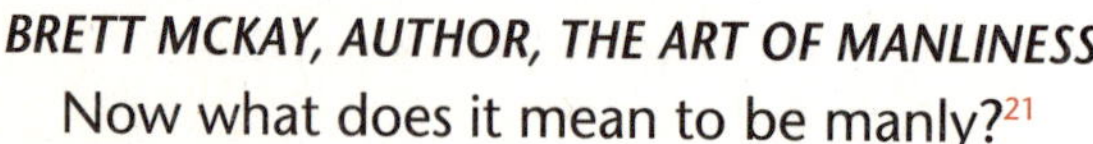

BRETT MCKAY, AUTHOR, THE ART OF MANLINESS

Now what does it mean to be manly?[21]

CAROL COSTELLO, CNN CORRESPONDENT

Brett McKay supports the retrosexual movement. Along with his wife, he wrote The Art of Manliness and says men can end the confusion by embracing the kind of machismo[22] that includes honor and self-reliance.[23]

BRETT MCKAY, AUTHOR, THE ART OF MANLINESS

I think it's just a reflection of this idea that men—young men particularly—want to grow up. They're tired of, you know, feeling like they're a teenager still.

CNN 特派员　卡萝·科斯特洛
你对这样的说法可能认同，也可能不认同，但对女性化的恐惧确实存在。也有其他男性正在抗拒这种现象，但不是借着研究这个问题，而是效法过去《广告狂人》这样的电视剧。

他们对 HBO 的《我家也有大明星》里缺乏男子气概的英雄嗤之以鼻，却拥护昔日那种雄赳赳的英雄人物，像老罗斯福及史蒂夫·麦克奎因。

《雄风的艺术》作者　布雷特·麦凯
究竟什么叫有男子气概？

CNN 特派员　卡萝·科斯特洛
布雷特·麦凯支持这项反型男运动。他和太太共同写了《雄风的艺术》一书，指出男人可以终结这种混淆，方法是拥抱包括荣誉和自立自强等的那种男性气魄。

《雄风的艺术》作者　布雷特·麦凯
我认为这只是反映了男人想长大的想法，尤其是年轻男性。他们已经厌倦觉得自己一直像个青少年了。

Notes & Vocabulary

15. retro [`rɛtro] *adj.* 复古的；怀旧的
There are many retro clothing styles you can choose from in the store.

16. à la [ɑ] [lɑ]
按照……的方式（法文）
The woman walked in the room and threw back her hair à la a Hollywood actress.

17. dismiss [dɪs`mɪs]
v. 摒弃；抛弃；不考虑
You should always listen to your coworkers and never simply dismiss what they say.

18. masculine [`mæskjəlɪn]
adj. 男子气概的；阳刚的
Boxing and rugby are very masculine sports where it is easy to get hurt.

19. embrace [ɪm`bres]
v. 拥抱；欣然接受
The school is finally embracing the policy of letting students not wear uniforms.

20. macho [`mɑtʃo]
adj. 大男人的；有气魄的
The little boy tried to be macho and lift the heavy box that his father had placed on the floor.

21. manly [`mænlɪ] *adj.* 有男子气概的
Kevin tried to be manly on his date with Doris by showing her how much he knew about cars.

22. machismo [mɑ`tʃizmo]
n. 男子气概

23. self-reliance [ˏsɛlfrɪ`laɪəns]
n. 自立；独立；靠自己

CAROL COSTELLO, CNN CORRESPONDENT

While a male studies class may help, Mckay says a good first step is simple.

BRETT MCKAY, AUTHOR, THE ART OF MANLINESS

You're gonna take the wide end, and you're gonna wrap it around.

CAROL COSTELLO, CNN CORRESPONDENT

Dress like a man. And men seem interested in going elegantly[24] macho. Both Banana Republic and Brooks Brothers are now selling retro looks. As for whether clothes or male studies will re-establish a manly man's place in the world, who knows?

As for what women think, in light of[25] the fact men still dominate[26] the top of the corporate[27] ladder and still dominate all three branches of government, some women are receptive,[28] others say it's just another slam[29] on feminism.[30v]

CNN 特派员　卡萝・科斯特洛
学习男性研究的课程虽然可能有帮助，但麦凯说，迈出良好的第一步其实很容易。

《雄风的艺术》作者　布雷特・麦凯
抓住领带宽的这一端，等一下会把它绕起来。

CNN 特派员　卡萝・科斯特洛
打扮得像个男人。男性似乎对优雅的阳刚装扮很感兴趣。香蕉共和国和布鲁克斯兄弟都推出了复古造型系列。至于服装及男性研究能否重新奠定男子汉在世界上的地位，谁知道呢？

至于女性的感受，有鉴于男性仍主宰着企业高层及政府的三权部门，有些女性接受这种主张，有些女性则认为这是对男女平等主义的另一个重大打击。

Notes & Vocabulary

24. elegantly [ˋɛləgəntlɪ]
adv. 优雅地；优美地

25. in light of
鉴于；根据；从……的观点
In light of some new information, the reporter decided to change his news story.

26. dominate [ˋdɑmə͵net]
v. 支配；主宰；控制
Few players have dominated tennis like Roger Federer is still doing.

27. corporate [ˋkɔrpərɪt]
adj. 大企业的；公司的
A corporate memo was sent to all of the employees at the company.

28. receptive [rɪˋsɛptɪv]
adj. 能接受的；能包容的
If you are nice to Susan, she will be more receptive when you ask her for a favor.

29. slam [slæm] *n.* 重创；重击

30. feminism [ˋfɛmə͵nɪzəm]
n. 女权主义；男女平等主义

非常体验 ⑫ 你知道空中小姐是怎么来的?

Elegant[1] Ambassadors[2] of the Air

A Historic Look at Flight Attendants[3]

图片提供：AP 达志

Ellen Church 艾立·丘奇

RICHARD QUEST, BUSINESS TRAVELLER

Flight attendants are trained to deal with all sorts of onboard[4] emergencies, especially when passengers are seriously ill. It's a little-known fact that the first flight attendant was actually a trained nurse. The airline believed in those early days that passengers would feel much more secure if they knew the staff were medically trained. Ayesha Durgahee explains.

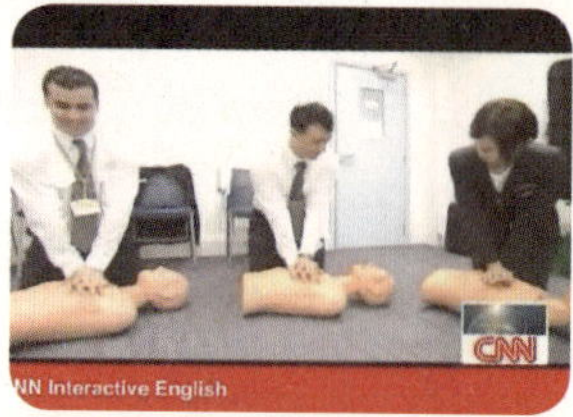

AYESHA DURGAHEE, CNN CORRESPONDENT

Richard, her name was Ellen Church, and it was 1935. Aviator,[5] medical aid—the woman who paved the way for[6] cabin crew as we know them today. It would be her profession as a nurse and not her pilot's license that led her to become the

12-F.MP3
12-S.MP3

《商务旅行家》 理查德·奎斯特

空中服务人员都受过充分训练，能妥善处理机上的各种紧急事故，尤其是乘客病重时。很少有人知道，史上第一位空中服务人员其实是专业护士。早期的航空公司认为，乘客若知道飞机上的工作人员受过医学训练，心里会更有安全感。请看爱伊莎·德加希的进一步说明。

CNN 特派员 爱伊莎·德加希

理查德，她叫艾伦·丘奇，拍照时间是1935年。丘奇是一名飞行员，也是医护人员，她为我们今天所知的空中服务人员奠定了基础。她能成为世上第一位空中服务人员，主要是因为她的护士身份，而非因为她

Notes & Vocabulary

1. elegant [ˋɛləgənt]
   adj. 优雅的；精致的
   Gina wore an elegant gown to the dance.
2. ambassador [æmˋbæsədɚ]
   n. 大使；使节；代表
3. flight attendant
   [flaɪt] [əˋtɛndənt] 空中服务人员
4. onboard [ˋɑn͵bɔrd]
   adj. 在船、车、飞机上的
   The car comes with a standard onboard GPS unit.
5. aviator [ˋevɪ͵etɚ] *n.* 飞行员
6. pave the way for
   为……铺好路、做好准备
   Jackie Robinson paved the way for minorities to play professional sports in the U.S.

史上第一位空中小姐

Ellen Church 艾伦·丘奇

早期的空中服务人员为男性，最早出现在1911年，名称沿用海运的 purser 或 steward“乘务员”，主要负责收费及协助乘客，20世纪20年代开始有所谓的 cabin boys 以及送餐的服务。

艾伦·丘奇1904年9月22日生于爱荷华州克里斯科，1930年成为史上第一位空中小姐。她当时25岁，是一名飞行员和合格护士，当时的 Boeing Air Transit 波音航空公司（United Airlines 美国联合航空公司前身）不愿聘请她当驾驶员，但接受她的建议聘请护士兼任空中服务人员，好协助安抚乘客。其他航空公司群起效尤，直到第二次世界大战爆发，护士被征召赴战场救护，空中服务人员的条件才放宽，不用具备护士资格。

world's first flight attendant, changing the onboard experience forever, where passengers were wined and dined and slept in bunk beds.[7]

FLIGHT CREW, EARLY AMERICAN AIRLINES AD

Did you have a nice trip?

PASSENGER, EARLY AMERICAN AIRLINES AD

Disappointed—over too quick.

AYESHA DURGAHEE, CNN CORRESPONDENT

Airlines quickly realized their cabin crew[8] could be the difference to make them stand out.[9]

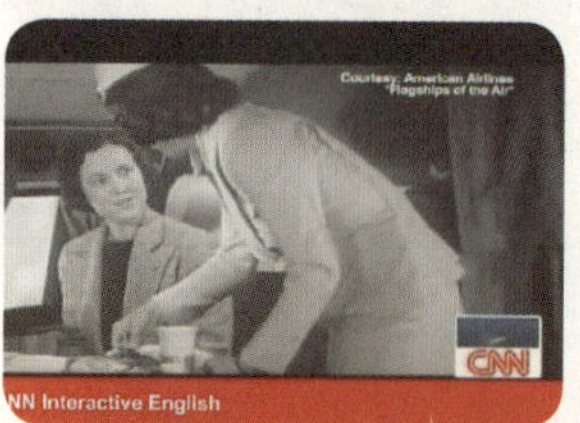

KEITH LOVEGROVE, AUTHOR, AIRLINE—IDENTITY, DESIGN & CULTURE

The cabin crew are an intrinsic[10] part of the corporate identity. I certainly think from the '50s and '60s, that's where it really started. That's where the jet set was born.

AYESHA DURGAHEE, CNN CORRESPONDENT

From Braniff babes to Singapore girls—the glamour,[11] the allure[12] of a flight attendant. Pat Pierce knows all too well. She was BA cabin crew for 35 years. Going through the different uniforms at the BA museum, the paper dresses bring back fond[13] memories.

PAT PIERCE, FORMER FLIGHT ATTENDANT

We only wore them for New York down to the Caribbean, so you put them on and then trotted[14] out onto a snowy tarmac[15] in New York with these little green shoes on down there, and this flower in your hair. You felt quite special in those days. It

持有飞行员驾照。她从此改变了乘机的经历，为乘客提供饮酒和餐点，并让他们睡在双层卧铺上。

早期美国航空公司广告　空中服务人员
您的旅程愉快吗？

早期美国航空公司广告　乘客
很失望……结束得太快了。

CNN 特派员　爱伊莎 • 德加希
航空公司很快就发现，空中服务人员可以成为他们在市场中突出的特色。

《航空公司——形象、设计与文化》作者　基思 • 洛夫格罗夫
空中服务人员是企业形象不可分割的一部分。我认为这种情形始于 20 世纪 50 及 60 年代，也就是富豪搭机客真正诞生的时代。

CNN 特派员　爱伊莎 • 德加希
从布拉尼夫航空的辣妹到新加坡航空的美女——空中服务人员总是光鲜亮丽，受人瞩目。帕特 • 皮尔斯最清楚不过了。她在英航担任空中服务人员长达 35 年。在英航博物馆看过了各式各样不同的制服，这些纸制服装勾起了美好的回忆。

前空中服务人员　帕特 • 皮尔斯
我们只会在纽约飞往加勒比海的航程上穿这种服装，所以我们会穿上这种衣服，然后踏上纽约覆盖着白雪的柏油路，脚上蹬着那种绿色小鞋，发际上插着这种花。那时你会觉

Notes & Vocabulary

jet set
富豪搭机客
jet 是“喷射机”的意思，set 在这里当名词，指“一伙、一帮人；阶层”。jet set 是指有经济能力常乘坐飞机旅行的人，也就是能过着奢华生活的有钱人、富豪阶级。

7. bunk bed [ˋbʌŋk] [bɛd]
行军床；上下铺

8. cabin crew [ˋkæbɪn] [kru]
座舱工作人员；空中服务人员（全体）

9. stand out 引人注目；脱颖而出
Jack stands out as the youngest student in his class.

10. intrinsic [ɪnˋtrɪnsɪk]
adj. 基本的；固有的
Risk is an intrinsic aspect of investing.

11. glamour [ˋglæmɚ]
n. 魅力；诱惑力

12. allure [əˋlʊr] *n.* 诱惑；引诱

13. fond [fɑnd] *adj.* 讨喜的；喜欢的
Ben has many fond memories of his trip to Spain.

14. trot [trɑt] *v.* 小跑步；疾行
When the rain stopped, the children trotted out of the schoolhouse and onto the bus.

15. tarmac [ˋtɑrˏmæk]
n. 柏油碎石子路

was a lovely time to be flying on DC-10s and 707s, and the aircraft didn't go as far as they go now, so you made more stops. Like, for instance, going to Australia, it was a three-week trip—London, Rome, Beirut, Bombay, Singapore, Sydney. When you're there living in the moment, I don't think you realize quite how special it was.

AYESHA DURGAHEE, CNN CORRESPONDENT

Cabin crew remain an integral[16] part of the onboard experience, setting the tone for passengers as soon as they hear the words "welcome aboard."

Braniff babes 布拉尼夫航空辣妹

Braniff International Airways 布拉尼夫航空公司于 1928 年创立，1982 年因油价上涨、不当扩张（expansion）等因素而破产停业。20 世纪 60 年代中期，为了摆脱航空业给人的单调印象，布拉尼夫率先找来知名建筑师设计飞机内饰（interior）及机身彩绘，并聘请知名时装设计师埃米利奥·普奇（Emilio Pucci）等人为员工设计制服，让空姐的制服开始成为焦点。

当年他们更推出“空中服务人员宽衣秀”（Air Strip），空姐们在机场时穿着大衣，到机舱后脱下大衣露出连衣裙，供餐时脱下连衣裙换上可爱便服。这样的宣传手法引来媒体争相报道，旅客增加了 49%，让布拉尼夫名噪一时，成为航空界的传奇。

得那样很特别。当时搭乘 DC-10 与波音 707 飞机是很愉快的经历，当时客机的航程没现在远，所以中途的停留站比较多。举例来说，若要到澳大利亚，就得花上三周：从伦敦、罗马、贝鲁特、孟买、新加坡到悉尼。你当时在那样的环境下，可能无法体会到那种经历有多么特别。

CNN 特派员 爱伊莎·德加希

空中服务人员至今仍是乘机体验的一部分，从乘客们一听到“欢迎登机”这句问候语开始，就奠定了他们对这次飞行的印象。

Notes & Vocabulary

set the tone for

为……奠定方向

tone 有“音调；调性”的意思，set the tone for 的字面意义是“为……定出调性”，可引申指“为……奠定方向”的意思。

· The keynote speaker's address set the tone for the conference.
那位主题演讲者的演说为会议确立了基调。

16. integral [ˋɪntəgrəl]
adj. 不可或缺的；必须的
Transparency is an integral part of any financial relationship.

非常体验 ⑬ 你知道飞机怎么停？CNN 记者亲自体验

Quest Parks[1] a Plane

Business Traveller Learns the Delicate Art of Marshaling

图片提供：photolibrary

RICHARD QUEST, BUSINESS TRAVELLER

The flying day is under way and there are 130 planes scheduled to land today. I'm going to marshal[2] one of them onto the stand[3] for real.

Learning to marshal begins in the office so I get the concept right.

KEVIN WINCELL, SENIOR AIRFIELD OPERATIONS CONTROLLER

This is the aircraft that's gonna come in, so it's not very far out. Within the next five minutes we'll be marshaling into the stand, and you'll be alright

13-F.MP3
13-S.MP3

《商务旅行家》 理查德·奎斯特
航空旅行的一天即将开始，共有 130 架次的飞机预订好要落地。我要亲自引导其中一架飞机回到停机位。

学习引导飞机要从办公室开始做起，好让我有正确的观念。

资深机场作业管制员 凯文·温塞尔
这是即将要进场的飞机，所以离机场不是太远。接下来五分钟内，我们就要把它引导到停机位上，你不会有问题的。

Notes & Vocabulary

for real 确实地
real 是“真正的”的意思，for real 则是副词短语，为口语用法，表示“真正地；认真地”。

- Jeff has flown planes in simulations, but he has never done it for real.
  杰夫玩过模拟飞行却从未开过真正的飞机。

延伸学习

Are you for real?
在美式美语的对话中常出现这句话，意思是“你是认真的吗？”，用来表示吃惊或不赞同。

- A: I've decided I want to cut off all my hair.
  我决定把头发全剪光了。
  B: Are you for real?!
  你是说真的吗？！

1. park [pɑrk] *v.* 停放（车辆、飞机等）
   Stan parked his car in a red zone and it was towed overnight.
2. marshal [ˋmɑrʃəl] *v.* 引领
   The captain marshaled the troops on the parade ground.
3. stand [stænd] *n.* 停机位；停车处

So what we've got is this is your stand over here. This is the apron road, and this is the taxiway[4] here. So when the aircraft is [has] crossed where the stand markings are for the box, you will raise your arms up in the air to signal[5] to that aircraft, this is the stand that you come into.

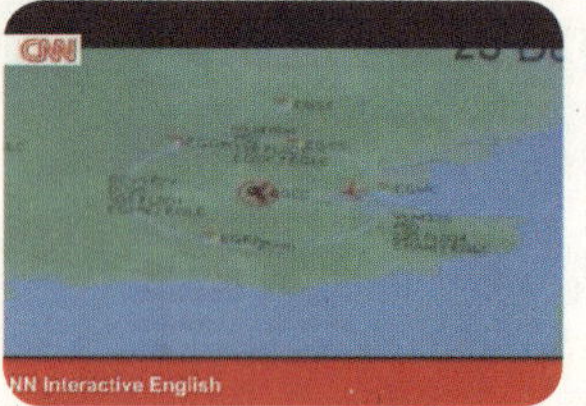

RICHARD QUEST, BUSINESS TRAVELLER

And then once he's on the second one, tell him to do that?

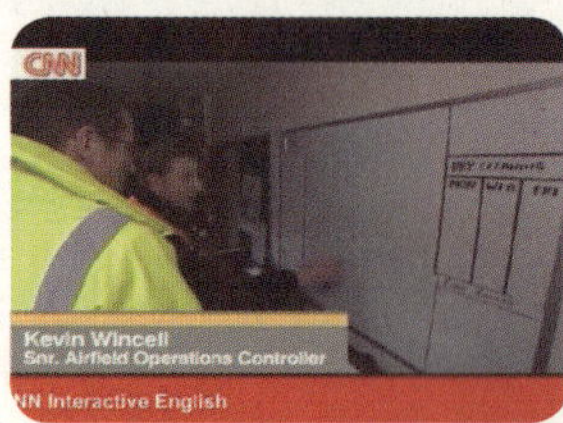

KEVIN WINCELL, SENIOR AIRFIELD OPERATIONS CONTROLLER

Yes. And what we need to do . . .

RICHARD QUEST, BUSINESS TRAVELLER

And then walk with him?

KEVIN WINCELL, SENIOR AIRFIELD OPERATIONS CONTROLLER

Walk with the nose, so keep looking at him.

RICHARD QUEST, BUSINESS TRAVELLER

Yeah.

KEVIN WINCELL, SENIOR AIRFIELD OPERATIONS CONTROLLER

Remember, we're gonna stay in the road, so you've got to keep going straight along there, and we will see that marshal in the corner. Have a look at him, hand over and just keep your arms up in the air until the wings are clear.

这里就是你的停机位，这里是停机坪道，这里则是滑行道。一旦飞机滑行超过机身的停机位标示点时，你就高举双臂向飞机打信号，告知他这里就是飞机要停靠的位置。

《商务旅行家》 理查德·奎斯特
等他到了第二个点的时候，叫他把飞机停好吗？

资深机场作业管制员 凯文·温塞尔
对，我们要做的是……

《商务旅行家》理查德·奎斯特
然后跟着他的飞机走？

资深机场作业管制员 凯文·温塞尔
跟着机鼻走，眼睛盯着他看。

《商务旅行家》 理查德·奎斯特
好。

资深机场作业管制员 凯文·温塞尔
记住，我们会在道路上，所以你一定要沿着那里直直地走，我们会看到角落那边那位引导员。看他一眼，把飞机交给他，双臂继续高举，直到机翼净空为止。

Notes & Vocabulary

4. taxiway [tæksi`we] *n.* 飞机滑行道
5. signal [`sɪgnəl] *v.* 发信号；打信号
The traffic officer signaled the cars to stop.

RICHARD QUEST, BUSINESS TRAVELLER

Just in case anybody is concerned ~~about~~ [for] what we are doing, we have the senior person here, who will be behind me. We have a second person, who will also be monitoring[6] what's happening and, of course, the captain has been warned that I'm doing this.

KEVIN WINCELL, SENIOR AIRFIELD OPERATIONS CONTROLLER

Alright, here he comes.

RICHARD QUEST, BUSINESS TRAVELLER

Here he is . . . there's a plane. That's the plane. Right, this is a first.

It may only be a little plane, but it suddenly seems very big as it's coming towards me.

KEVIN WINCELL, SENIOR AIRFIELD OPERATIONS CONTROLLER

Fantastic.[7] Well done.

RICHARD QUEST, BUSINESS TRAVELLER

So, were my instructions of any use to the pilot?

Captain?

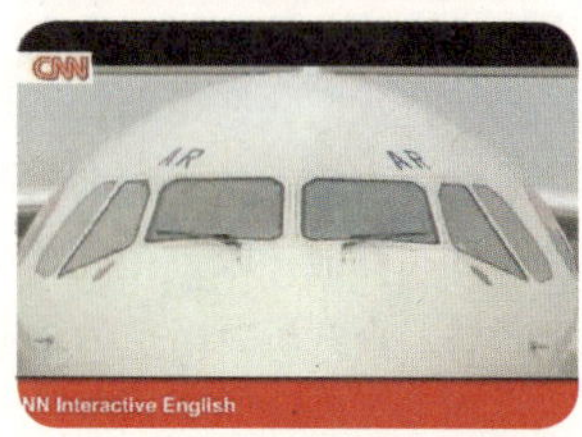

JOHN MCGHEE, PILOT

How are you doing?

RICHARD QUEST, BUSINESS TRAVELLER

Thank you very much.

JOHN MCGHEE, PILOT

No problem. Nice and easy.

RICHARD QUEST, BUSINESS TRAVELLER

Well, you did the hard bit.

《商务旅行家》 理查德·奎斯特
万一有人对于我们要做的事感到担忧，我们这里有资深人员会站在我的身后。我们有第二个人会监控一切过程，当然，机长已经接获警告，知道会由我来做这件事了。

资深机场作业管制员 凯文·温塞尔
好的，飞机来了。

《商务旅行家》 理查德·奎斯特
他来了……一架飞机。就是那架飞机，没错，这是头一次。

这也许只是一架小飞机，但当它朝着我驶来时，却忽然间看起来非常大。

资深机场作业管制员 凯文·温塞尔
太好了，干得好。

《商务旅行家》 理查德·奎斯特
我的指挥对飞行员而言有用吗？

机长吗？

飞行员 约翰·麦基
你好吗？

《商务旅行家》 理查德·奎斯特
非常感谢你。

飞行员 约翰·麦基
不客气。你做得很好。

《商务旅行家》 理查感·奎斯特
嗯，你做的才是难的部分。

Notes & Vocabulary

of any use 有用处的

of any use 表示“有用处的；帮得上忙的”，意思相当于 useful，较常用于表示质疑。

- Ted couldn't find any books that were **of any use** to him in remodeling his house.
泰德找不到任何对改建他的房屋有用处的书。

6. **monitor** [`mɑnətɚ] *v.* 监控；监测
All of the news networks monitored the election results.

7. **fantastic** [fæn`tæstɪk]
adj. 了不起的；极好的
Dina did a fantastic job planning the party.

JOHN MCGHEE, PILOT

I just watch for you to tell me what to do, and then I ~~will~~ [do it].

RICHARD QUEST, BUSINESS TRAVELLER

Does the marshaling . . . is it actually useful to you?

JOHN MCGHEE, PILOT

Very much. Well, it's not just useful, it's necessary. The wings themselves, between the other aircraft, we can't . . . one, see them, and what we can't see over, we can't judge, so we rely on the job of the marshals 100 percent.

RICHARD QUEST, BUSINESS TRAVELLER

You did a good job. Thank you very much.

JOHN MCGHEE, PILOT

Thank you.

RICHARD QUEST, BUSINESS TRAVELLER

Was I really doing that or was there somebody else doing it?

KEVIN WINCELL, SENIOR AIRFIELD OPERATIONS CONTROLLER

No, you were doing it all yourself, entirely yourself.

I would have only jumped in if he had started running over your toes.

RICHARD QUEST, BUSINESS TRAVELLER

That was so cool.

KEVIN WINCELL, SENIOR AIRFIELD OPERATIONS CONTROLLER

It is. It's fantastic stuff. You did a really good job.

13-F.MP3 / 13-S.MP3 | *Quest Parks a Plane*

飞行员　约翰・麦基
我只是看着你告诉我该如何做，然后我就照做。

《商务旅行家》　理查德・奎斯特
引导工作……真的对你有用吗？

飞行员　约翰・麦基
非常有用。不只是有用，而且有必要。这些机翼，和其他的飞机之间，我们无法……第一，我们看不到距离，然后既然我们看不到周围的距离，就无法做判断，所以我们百分之百依赖引导员的指引。

《商务旅行家》　理查德・奎斯特
你配合得很好，感激不尽。

飞行员　约翰・麦基
谢谢你。

《商务旅行家》　理查德・奎斯特
真的是我在引导吗？还是别人引导的？

资深机场作业管制员　凯文・温塞尔
没有，是你自己引导的，都是你做的。

如果他开始要碾过你的脚指头了，我才会介入。

《商务旅行家》　理查德・奎斯特
太酷了。

资深机场作业管制员　凯文・温塞尔
的确，这真是太棒了，你做得非常好。

Notes & Vocabulary

非常体验 ⑭ 总统背后的守护者——美国反狙击特勤小组

Obama's Guardian[1] Angels

Countersnipers Hunt Would-Be Presidential Assassins[2]

图片提供：photolibrary

CNN ANCHOR

Those charged with protecting the president have quite a job on their hands. Now Secret Service agents will be stationed[3] everywhere, ready to react in the blink of an eye. CNN's Jeanne Meserve has more.

U.S. SECRET SERVICE SPOTTER

First man on the gun, target one.

U.S. SECRET SERVICE SNIPER

Target one.

14-F.MP3
14-S.MP3

CNN 主播
那些被赋予保护总统任务的人有份不简单的工作。现在特勤局特工将会部署在各处，准备在瞬间做出反应。请看本台特派员吉妮·梅瑟夫的进一步报道。

美国特勤局着弹点观测员
第一位射手，一号目标。

美国特勤局狙击手
一号目标。

Notes & Vocabulary

标题扫描

would-be

可能成为的

would-be 在这里作形容词，表示“有可能成为……的”，也就是英文单词 potential 的意思。

- The would-be thief was frightened away by the barking dog.
  那个小偷嫌疑犯被吠叫的狗给吓跑了。

in the blink of an eye

一眨眼间

blink 原指“眨眼的动作”，in the blink of an eye 也就是“在一眨眼之间”，用来形容“在极短的时间内”。

- When the market collapsed, Doug saw his life savings vanish in the blink of an eye.
  股市崩盘时，道格看着他一辈子的积蓄在一眨眼间全没了。

1. guardian [`gɑrdiən]
   n. 保护者；守护者
2. assassin [ə`sæsən]
   n. 暗杀者；刺客
3. station [`steʃən] *v.* 部属
   After joining the Army, Trent was stationed in Baghdad.

名流轶事 非常体验 生活咀嚼 天地之间

U.S. SECRET SERVICE SPOTTER

Center! Hit!

JEANNE MESERVE, CNN HOMELAND SECURITY CORRESPONDENT

They shoot with great accuracy[4] at great distances.

U.S. SECRET SERVICE SPOTTER

Hit, right eye!

JEANNE MESERVE, CNN HOMELAND SECURITY CORRESPONDENT

And call it a blend[5] of art and science. They are the countersnipers of the U.S. Secret Service.

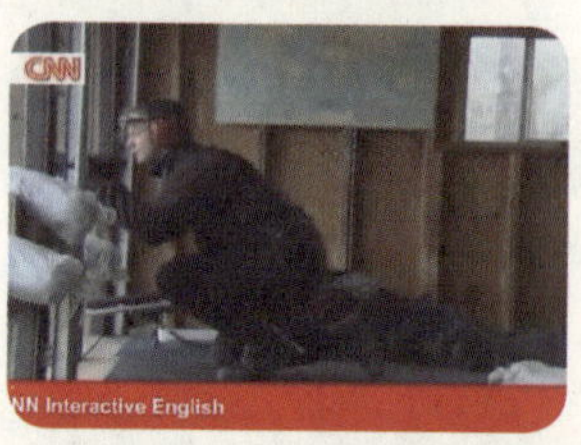

MARK SULLIVAN, DIRECTOR, U.S. SECRET SERVICE

They're very good, and I would put them among the best in the world at what they do.

JEANNE MESERVE, CNN HOMELAND SECURITY CORRESPONDENT

The countersnipers consider themselves the most elite[6] unit in the uniformed Secret Service. Nine weeks of intense[7] training turns them into Olympic-quality shooters. They have to requalify[8] monthly. Standards are so high, half of the officers accepted for training wash out.[9]

U.S. SECRET SERVICE SPOTTER

Hit, left lung!

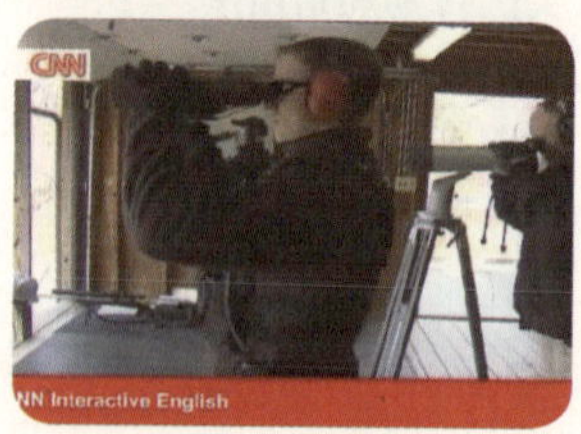

美国特勤局着弹点观测员
正中靶心！命中！

CNN 国土安全部特派员　吉妮·梅瑟夫
他们能远距离精确射中目标。

美国特勤局着弹点观测员
命中，右眼！

CNN 国土安全部特派员　吉妮·梅瑟夫
可称之为艺术与科学的结合。他们是美国特勤局的反狙击手。

美国特勤局局长　马克·苏利文
他们非常棒，我会说他们是全世界这个领域中的佼佼者。

CNN 国土安全部特派员　吉妮·梅瑟夫
这些反狙击手自认为是制服特勤特工中的精锐部队。九个星期的密集训练，使他们成为奥林匹克级的射手。他们必须每个月考核一次。标准之高，以至于有半数接受训练的军官都遭到了淘汰。

美国特勤局着弹点观测员
命中，左肺！

Notes & Vocabulary

4. accuracy [ˋækjərəsɪ]
n. 正确（性）；准确（性）

5. blend [blɛnd] *n.* 混合

6. elite [iˋlit] *n.* 精英；优秀分子

7. intense [ɪnˋtɛns]
adj. 强烈的；剧烈的
Many students face intense pressure to do well on exams.

8. requalify [rɪˋkwɑləfaɪ]
v. 重新取得资格
Wanda requalified as a nurse practitioner after taking an annual exam.

9. wash out [wɑʃ] [aʊt] 淘汰
Don wanted to be a police officer, but he washed out of the academy.

JEANNE MESERVE, CNN HOMELAND SECURITY CORRESPONDENT

Each countersniper uses a rifle[10] customized[11] for his height and arm length. They work in two-man teams. Though both are expert marksmen,[12] only one shoots at a time. The other gauges[13] the wind which can change a bullet's trajectory.[14]

U.S. SECRET SERVICE SPOTTER

Hit, high in the forehead!

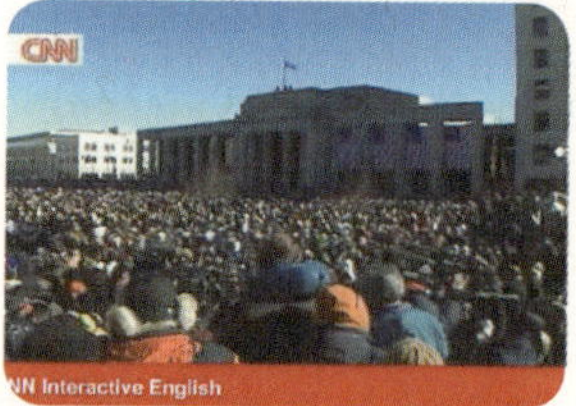

LT. BERNARD HALL, U.S. COUNTER-SNIPER UNIT

There are different methods: smoke from chimneys, undulations[15] and the mirage[16] from heat, foliage[17] on the trees, flag poles.

JEANNE MESERVE, CNN HOMELAND SECURITY CORRESPONDENT

When a president is going to move along a public route,[18] the countersnipers scout it out[19] to assess[20] the threat and find good vantage[21] points for themselves.

On Inauguration[22] Day, some will position[23] themselves on rooftops with a view of the parade route, the crowd and other buildings where snipers could be hiding. The cold will be biting, but the countersnipers can wear lightweight gloves, and they have tricks for keeping mental focus no matter what the weather.

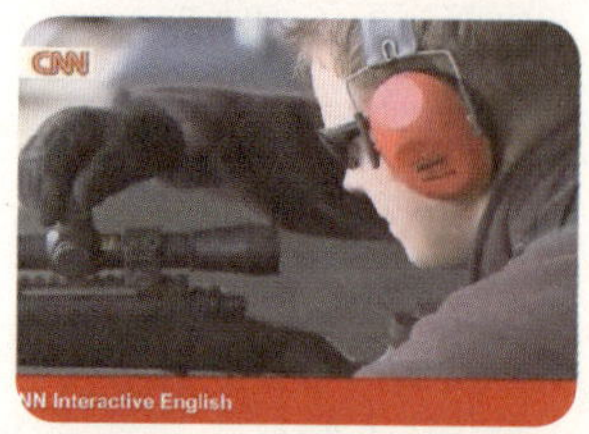

CNN 国土安全部特派员　吉妮·梅瑟夫

每一位反狙击手都会使用一把为个人身高和臂长定做的步枪，两人为一组。虽然两人都是神射手，但每次只有一人负责射击。另一人则负责测量风速，因为风速会改变弹道。

美国特勤局着弹点观测员

命中，前额上方！

美国反狙击小组　柏纳德·霍尔中尉

有各式各样的方法：烟囱冒出来的烟、热气产生的波纹和幻影、树上的枝叶、旗杆。

CNN 国土安全部特派员　吉妮·梅瑟夫

一旦总统要沿着公共道路行进时，反狙击手便会进行侦察，以评估威胁并为自己找到有利位置。

在就职日当天，有些反狙击手会部署在屋顶上，眼睛观察游行路线、群众，以及其他可能藏匿狙击手的建筑物。天气将如刺骨般的寒冷，反狙击手可以戴轻薄的手套，而且他们有在任何天气状况下保持专心的妙招。

Notes & Vocabulary

10. rifle [`raɪfl̩] *n.* 步枪；来复枪
11. customize [`kʌstə͵maɪz]
    v. 定做
    Phil customized his car with new paint and chrome wheels.
12. marksman [`mɑrksmən]
    n. 射手；神射手
13. gauge [gedʒ] *v.* 测量；判断
    The singer gauged the mood of the audience before going on stage.
14. trajectory [trə`dʒɛktərɪ] *n.* 弹道
15. undulation [͵ʌndjə`leʃən]
    n. 波动
16. mirage [mə`rɑʒ]
    n. 雾气；蜃景；海市蜃楼
17. foliage [`foliɪdʒ] *n.* 树叶；植物
18. route [rut] *n.* 路线；路程
19. scout out [skaʊt] [aʊt]
    搜寻；找寻
    The film crew scouted out locations for an important scene.
20. assess [ə`sɛs] *v.* 进行评估
    The accountants assessed the expenses needed to expand the business.
21. vantage [`væntɪdʒ] *n.* 优势
22. inauguration [ɪ͵nɔgjə`reʃən]
    n. 就职；就职典礼
23. position [pə`zɪʃən]
    v. 把……放在适当位置
    Bill positioned himself to get the best view of the parade.

LT. BERNARD HALL, COUNTER-SNIPER UNIT

When it's hot in the summer, we think about the cold days in January, and then in January, we're thinking about what's happening in August.

JEANNE MESERVE, CNN HOMELAND SECURITY CORRESPONDENT

The countersnipers make no effort to hide their location. They want the bad guys to know they're there ready to shoot if necessary.

countersniper 反狙击手

countersniper "反狙击手" 是从 sniper "狙击手" 延伸而来，"counter-" 有 to oppose / to defeat "使对抗；使击败" 的意思。

反狙击手的职责在于找出敌方的狙击手，或有暗杀（assassination）意图的歹徒。美国特勤局反狙击手小组成立于 1971 年，目前尚未在保护（safeguard）任务中击发过一颗子弹。反狙击手必须经历九周的严格训练，大约有半数会被淘汰（eliminate）。该小组自成立以来，参加训练的人数不到 200 人，成员在百人以下，其基本条件包括：

- 具有美国公民身份。
- 年龄在 21~40 岁之间。
- 具有高中以上学历。
- 健康状况良好。
- 未矫正裸视（naked eye）不得低于20/60（即0.5），矫正后不得低于20/20（即 1.5）。
- 接受家庭背景调查（background investigation），包括驾驶纪录检查（driving record check）、药物检测（drug screening）、健康检查（medical examinations）等。
- 通过笔试及测谎（polygraph examinations）。

美国反狙击小组　柏纳德·霍尔中尉

夏天热的时候，我们就想象一月的冷天，一月的时候，我们就想象八月的状况。

CNN 国土安全部特派员　吉妮·梅瑟夫

反狙击手不会刻意隐藏他们的位置。他们要坏人知道，他们已经就位，必要时将随时准备开火射击。

sniper 狙击手

美国官方也常用一些较为委婉的名词来代替 sniper 这个词，例如 precision marksman、tactical marksman、sharpshooter、precision rifleman 与 precision shooter 等。

最远狙击距离的世界纪录：

目前创下世界最远狙击射程（range）的是加拿大的佛龙下士（Corporal Rob Furlong），他以麦克米兰 TAC-50 口径步枪于 2430 米外一枪击毙一名塔利班（Taliban）武装分子。

TAC-50

Notes & Vocabulary

make no effort

毫不费力

名词 effort 是"努力；尽心"的意思，而 make no effort to do sth. 则是"毫不费力做某事"。

- Many people believed Nathan was a spy, and he made no effort to dissuade them.
  很多人相信纳森是间谍，而他完全不解释。

非常体验 ⑮ 环游世界十三年

Pedaling[1] around the World

British Adventurer Completes 13-Year Circumnavigation

图片提供：EXPEDITION 360

CNN ANCHOR

Well now for a story that might make your feet hurt just hearing about it. Now, this guy's been on the road, so to speak, for 13 years.

CNN ANCHOR

And when Jason Lewis finally returns to Greenwich, England in a couple of days, he will have circumnavigated[2] the globe.

CNN ANCHOR

Using foot-power for all 76,000 kilometers of his journey. Neil Connery has his saga.[3]

15-F.MP3
15-S.MP3

CNN 主播
接下来的报道，可能会让你光听就觉得脚痛。这家伙已经旅行跋涉了 13 年。

CNN 主播
过几天杰森 • 路易斯终于要回到英格兰的格林尼治，那也将是他完成环游世界的壮举之时。

CNN 主播
全程 76 000 千米都只靠双脚。尼尔 • 康纳利将报道他的经历。

Notes & Vocabulary

1. pedal [ˋpɛdl̩] *v.* 踩踏板
   Jan pedaled her bike to the park.
2. circumnavigate [ˋsɜkəmˋnævə͵get] *v.* 绕行一周；环航
   Magellan was the first explorer to circumnavigate the globe.
3. saga [ˋsɑgɑ] *n.* 英雄事迹；冒险故事

NEIL CONNERY, ITV NEWS CORRESPONDENT

The country Jason Lewis left 13 years ago is a very different place to the one he's returned to. In 1994, John Major was prime minister, Wet Wet Wet's single "Love is All Around" was number one, and the average house price was 50,000 pounds.

After all the challenges Jason's overcome on his grueling[4] journey, powering himself around the world using his own strength, there were just a few more obstacles[5] to navigate[6] around as he headed into Dover.

JASON LEWIS, ADVENTURER

I can see the white cliffs[7] of Dover over there. I'm pedaling towards them right now. And this sort of theoretical[8] place on the map that I've been pedaling towards for all these years, England, is now in my sights, and it's getting bigger by the hour, by the minute. It's very exciting.

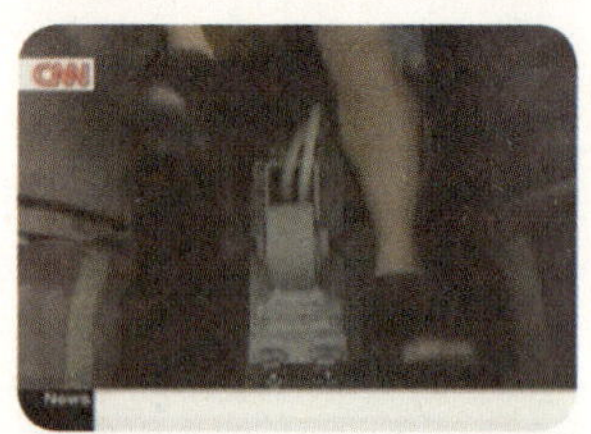

NEIL CONNERY, ITV NEWS CORRESPONDENT

Jason's journey began at the age of 26, when he set off on his 46,000-mile trip from Greenwich. He cycled across Europe in his bid to become the first man to circumnavigate the planet using only human power. He crossed the Atlantic in his 26-foot pedal boat Moksha and traveled across America on roller blades[9]. Yesterday, the 40-year-old arrived in Dover, having set off from Cape Gris Nez near Calais on the last leg of his journey, which he'll complete by pedaling up the Thames.

ITV 新闻台特派员　尼尔·康纳利

杰森·路易斯在 13 年前离开了祖国，与他现在归来所见到的英国已经非常不一样。1994 年，约翰·梅杰还是首相，湿湿湿合唱团的单曲《爱无所不在》是排行榜冠军歌曲，当时平均房价是 5 万英镑。

杰森在艰苦的旅程中克服了各种挑战，靠着自身的力量环游了世界一周。但他进入多佛之后，还必须通过几道障碍。

冒险家　杰森·路易斯

我可以看到多佛的白色悬崖。我正朝着那片悬崖迈进。地图上的这个地点，可以说就是我这些年来奔走的最终目标。英格兰如今已经在我眼前了。随着每一小时、每一分钟的流逝，英格兰不断变得愈来愈大，实在很令人兴奋。

ITV 新闻台特派员　尼尔·康纳利

杰森在 26 岁开始这趟旅程，从格林尼治出发，踏上 46 000 英里的长征。他骑自行车横跨欧洲，企图成为世界上第一个单靠人力环游世界的人。他驾驶 26 英尺长的脚踏船“解脱号”航越大西洋，接着又溜着单排轮滑跨越美洲。昨天，40 岁的杰森抵达多佛，他从加莱附近的格里斯尼兹角踏上旅程的最后这一段路。他将驾驶脚踏船沿泰晤士河而上，完成环游世界之旅。

Notes & Vocabulary

in one's bid

付出某人的全部心力

bid 当名词原本是指“出价；投标”或“叫牌”，引申为“为达目的而做的企图或努力”，类似 attempt 或 effort 的意思。in one's bid 则表示某人为了某事付出全部心力。

- David bought Helen a diamond **in his bid** to win her heart.
  大卫买了钻戒送海伦，以求能一举赢得她的芳心。

4. grueling [ˋgruəlɪŋ] *adj.* 累垮人的
   The runners faced a grueling climb up the mountain.
5. obstacle [ˋɑbstɪkl̩] *n.* 障碍；困难
6. navigate [ˋnævəˏget]
   v. 使通过
   The pilot navigated the ship into the busy harbor.
7. cliff [klɪf] *n.* 悬崖
8. theoretical [ˏθiəˋrɛtɪkl̩]
   adj. 假设的；理论上的
   The professor is an expert in theoretical physics.
9. roller blades [ˋrolɚ] [bledz]
   直排轮；单排轮滑

JASON LEWIS, ADVENTURER

That simple idea of circumnavigating the world using only just the power of the human body and mind and spirit has always fascinated[10] me. You know, it's been done by sailing boats, of course, and motor boats and everything like this, but no one's done it just using their own body.

NEIL CONNERY, ITV NEWS CORRESPONDENT

There's still a few days left to make it to London, but for now, Jason is relieved to be near journey's end.

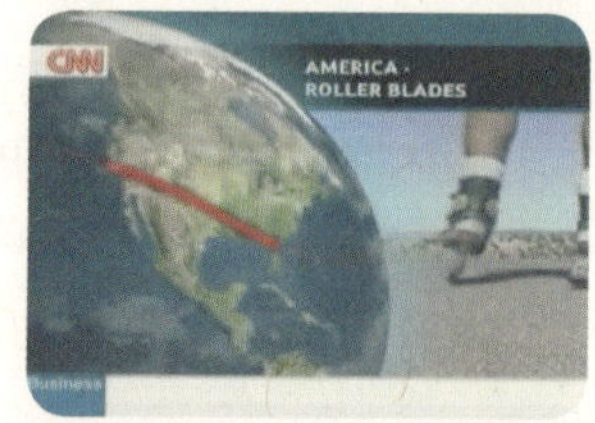

So, after 13 years, Jason Lewis finally arrives back in Britain after his epic[11] solo-powered global circumnavigation. Much has changed while he's been away, but at least he's come back to find that the British weather is, well, pretty much the same.

冒险家　杰森•路易斯
只靠着人的身体、意志和精神的力量环游世界，虽然是个很简单的概念，却一直让我深深着迷。当然，有很多人靠着帆船和汽艇等各种工具完成环游世界，但都不是只依赖自己的体力（注 1）。

ITV 新闻台特派员　尼尔•康纳利
还有几天才会抵达伦敦。不过，杰森对于旅程将近尾声已经感到相当宽慰。

于是，历经 13 年，杰森•路易斯终于完成单人自力环游世界的壮举返回英国（注 2）。在他离开的这段时间，许多人和事已物换星移，但他回来时至少会发现，英国的天气还是没什么变化。

注 1：杰森•路易斯在接近澳大利亚时，因天气不佳可能会被撞上大堡礁，因此靠机动船拖行约 20 英里靠岸，然后就继续澳洲大陆上的自行车旅程。虽然他后来回来弥补这段航程，但因旅程不连续，吉尼斯世界纪录不予承认。

注 2：杰森•路易斯在横渡大西洋及太平洋时，曾分别与队友 Steve Smith 及 April Abril 轮流踩人力船，并不是单人完成。

Notes & Vocabulary

on the/one's last leg
最后阶段、旅程

leg 不是指"腿"，而是"全部行程中的一部分"，例如一段旅程、赛程或一个阶段。on the/one's last leg 还可以表示"走到最后的地步"，类似中文"穷途末路"、"苟延残喘"的意思。

- Matt's car is on its last leg. It could break down at any moment.
  麦特的汽车已经快不行了，随时可能抛锚。

其他与 leg 连用的词组

a leg to stand on
有正当理由、立场

- Jim tried to explain his mistake, but he didn't have a leg to stand on.
  吉姆为他的过错辩解，但他提不出任何正当理由。

a leg up
优势；助力

- Mindy's connections gave her a leg up when she opened her own business.
  明迪的人脉在她创业时成为助力。

10. fascinate [ˋfæsəˏnet]
v. 令……着迷；吸引
Wildlife programs fascinate Glen.

11. epic [ˋɛpɪk] *adj.* 史诗的；英雄的
Beowulf is an epic poem that is considered one of the first works of English literature.

Circumnavigation 环球航行

circumnavigation 由前缀 circum“环绕；在……周围”和 navigation“航行；导航”组合而成，是指“环绕地球一圈的旅行”。公认的环球航行必须经过地球上的一组对跖点（antipodes），通过所有的子午线（meridian），且终点必须重回到出发点。

人力环球航行必须以人力为动力，通过步行、自行车、划船等方式，路程至少 36 787.559 千米（即北回归线 Tropic of Cancer 的长度），须通过赤道（equator），不须通过对跖点，但每段旅程须从前一段的终点出发。

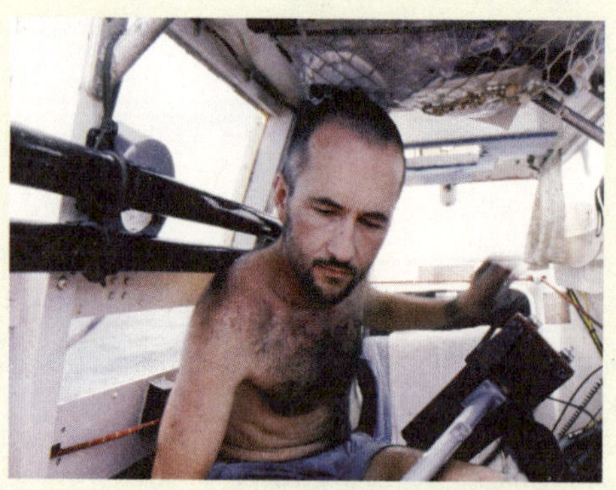

Jason Lewis 的 Expedition 360 环航之旅

1995-1996 北美洲 以自行车及单排轮滑穿越美国。途中因车祸双腿骨折疗养9个月，1996年9月抵达旧金山。

1995 大西洋 从拉各斯（Lagos）航行111天共4300英里抵达迈阿密。

2007 欧洲 骑自行车于10月抵达比利时奥斯坦德（Oostende），踩人力船过海峡，10月6日返回格林尼治完成环航。

2007 非洲 过海到东非吉布提（Djibouti），靠自行车及独木舟于7月抵达土耳其伊斯坦布尔（Istanbul）。

2006 亚洲 骑自行车往北进入中国青藏高原（Tibetan Plateau），攀越喜马拉雅山往南到印度孟买（Mumbai）。

1997 中美洲 靠自行车及独木舟（kayak）抵达洪都拉斯，因厄尔尼诺现象（El Nino）改回旧金山出海。

1994 欧洲 7月12日从格林尼治骑自行车启程，靠人力脚踏船 Moksh 号通过英吉利海峡到法国，再骑自行车到葡萄牙。

2005 进入亚洲 弥补抵澳前中断的航程后，从达尔文过海到东帝汶（East Timor），靠自行车及独木舟到新加坡。

2001 澳大利亚 骑自行车到达尔文（Darwin），暂停旅行进行募款及工作赚钱。

1998-2000 太平洋 从旧金山出发，队友 Steve Smith 在夏威夷退出。在澳大利亚外海由机动船拖行到蜥蜴岛（Lizard Island）。

资料来源：EXPEDITION 360

次郎
次郎

生活咀嚼

生活咀嚼 ⑯ 当心上网成为个人隐私的漏洞

The Death of Privacy

Social Networking Sites Expose Personal Information to Prying[1] Eyes

PAULINE CHIOU, CNN ANCHOR

It seems just about everyone online shares information with their friends on sites like Facebook and Twitter, but it's often more than just friends who see it, whether the users realize it or not. Jeanne Meserve reports on the risks of social networking sites.

JEANNE MESERVE, CNN HOMELAND SECURITY CORRESPONDENT

Dick Hardt put photos of his Hawaiian wedding on Facebook to share with close friends, but when he made mention of it on Twitter, he didn't know a link would be attached, giving more than 3,000 followers access to some rather intimate[2] images.

16-F.MP3
16-S.MP3

CNN 主播　邱波林

似乎每个上网的人都在脸书和推特这类网站上和朋友分享信息，但不管使用者知不知情，看到这些信息的常常不只是朋友。吉妮•梅瑟夫要报道社交网站的风险。

CNN 国土安全部特派员　吉妮•梅瑟夫

迪克•哈特把他在夏威夷的婚礼照片放在脸书上与密友分享。但是当他在推特上提及此事时，他不知道有个链接将被附加在推特上，这让他的 3000 多名推特粉丝得以观赏他的一些相当私密的照片。

Notes & Vocabulary

1. prying [ˋpraɪɪŋ] *adj.* 窥探的
   The celebrity couple vacationed far from the prying eyes of the paparazzi.
2. intimate [ˋɪntəmət]
   adj. 个人隐私的；私密的
   The biography contained the intimate details of the actress' life.

DICK HARDT, PUT PHOTOS ON FACEBOOK

We didn't think they were offensive in any way, but my wife didn't prefer for everybody to see those photos.

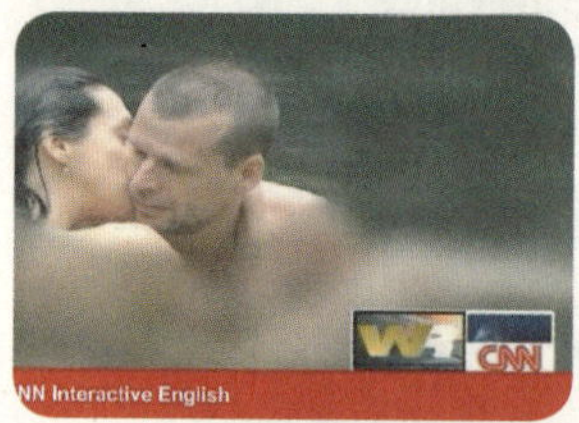

JEANNE MESERVE, CNN HOMELAND SECURITY CORRESPONDENT

While his case was embarrassing, others are downright[3] dangerous. Sarah Downey was horrified when a picture of her young daughter was hijacked from her Flickr account and used in a sexually suggestive[4] Portuguese-language profile on orchid. com, a social networking site.

SARAH DOWNEY, PRIVACY WAS EXPLOITED

It broke my heart. It broke my heart.

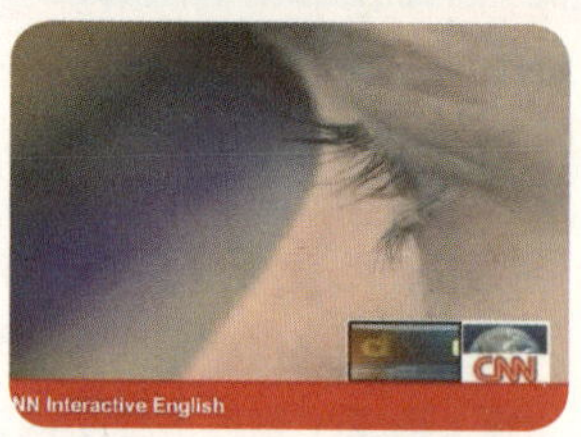

JEANNE MESERVE, CNN HOMELAND SECURITY CORRESPONDENT

Downey posted a translation to warn other Flickr users, but then she says total strangers exploited[5] the Internet to find her phone number and, worse, her home address.

SARAH DOWNEY, PRIVACY WAS EXPLOITED

We would go to the grocery store and I'd wonder, has this person seen my daughter? Are they here, you know, trying to find us? Trying to, you know, get close with [to] my daughter?

将照片放上脸书者　狄克·哈特

我们不认为这些照片有哪里让人不舒服，但我妻子不喜欢让大家看到这些照片。

CNN 国土安全部特派员　吉妮·梅瑟夫

他的例子只是让人难为情，其他的情况却是相当危险。当莎拉·道妮看到她小女儿的照片从 Flickr 账号被劫取，并放在社交网站 orchid.com 上一则有性暗示含义的葡萄牙语个人档案时，她吓坏了。

隐私遭剥削者　莎拉·道妮

我的心都碎了。

CNN 国土安全部特派员　吉妮·梅瑟夫

道妮登载了一则翻译启事，向其他 Flickr 使用者提出警告，但后来她表示素昧平生的人利用网络找到了她的电话号码，更糟的是，连她家的地址都找到了。

隐私遭剥削者　莎拉·道妮

我们去杂货店买东西时我就会想，这家伙看过我女儿吗？他们是不是正设法要找到我们，并企图接近我的女儿？

Notes & Vocabulary

3. downright [ˋdaun͵raɪt]
adj.（反面的）十足的；彻头彻尾的
After several warm days, the weather turned downright cold.

4. suggestive [səgˋdʒɛstɪv]
adj.（性）暗示的；挑逗性的
The singer's latest single contained suggestive lyrics.

5. exploit [ɪkˋsplɔɪt]
v. 利用；剥削
The virus exploits a security flaw in the software.

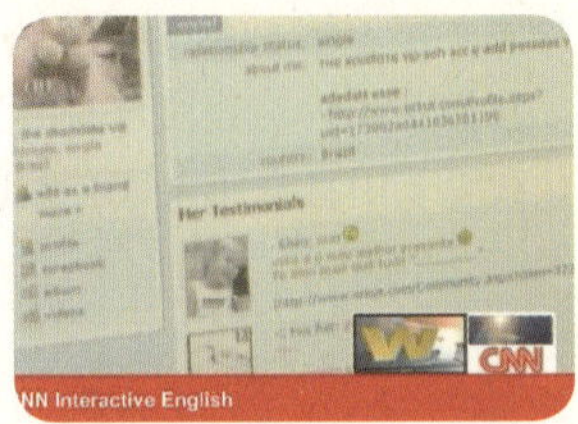

JEANNE MESERVE, CNN HOMELAND SECURITY CORRESPONDENT

Since then, Downey has tried to protect her private information. Has it worked? With her permission, we gave her name to Steven Rambam, a private investigator who harvests[6] information from the Internet. In less than 90 seconds, he turns up[7] 100 pages of possible links.

STEVEN RAMBAM, PRIVATE INVESTIGATOR

Frankly, anything you'd want to know about this young lady seems to be available on the Web.

JEANNE MESERVE, CNN HOMELAND SECURITY CORRESPONDENT

On sites like YouTube, Facebook, MySpace and Twitter, more and more Americans are making their private information public. Put it together with public documents like newspaper accounts and property records and a portrait emerges.

Take Supreme Court Justice Antonin Scalia. Using free, publicly available information on the Internet, a Fordham University law school class came up with[8] 15 pages of information, including Scalia's home address and phone number, even the movies and foods he likes.

JOEL REIDENBERG, FORDHAM UNIVERSITY LAW SCHOOL

If we were willing to spend $100 for the project, we would have been able to acquire far more intrusive,[9] far scarier information.

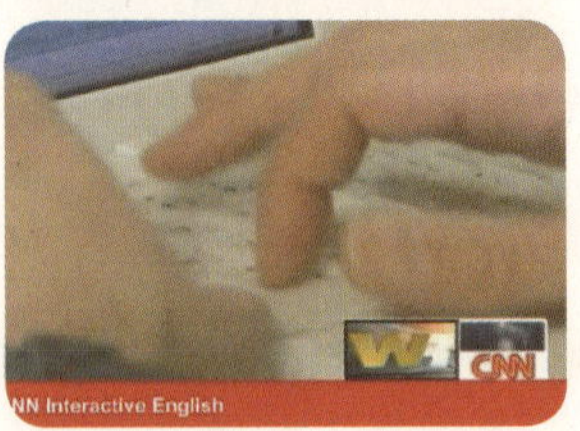

CNN 国土安全部特派员　吉妮·梅瑟夫

自此之后，道妮就想办法保护她的私人信息。有用吗？在她的允许下，我们将她的名字给了专门从网络上收集信息的私家侦探史蒂夫·兰巴姆。还不到 90 秒，他就找到了 100 页的可能链接。

私家侦探　史蒂夫·兰巴姆

老实说，关于这个小女孩的所有信息，网络上似乎都找得到。

CNN 国土安全部特派员　吉妮·梅瑟夫

越来越多的美国人在 YouTube、脸书、MySpace 和推特这类网站上公开他们的个人信息。将这些信息和类似新闻报道及财产记录这类公开文件相结合，你整个人的轮廓就随之浮现了。

就以最高法院法官安东尼·斯卡利亚为例。利用网络上的免费公开信息，佛敦大学法学院的一个班级就找到了 15 页与他有关的信息，包括斯卡利亚的家庭住址和电话号码，甚至连他喜欢的电影和食物都有。

佛敦大学法学院　乔伊·雷登堡

如果我们愿意为这个研究支付 100 美元，我们就能买到更深入、更骇人的信息。

Notes & Vocabulary

6. harvest [ˋhɑrvɪst] *v.* 收集；捕获
   The spam email was a ploy to harvest personal information from users' computers.

7. turn up 发现；注意到
   Gina turned up some old photos in the attic.

8. come up with sth.
   得出；找到；准备好
   Phil came up with several reasons to stay home this weekend.

9. intrusive [ɪnˋtrusɪv]
   adj. 侵入的；侵扰的
   The questionnaire asked several intrusive questions.

JEANNE MESERVE, CNN HOMELAND SECURITY CORRESPONDENT

Private investigator Rambam says any time you hit the "send" button, your information is no longer your own. He says your frequent flier program, movie account, book purchases, even some searches can be tracked stored and sometimes sold.

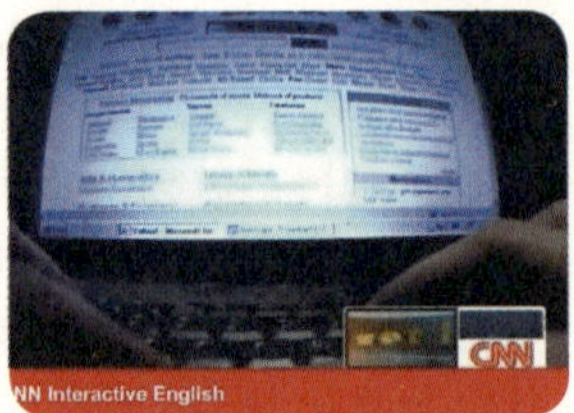

STEVEN RAMBAM, PRIVATE INVESTIGATOR

I have a window into your soul. I know what you believe. I know what you think. I know who your family is. I know who your friends are. I know your politics.[10]

JEANNE MESERVE, CNN HOMELAND SECURITY CORRESPONDENT

Orchid.com says it has updated its policies and tools to find and remove fake profiles like the one of Sarah Downey's daughter. And Google says it gives customers the tools they need to protect their personal information. Many of us could be more careful.

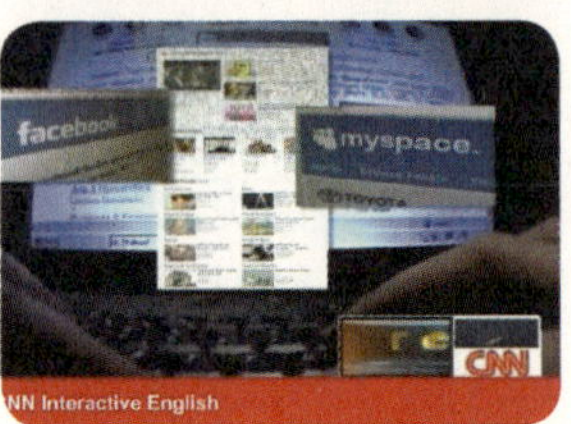

In addition, some privacy experts would like to see standardized and simplified Web site privacy policies or even government restrictions on secondhand use of private information.

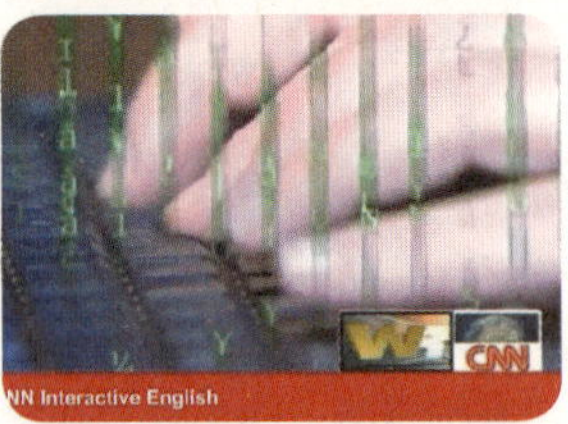

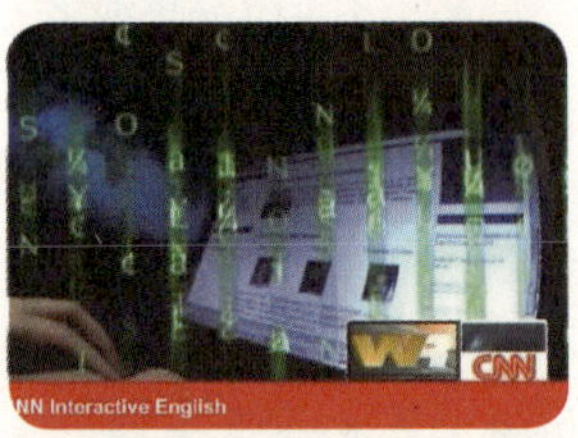

JEANNE MESERVE, CNN HOMELAND SECURITY CORRESPONDENT

Steven Rambam sees a lot of positives[11] to having so much information on the Internet and says the genie is already out of the bottle.

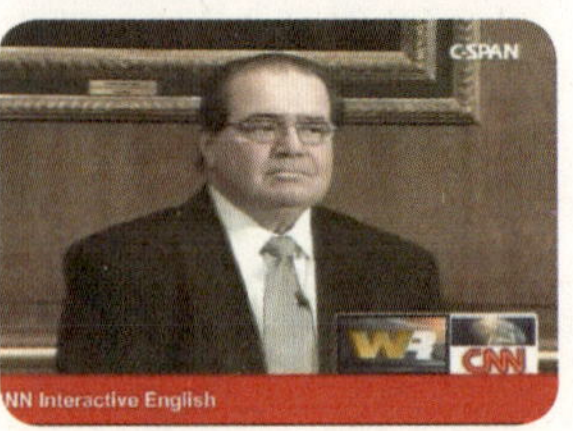

CNN 国土安全部特派员　吉妮·梅瑟夫

私家侦探兰巴姆表示，不管什么时候只要你按下“发送”键，你的个人信息就不再是你自己的了。他表示包括你的飞行里程酬宾计划、电影账户、书籍购买，甚至一些你做过的搜索都可能被追踪、储存，甚至有时还会被加以售出。

私家侦探　史蒂夫·兰巴姆

我有一扇望向你灵魂的窗口，我知道你相信些什么，我知道你在想什么，我知道你的家人是谁，我知道你的朋友有谁，我知道你的政治观点。

CNN 国土安全部特派员　吉妮·梅瑟夫

Orchid.com 网站表示他们已更新其使用政策并且把寻找和卸载莎拉·道妮女儿个人资料的工具升级。Google 则表示，他们给予顾客需要的工具来保护他们的个人信息。许多人应该更加谨慎。

此外，有些隐私专家希望能有标准化、简化的网站隐私政策，甚至还希望政府能对私人信息的再利用加以设限。

CNN 国土安全部特派员　吉妮·梅瑟夫

史蒂夫·兰巴姆认为网络上信息如此丰富好处多多，而且也已经一发不可收拾了。

Notes & Vocabulary

let the genie out of the bottle

让灾祸一发不可收拾

此谚语的典故出自瓶中精灵对将解救他的人恩将仇报的故事，后来英文便以 let the genie out of the bottle 比喻“让灾祸发生且无法回复或修正”。

- When scientists invented the atom bomb, the nuclear genie was out of the bottle.
  科学家发明原子弹后，世人就再也无法摆脱核武器的阴影了。

10. politics [ˋpɑlə͵tɪks]
    n.（个人的）政治观点、信仰（恒为复数）
11. positive [ˋpɑzətɪv] *n.* 优点

STEVEN RAMBAM, PRIVATE INVESTIGATOR

Ten years from now, you're gonna have a choice of getting used to minimal privacy or subleasing[12] the Unabomber's cabin. ~~That's~~ [Those are] going to be your two choices. The fact of the matter is there's nowhere to hide.

JEANNE MESERVE, CNN HOMELAND SECURITY CORRESPONDENT

As Rambam puts it, privacy is dead. Get over[13] it.

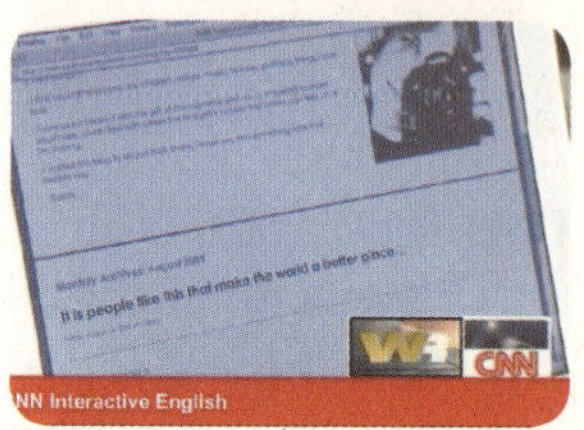

私家侦探 史蒂夫·兰巴姆

十年前，你可以选择习惯几乎没有隐私的情况，或者去向炸弹客（注）分租他的小木屋。这会是你的两个选择。不过事实就是你已无处可躲。

CNN 国土安全部特派员 吉妮·梅瑟夫

诚如史蒂夫·兰巴姆所说，隐私已死。认了吧。

注：炸弹客（Unabomber）是媒体为卡钦斯基（Theodore John Kaczynski）取的外号。他原本是大学助理教授，因为对人类文明及科技反感而毅然辞职，隐居在乡间过着离群索居、无水无电的原始生活。后来卡钦斯基的隐居地因开发受到破坏，遂决定采取激烈行动彻底解决工业、科技造成的问题。自 1978 年起，他在 20 年间陆续以匿名方式寄出炸弹，共造成 3 人死亡、20 余人伤残。最后他被弟弟指认出身份，被判处终身监禁。

Notes & Vocabulary

12. sublease [ˋsʌbˏlɪs] *v.* 分租
Will subleased his apartment while he was out of town for the summer.

13. get over 克服；妥协于；习惯于
After several weeks, Ron got over his ex-girlfriend.

生活咀嚼 ⑰ 狂发手机短信　当心意外临头

Texting[1] Traumas[2]

Fans of Mobile Messaging[3] May Be Walking into Trouble

图片提供：photos.com

CNN ANCHOR

So, let's imagine this. You're walking down the street, and you fall into a manhole[4] left unattended[5] by city workers. The city's fault—open-and-shut—right? Well, not so fast. What if you happen to be texting when you fall? Now that changes the entire story. Our Jeanne Moos has that and other unfortunate text-related accidents.

JEANNE MOOS, CNN CORRESPONDENT

It's one of those stories that almost sounds like a joke.

Did you hear about the girl that fell in the manhole . . .

17-F.MP3
17-S.MP3

CNN 主播
想象这个情景。你走在街上，结果跌进市政府工人忘了盖上的检修孔里。这是市政府的错，就这么简单，对吧？别那么快下定论。如果你跌进去的时候刚好在发短信呢？这么一来，整个情况就完全不一样了。本台的吉妮·莫斯带来的这个报道，还有其他与短信相关的不幸意外。

CNN 特派员 吉妮·莫斯
这件事故听起来就像是笑话一样。

你有没有听说有个女孩跌进了检修孔里……

Notes & Vocabulary

标题扫描

walk into 踏入（陷阱）；不小心遇上

walk into 字面上指“走进某处”，也可抽象比喻为“踏入陷阱（骗局、圈套等）”，另外还有“不小心遇上；巧遇”的意思。

- The investigators walked into a maze of government corruption when they took the case.
  调查人员承办该案件时发现了政府贪污的乱象。

open-and-shut
简单明了的；一目了然的

字面上是“打开后就关上”，形容某事物“简单明了；清楚易断”，好像只需看一眼就能明白，不用多考虑、很容易就能做出决定。

- The murder investigation was an open-and-shut case since the prime suspect confessed to the crime.
  由于主嫌犯已经认罪，该起谋杀侦查的结果已经很明白了。

1. text [tɛkst] *v.*（用手机）发短信
   Alan texted his friends the directions to the party.
2. trauma [ˋtraumə]
   n. 外伤；（心理）创伤
3. message [ˋmɛsɪdʒ] *v.* 传送信息
   Ben messaged his wife that he would be working late tonight.
4. manhole [ˋmænˏhol]
   n.（下水道等）入孔；检修孔
5. unattended [ʌnəˋtɛndɪd]
   adj. 没人照顾的；未被注意的
   Marge's purse was stolen when it was left unattended on the park bench.

名流轶事 非常体验 生活咀嚼 天地之间

UNIDENTIFIED FEMALE

Oh, my god.

JEANNE MOOS, CNN CORRESPONDENT

. . . while texting?

UNIDENTIFIED FEMALE

Oh, my god.

JEANNE MOOS, CNN CORRESPONDENT

This 15-year-old from Staten Island fell six feet into this manhole.

ALEXA LONGUEIRA

Like, there was no warning of a big open hole.

KIM LONGUEIRA, MOTHER OF ALEXA LONGUEIRA

How could my kid fall down a manhole?

JEANNE MOOS, CNN CORRESPONDENT

Well, for one thing, workers left the manhole open, her mom says, while they went to get safety cones.[6] But the daughter was also checking out a text message on a friend's cell phone. And when folks heard texting was involved,[7] insults[8] like "idiot moron[9]" started to fly. People posted joke text messages. This one translates to, "Oh my god. Be right back. I landed in sewer![10] Talk to you later once I'm out of here!!!"

The people who themselves text while walking shouldn't throw stones.

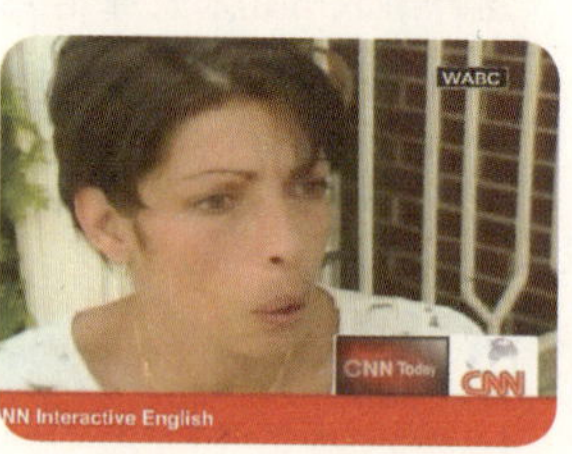

不知名女子
噢，我的天哪。

CNN 特派员　吉妮・莫斯
……而且当时她正在发短信？

不知名女子
噢，我的天哪。

CNN 特派员　吉妮・莫斯
这名来自史斯塔恩岛的 15 岁女孩，跌进了这个深达 6 英尺的检修孔里。

艾莉克莎・朗盖拉
这个敞开的大洞旁边根本没有警告标示。

金姆・朗盖拉　艾莉克莎・朗盖拉的母亲
我的孩子怎么会跌进入检修孔里？

CNN 特派员　吉妮・莫斯
她妈妈说，工人去拿安全锥的时候没有把检修孔盖上。不过，当时她女儿也正在看朋友手机上的短信。大家一旦听到这场意外和发短信有关，“智障白痴”这类侮辱性言词就都纷纷出笼了。大家在网络上发布玩笑短信。这一则火星文（编注：原文为 omg brb I landed in sewer! ttyl 1ce im out of er!!!）翻译成白话是：“天啊，马上回来。我跌进下水道了！等我爬出来再跟你聊！！！”

自己也会边走边发短信的人，不要在那里五十步笑百步了。

Notes & Vocabulary

People who . . . shouldn't throw stones.
出自谚语 “People who live in glass houses shouldn't throw stones.”，直译是“住在玻璃屋里的人最好不要扔石头。”，因为会把自己的房子砸碎，反而使自己遭殃。这个谚语是教人“自己有弱点就不要攻击别人”，免得自己难看，类似中文的“不要五十步笑百步”、“不要龟笑鳖无尾”。

6. safety cone [ˋseftɪ] [kon]
   安全锥
7. involved [ɪnˋvɑlvd]
   adj. 有关的；牵涉的
   The property developer has been involved in several large building projects.
8. insult [ˋɪnˏsʌlt] *n.* 侮辱；羞辱
9. moron [ˋmɔrˏɑn]
   n. 白痴；低能者
10. sewer [ˋsuɚ]
   n. 下水道；污水管；阴沟

名流轶事　非常体验　生活咀嚼　天地之间

UNIDENTIFIED MALE

I tripped over a cone.

UNIDENTIFIED FEMALE

I had a tree branch. I snapped[11] a tree branch like that.

JEANNE MOOS, CNN CORRESPONDENT

I run into these.

UNIDENTIFIED FEMALE

A pole[12]? We call this a pole.

UNIDENTIFIED FEMALE

I think I've walked into the middle of, like, dog leashes.[13]

UNIDENTIFIED MALE

And I ran into a bicyclist two days ago.

JEANNE MOOS, CNN CORRESPONDENT

How about a motorcyclist texting while driving on an expressway? In an age when texting occurs at 12,000 feet while free-falling, not to mention while falling asleep, someone coined[14] this term. . .

UNIDENTIFIED MALE

The techno-sexual.

JEANNE MOOS, CNN CORRESPONDENT

. . . in a mock[15] public service announcement from Web site Gizmodo. We all have our excuses.

不知名男子
我绊到过安全锥。

不知名女子
我是撞到了树枝，把一根树枝撞断了。

CNN 特派员　吉妮·莫斯
我撞到过这个。

不知名女子
路灯柱吗？我们叫这个路灯柱。

不知名女子
我想我踩进了一团狗链一类的东西。

不知名男子
我两天前撞到一位骑自行车的人。

CNN 特派员　吉妮·莫斯
那么骑摩托车的人在高速公路上一边骑车一边发短信呢？这个时代，在 12 000 英尺高空玩自由落体运动的时候也不忘发短信，更别说入睡的时候，于是有人创造了这个术语……

不知名男子
机械恋。

CNN 特派员　吉妮·莫斯
……出现在“小发明”网站一则假的公告中。每个人都有自己的借口。

Notes & Vocabulary

11. snap [snæp]
v. 啪地关上；啪地折断
The big dog easily snapped the bone he was chewing on.

12. pole [pol] *n.* 柱；竿

13. leash [liʃ]
n.（拴动物用）链条；皮带

14. coin [kɔɪn] *v.* 铸造；创造；杜撰
The comedian was known for coining several popular catchphrases.

15. mock [mɑk] *adj.* 假装的；模拟的
The students created a mock United Nations for their political science class.

UNIDENTIFIED FEMALE

I was checking a date.

JEANNE MOOS, CNN CORRESPONDENT

I read. I go through, and I delete e-mails.

UNIDENTIFIED FEMALE

I'm embarrassed by my texting. There should be a black line over it.

JEANNE MOOS, CNN CORRESPONDENT

Delete?

At the rate we're going, maybe we could use a little sonar[16] in our cell phones, as demonstrated[17] by this Hungarian research group.

Have you ever had any mishaps[18] texting while walking?

UNIDENTIFIED FEMALE

Yeah, I stepped in dog poo.[19]

JEANNE MOOS, CNN CORRESPONDENT

At least she didn't end up getting banged up[20] in a manhole with four inches of sewage.[21] LOL[22] it ain't.

不知名女子
我当时正在确认一个约会。

CNN 特派员　吉妮 • 莫斯
我会看内容，浏览一下，还有删除电子邮件。

不知名女子
我对自己发短信这件事觉得很不好意思。应该用一道黑线把手机屏幕遮起来。

CNN 特派员　吉妮 • 莫斯
要删除吗?

按照我们发生短信事故的频率来看，也许我们的手机应该装上小声呐，就像这个匈牙利研究小组的研究结果。

你有没有在边走边发短信时发生过意外?

不知名女子
有啊，踩到狗大便。

CNN 特派员　吉妮 • 莫斯
至少她没摔进污水深达 4 英寸的检修孔里而受伤。那可是一点都不好笑。

Notes & Vocabulary

16. sonar [ˋso͵nɑr] *n.* 声呐
17. demonstrate [ˋdɛmən͵stret]
v. 示范；展示
Alan demonstrated considerable skill in the kitchen when he was asked to cook dinner.
18. mishap [͵mɪsˋhæp]
n. 意外；不幸
19. poo [pu] *n.*【口】【儿】屎
20. bang up [bæŋ] [ʌp]
严重损坏；毁坏
The car was severely banged up in the accident.
21. sewage [ˋsuɪdʒ] *n.* 污水
22. LOL [ˋɛlˋoˋɛl]
大笑；狂笑（= laugh out loud）

Automated[1] Eats

German Efficiency[2] Eliminates[3] the Middleman[4] from Restaurant Dining

CNN ANCHOR

It is fast food, German style. What's been called the world's first fully automated restaurant has opened in the city of Nuremberg.

CNN ANCHOR

Very efficient[5] folk there. As Fredrik Pleitgen tells us, you might find the service a little bit robotic, but then again, you don't have to worry about the tip.

FREDRIK PLEITGEN, CNN CORRESPONDENT

Hello. Can I have a table for one, please?

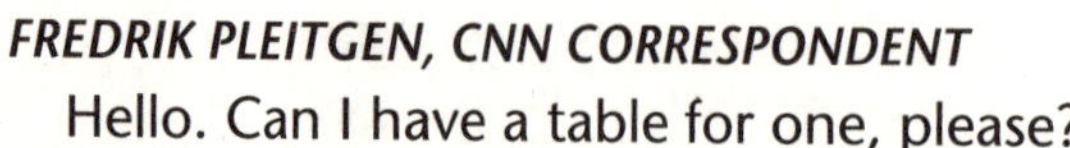

SONJA, HOSTESS, BAGGERS

Sure, no problem.

18-F.MP3
18-S.MP3

CNN 主播

这是一种德国式的快餐。被称作全球第一家全自动化的餐厅在纽伦堡开业了。

CNN 主播

那里的员工非常有效率。据弗雷德里克·普里根报道，您可能会觉得那里的服务有点机械化，但是话说回来，您不必担心付小费的事。

CNN 特派员　弗雷德里克·普里根

你好，请帮我找一个人的座位。

女服务员　索妮亚

没问题。

Notes & Vocabulary

1. automated [ˋɔtəˋmetɪd]
   adj. 机械化的；自动化的
   Automated assembly lines have replaced many workers in the automotive industry.

2. efficiency [ɪˋfɪʃənsɪ]
   n. 效率；效能；功效

3. eliminate [ɪˋlɪmə͵net]
   v. 淘汰；消除
   Marge eliminated all red meat from her diet.

4. middleman [ˋmɪdl̩͵mæn]
   n. 中间人

5. efficient [ɪˋfɪʃənt]
   adj. 效率高的
   Shelly is an efficient worker.

FREDRIK PLEITGEN, CNN CORRESPONDENT

Thank you very much.

That was Sonja, and she's pretty much the last staff member I'll be seeing at the 's Baggers restaurant in Nuremberg. Inside, it's pots, cups and bottles on a rollercoaster ride. The owners say they've designed what they believe is the world's first fully automated food ordering and delivery system. Here's how it works.

Let's just see what we'll have today. Why not a steak? And we are ready to go.

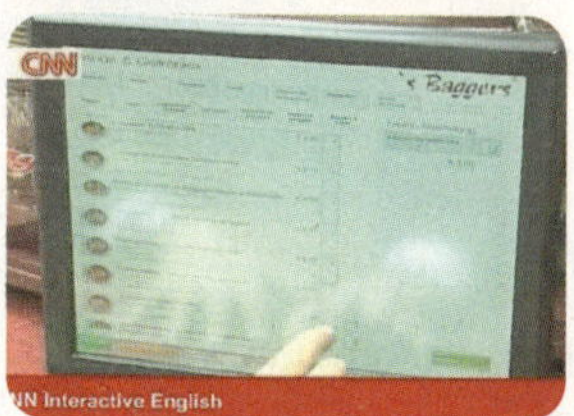

And that sets these guys in motion. A little sauce, some salad, then they put it into this specially designed . . . well, let's just call it a food sled,[6] and it's off to the races, straight to my table.

[Take] this out of here, ready to eat.

Easy enough. Most customers tell us they came for the entertainment value.

"I've never seen anything like this before," this woman says. "I think it's really funny."

"It makes eating an adventure," he says. "Certainly something totally different."

But the restaurant's creator says what looks like a cute gimmick[7] makes pretty good business sense, as well.

CNN 特派员 弗雷德里克·普里根

多谢。

见过索妮亚，她将是我在纽伦堡这家’s Baggers 餐厅所看到的最后一名员工。餐厅里会看到锅子、杯子和瓶子乘坐着过山车。餐厅主人说，他们设计出自认为是全球首家全自动化点餐及上菜系统。其运作方式如下。

来瞧瞧今天要吃些什么。何不来块牛排？我们准备好要点餐了。

这么一来，这些家伙就开始运转了。一点酱汁、些许色拉，然后放进这个特别设计的……咱们就称它为食物雪橇吧，接着就快速跑了起来，直接到达我桌上。

把这拿出来，准备吃吧。

简单得很。大部分客人告诉我们他们是冲着其娱乐价值而来的。

这位女士说：“我从未见过这种东西。我觉得这真的很有趣。”

这位男子则说：“这让吃东西变成一次冒险，绝对是截然不同的体验。”

但是餐厅创始人表示，这个看似一个可爱机关的东西，其实也很符合商业概念。

Notes & Vocabulary

set . . . in motion
使……开始进行

motion 意为“运动；移动”，短语 set sth. in motion 意为“使某事开始进行”。

- The inspiring speech **set** Natalie **in motion** to improve her career options.
  这场激动人心的演讲促使纳塔利决心加强她的职业选择。

6. sled [slɛd] *n.* 雪橇
7. gimmick [ˋgɪmɪk] *n.* 巧妙的小玩意儿

"In a fast-food restaurant, imagine[8] customers don't have to go to the counter," Michael Mack says. "You don't need an employee to take orders, or for the payment process, and then, the food just slides[9] to the table. It all becomes much more efficient with less staff."

Efficiency is what it's all about—no waiters and, of course, no tip.

's Baggers restaurant

`s Baggers®
Die fränkische Antwort
auf die globale
Herausforderung

图片提供：HeineMackGmbH

迈克尔•麦克说："想想看，客人在快餐厅里不需要走到柜台去。你不需要有员工来帮你点餐或结账，然后食物就滑到桌上。员工越少，效率就越高。"

这一切都是为了效率——没有服务生，当然也不用付小费。

Notes & Vocabulary

8. imagine [ɪˋmædʒɪn] *v.* 想象
It's hard to imagine how you got yourself stuck in the hole.

9. slide [slaɪd] *v.* 滑；滑动
It's dangerous to slide down the banister.

创办人：Michael Mack
总公司：HeineMack GmbH
餐厅设计师：Klaus Kiener & Michael Mack
开业时间：2007 年 4 月 4 日

- 选用高品质食材（high-quality ingredients），点餐前让客人清楚了解餐点的品质与来源。
- 餐点从厨房通过店内特别设计的轨道送到客人的餐桌上。
- 可使用授权自动扣缴（direct debit）付账，可月结。
- 熟客（regular customer）或推荐者可获得折价优惠（bonus）。
- 以电子邮件通知顾客餐厅的最新消息（newsletter）。
- 用餐后可在计算机上做食物与服务质量评价（review），也可看到其他顾客的评价。
- 个人偏好餐点（favorites）会记录在计算机中。
- 可为顾客特定活动（occasion）做场地设计。

生活咀嚼 ⑲ 生死一瞬间 空难逃生要诀

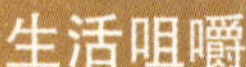

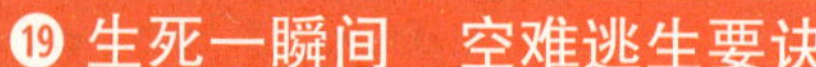

Sudden Impact

Learning to Survive a Plane Crash

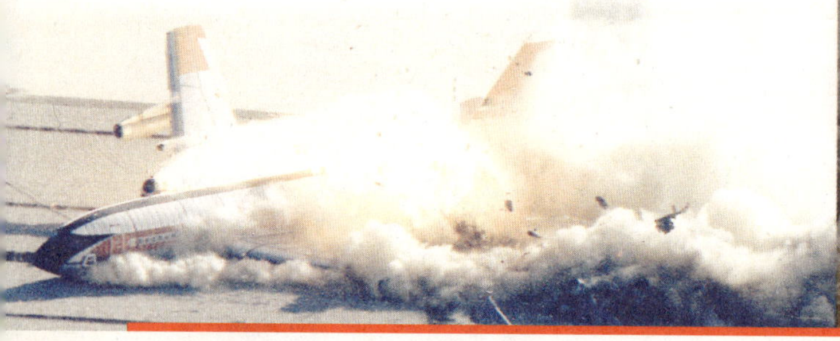

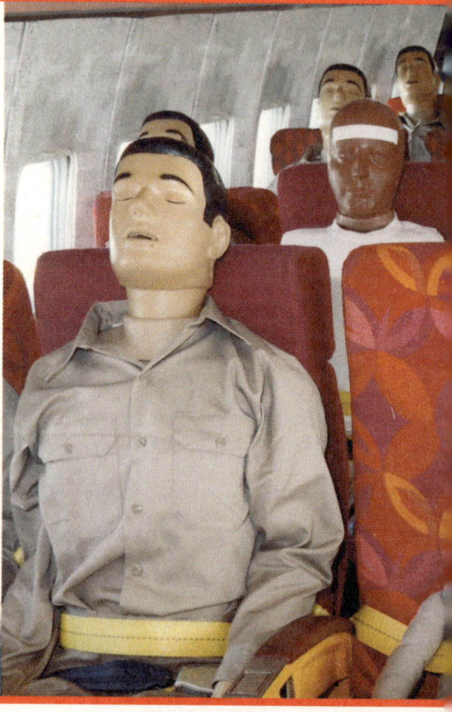

CNN ANCHOR

Thankfully, few of us will ever experience the horror of a plane crash, but you can prepare for potential[1] disaster. Our Deborah Feyerick learns how to survive a plane crash.

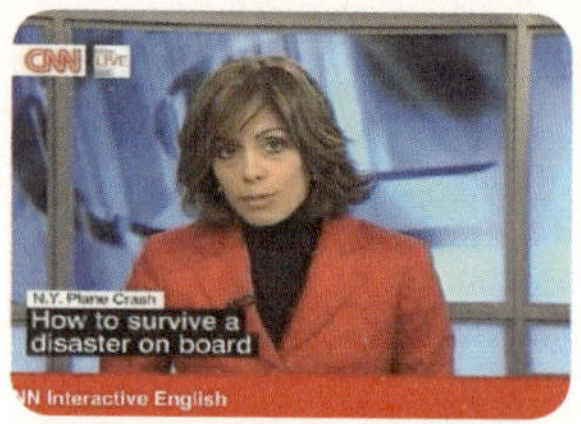

TRACY GROSS, FLIGHT ATTENDANT

The captain has just informed me that we have an engine fire, and it's on this side of the aircraft. We're gonna return back to the field and land, and evacuate[2] through the main cabin door once we've come to a complete stop.

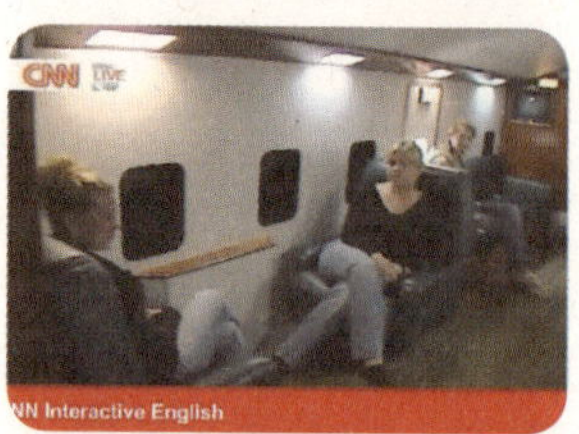

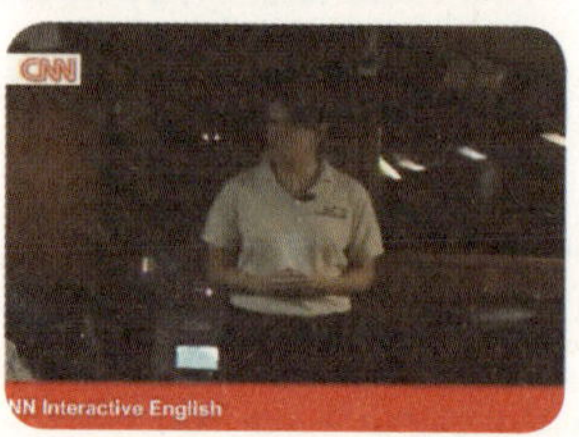

19-F.MP3
19-S.MP3

CNN 主播

感谢老天，很少有人会遇到坠机的恐怖经历。不过，你还是可以为可能发生的灾难预先做准备。本台的黛博拉·费瑞克学习了该怎么在坠机状况中存活下来。

空中服务人员　特蕾西·格罗丝

机长刚才通知我，我们的引擎起火了，是在飞机的这一侧。我们要返回机场降落，等飞机完全停下来之后，大家再从主机舱门疏散。

Notes & Vocabulary

come to

达到；及

come to 是指“达到；及”，后面接名词，意思和 reach 或 arrive at 相同，可表示具体或抽象的含义。如文中的 come to a complete stop “完全停止”，指行进中的人、车等停止下来，其他还有 come to an agreement “达成协议”等。

- The hikers came to a fork in the path.
  徒步旅行者来到一个分岔路口。

1. potential [pəˋtɛnʃəl]
   adj. 可能的；潜在的
   That toy with the small parts is a potential choking hazard.

2. evacuate [ɪˋvækjəˏet]
   v. 疏散；避难
   The firefighters evacuated the building until they figured out where the smoke was coming from.

DEBORAH FEYERICK, CNN CORRESPONDENT

Everyone is quiet as the flight attendant[3] tells us what's happening and what we need to do.

TRACY GROSS, FLIGHT ATTENDANT

Put your seat belts on nice and tight, very, very snug[4] against your hips.

BLAIN STANLEY, EVACUATION EXPERT

Pandemonium[5] and chaos[6] and mayhem[7] ~~is~~ [are] not the norm[8] per se. People look for direction. They get quiet. They look at the crew members, and they want to be led.

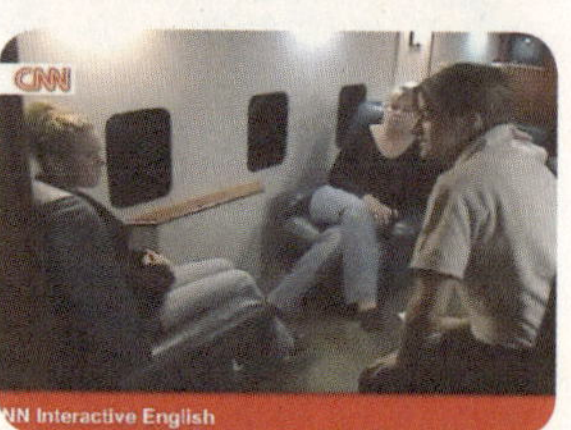

DEBORAH FEYERICK, CNN CORRESPONDENT

The pilot keeps talking to the flight attendant; the flight attendant keeps talking to us. Evacuation expert Blain Stanley, who's running the drill,[9] says communication is critical.[10]

BLAIN STANLEY, EVACUATION EXPERT

Without the communication, nobody has a plan to follow. You all need to be reading off the exact same sheet of music in order to be able to be successful in evacuating.

DEBORAH FEYERICK, CNN CORRESPONDENT

Tracy Gross, our flight attendant, shows me how to open the emergency exit.

CNN 特派人员　黛博拉·费瑞克
每个人都静静地听着空中服务人员报告目前的状况并且指示我们该怎么做。

空中服务人员　特蕾西·格罗丝
请系紧安全带，稳稳地固定住臀部。

疏散专家　布雷恩·史丹利
混乱、失控、暴乱可不是基本原则。一般人都会寻求指示，他们会安静下来，看向机组人员，希望有人引导他们。

CNN 特派员　黛博拉·费瑞克
飞行员持续指示空中服务人员，空中服务人员持续转达给我们。主导这场演习的疏散专家布雷恩·史丹利说，沟通至关紧要。

疏散专家　布雷恩·史丹利
如果没有沟通，大家就没有计划可以遵循。大家都必须完全遵照同样的指示，才能疏散成功。

CNN 特派员　黛博拉·费瑞克
我们的空中服务人员特蕾西·格罗丝教我怎么打开紧急出口。

Notes & Vocabulary

per se 就其本质而言

per se 是拉丁语，意思是 in itself 或 by itself “就其本质而言”，等于单词 intrinsically。

· Owning an endangered animal isn't illegal, per se, but their ownership is severely restricted.
拥有濒临绝种动物这件事不违法，但是其拥有资格限制得非常严格。

read off the same sheet of music 有共识

read off 是“宣读”的意思，sheet of music 就是“乐谱”，整句话字面上的意思是“宣读同一张乐谱”，表示有“相同的认知或是共识”，也等于 be on the same page。

· Beth and Tom were reading off the same sheet of music when planning their wedding together.
贝丝和汤姆在筹划他们的婚礼时有共同的认识。

3. attendant [əˋtɛndənt]
n. 服务员；随员
4. snug [snʌg] *adj.* 贴身的；舒适的
When the children were snug in their beds, the parents finally got a chance to relax.
5. pandemonium
[ˏpændəˋmoniəm] *n.* 地狱；大混乱
6. chaos [ˋkeˏɑs] *n.* 混乱；杂乱
7. mayhem [ˋmeˏhɛm]
n. 有意的破坏或暴行
8. norm [nɔrm] *n.* 基准；规范
9. drill [drɪl] *n.* 演习
10. critical [ˋkrɪtɪkəl] *adj.* 紧要的
The machine was missing several critical parts.

TRACY GROSS, FLIGHT ATTENDANT

Can you repeat that back to me?

DEBORAH FEYERICK, CNN CORRESPONDENT

I remove the cushions,[11] I take the panel[12] off, then I pull the handle and do leg body leg.

It's important that all bags be tucked away tightly.

BLAIN STANLEY, EVACUATION EXPERT

That laptop bag weighing in at eight, 10, 12 pounds, in a crash where you're pulling nine, 10, 12, 14 G's, turns into a gigantic[13] catapult[14] that will take your head off.

TRACY GROSS, FLIGHT ATTENDANT

You two, all the way over. Grab your arms in the backside[15] of your leg. Do it quick.

DEBORAH FEYERICK, CNN CORRESPONDENT

We get ready for impact.

TRACY GROSS, FLIGHT ATTENDANT

All right, everybody brace! Brace! Hold tight!

DEBORAH FEYERICK, CNN CORRESPONDENT

The next drill deals with smoke. That and fire are the two things many pilots and crew members fear most.

空中服务人员　特蕾西·格罗丝
你能跟我重复一遍吗？

CNN 特派员　黛博拉·费瑞克
我把椅背搬开，打开面板，拉手把，然后用腿和身体推撞出口。

重要的是所有的行李都要稳稳收好。

疏散专家　布雷恩·史丹利
笔记本电脑包有 8 、10 、12 磅重。坠机的时候，重力常数高达 9 、10 、12 、14 ，这时电脑包就会变成一个巨大的投石机，可以把你的头砍掉。

空中服务人员　特蕾西·格罗丝
你们两个，全身弯下去，双手环抱双腿。快点。

CNN 特派员　黛博拉·费瑞克
我们准备迎接迫降的冲击。

空中服务人员　特蕾西·格罗丝
好了，大家准备好！准备好！抓紧！

CNN 特派员　黛博拉·费瑞克
下一场演习要模拟浓烟。浓烟和大火是许多飞行员和机组人员最害怕的两样东西。

Notes & Vocabulary

weigh in
秤重；重达
weigh in 原本用在测量运动员的体重是否在标准范围之内，如拳击手因体重而有轻重量级之分，后面接 at 加上体重的数值。在其他情形下，weigh in 用 weigh 表达即可。

- David's dog weighs in at 60 kilograms.
  大卫的狗重达 60 千克。

11. cushion [ˋkuʃən]
    n. 坐垫；靠垫
12. panel [ˋpænəl]
    n. 镶板；壁板
13. gigantic [dʒaɪˋgæntɪk]
    adj. 巨大的；庞大的
    Maxine stepped into a gigantic puddle when she got out of the taxi.
14. catapult [ˋkætəˏpʌlt]
    n. 弹射器；投石机
15. backside [ˋbækˏsaɪd]
    n. 背部；后方；臀部

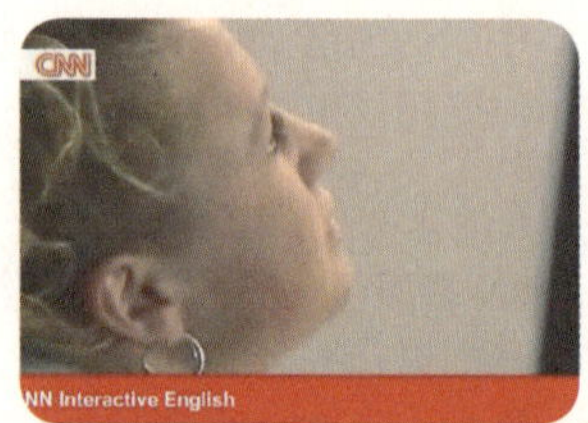

BLAIN STANLEY, EVACUATION EXPERT

Most people who are alive when the airplane comes to a stop but end up dead die because of smoke inhalation.[16] They are consumed by the smoke and fire because the evacuation does not proceed[17] rapidly enough.

TRACY GROSS, FLIGHT ATTENDANT

Does everyone see this exit?

DEBORAH FEYERICK, CNN CORRESPONDENT

It's important to know exactly where the closest exit is. The smoke is blinding.[18]

On commercial planes equipped with emergency chutes,[19] you can't just sit and slide. You have to run and jump, says flight attendant Denise Goubin.

DENISE GOUBIN, FLIGHT ATTENDANT

It's a time factor. You have to be able to exit an aircraft within 90 seconds.

DEBORAH FEYERICK, CNN CORRESPONDENT

With a water landing, it's important not to inflate[20] your vest until after you're out of the aircraft.

BLAIN STANLEY, EVACUATION EXPERT

Once you get that vest on, and you inflate it fully, it blows up to about twice your normal body size up front. Now, as you move towards the exit, if the exit is too small, you can't fit through.

疏散专家 布雷恩·史丹利
许多人在飞机降落的时候还活着，最后却因为吸入浓烟而死亡。这些人都是因为疏散速度不够快，才会被浓烟和大火吞噬。

空中服务人员 特蕾西·格罗丝
大家都看到这个出口了吗？

CNN 特派员 黛博拉·费瑞克
一定要确切知道最近的出口在哪里，浓烟会让人看不清楚。

在配备有救生滑道的商业客机上，你不能只是坐下来往下滑。空中服人务员丹尼斯·高宾说，要跑，然后跳。

空中服务人员 丹尼斯·高宾
这是时间的问题。你必须在 90 秒内离开飞机。

CNN 特派员 黛博拉·费瑞克
若是迫降水面，重要的是要到了飞机外面方可把救生衣充气。

疏散专家 布雷恩·史丹利
一旦穿上救生衣，又充满了气，它的正面面积会胀大到你正常身体大小的两倍左右。然后你往逃生门移动，假如出口不够大，你就过不去了。

Notes & Vocabulary

consume 吞噬；烧毁
consume 的原意是“消耗”或“吃；喝”，也可用来表达抽象的意思，例如 time-consuming “耗时的”、be consumed with guilt “深感内疚的”，文中解释为“被大火吞噬或烧毁”。

- Flames consumed several homes in the neighborhood.
  火焰烧光了邻区好几户人家。

blow up 胀大；膨胀
blow up 在文中是“某物体自身膨胀”的意思，但是 blow up 也可以是“给……充气；打气”的意思。

- Annie had always been thin, but she blew up during her pregnancy.
  安妮原本一直很瘦，但她怀孕时整个人胀大了起来。
- Danny blew up a lot of balloons for the party.
  丹尼为派对吹了好多气球。

16. inhalation [ˌɪnhəˋleʃən]
n. 吸入

17. proceed [proˋsid]
v. 进行；开展
The fire drill proceeded without a problem.

18. blinding [ˋblaɪndɪŋ]
adj. 使看不见的
There was a blinding flash when the fuel tank exploded.

19. chute [ʃut] *n.* 陡坡道；降落伞

20. inflate [ɪnˋflet]
v. 使充气；使膨胀
Jeff inflated the air mattress for his guests to sleep on.

DEBORAH FEYERICK, CNN CORRESPONDENT

As for us, on our smoky plane . . .

ANNOUNCER

Ten seconds, 10 seconds!

TRACY GROSS, FLIGHT ATTENDANT

Hold tight!

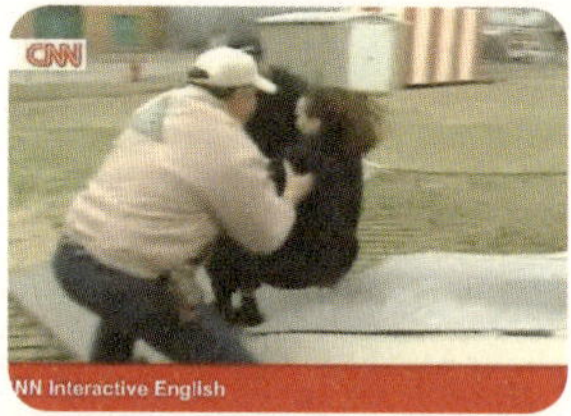

DEBORAH FEYERICK, CNN CORRESPONDENT

As our plane crashes, we climb out the window, hearts racing, even though it's just a drill.

CNN 特派员　黛博拉·费瑞克
至于我们，在这架满是浓烟的飞机上……

广播
10 秒，10 秒！

空中服务人员　特蕾西·格罗丝
抓紧！

CNN 特派员　黛博拉·费瑞克
飞机迫降之后，我们爬出窗户。虽然只是演习，还是让我们的心脏怦怦直跳。

机上紧急逃生设备

- emergency exit　紧急出口
- evacuation slide　逃生梯
- oxygen mask　氧气罩
- life vest　救生衣
- life raft　救生筏
- flotation devices (ex: seat cushion)
漂浮装置（如：椅垫）
- emergency floor lighting
紧急楼层照明

生活咀嚼 ⑳ 音乐新体验——无乐器人声乐团

Naturally in Tune

A Cappella Group Naturally 7 Rocks with Nary[1] an Instrument

图片提供：AP

CNN ANCHOR

If you haven't heard of them yet, then you're about to. The Naturally 7 music ensemble[2] has risen to international acclaim[3] over the past few years. The group boasts[4] a guitarist, a keyboard player, a drummer and a trumpeter, but as Shannon Cook now reports, they create their signature[5] sound without their instruments.

SHANNON COOK, CNN CORRESPONDENT

You're not the typical a cappella group because you're all instrumentalists[6] as well, aren't you?

20-F.MP3
20-S.MP3

CNN 主播

如果您没听过他们的声音，您很快就要听到了。过去几年来，Naturally 7 合唱团已成为国际上家喻户晓的团体。该乐团由一名吉他手、一名键盘手、一名鼓手和一名小喇叭手组成。但根据特派员夏侬·库克的报道，他们不用乐器就能制造出他们的招牌声音。

CNN 特派员　夏侬·库克

你们不是典型的人声乐器团体，因为你们也都是乐器演奏家，对吧？

Notes & Vocabulary

标题扫描

in tune 合调；协调一致

tune 在这里作名词，是“曲调”的意思，in tune 是指在音乐旋律与节奏上配合得很好。另外 in tune 加上 with 解释为“与……协调；意见一致”。

- The three singers were in tune after just one rehearsal.
  这三位歌手只经过一次排练就配合得很好了。
- It' s hard for the politicians to be in tune with one another.
  要政治人物们彼此意见相同是件困难的事。

其他与 tune 连用的词组

tune in 收听（广播）；收看（电视）

- Melba tunes in her favorite radio show every night.
  梅芭每晚都收听她最喜欢的广播节目。

tune up 给（乐器）调好音

- The singer tuned up his guitar before beginning his song.
  那位歌手在唱歌前先给他的吉他调音。

1. **nary** [`nɛrɪ]
   adj. 连……也没有（常与 a/an 连用）
   John lives by himself with nary a friend.
2. **ensemble** [ɑn`sɑmbḷ]
   n. 小型合奏（或合唱）团
3. **acclaim** [ə`klem]
   n. 欢呼；喝彩；称赞
4. **boast** [bost] *v.* 包含；拥有
   The resort boasts a golf course and a spa.
5. **signature** [`sɪgnətʃə]
   n. 特征；特色
6. **instrumentalist**
   [ˏɪnstrə`mɛntḷɪst] *n.* 乐器演奏者

名流轶事
非常体验
生活咀嚼
天地之间

ROGER THOMAS, ARRANGER & FIRST BARITONE, NATURALLY 7
We like to consider ourselves that.

SHANNON COOK, CNN CORRESPONDENT
Yet you have no instruments.

ROGER THOMAS, ARRANGER AND FIRST BARITONE, NATURALLY 7
This is also true.

Drums, bass, guitar, horns, DJ scratching—anything we can get . . . wrap our minds around we'll try to make our vocal chords[7] do it.

SHANNON COOK, CNN CORRESPONDENT
Who does the guitar, the electric guitar?

ROGER THOMAS, ARRANGER AND FIRST BARITONE, NATURALLY 7
Uh, Warren does a mean[8] electric . . . give them a little . . .

SHANNON COOK, CNN CORRESPONDENT
Wow. Now how did you find that sound?

WARREN THOMAS, GUITAR AND DRUMS, NATURALLY 7
Oh, wow, just uh . . . I guess in the shower one day.

SHANNON COOK, CNN CORRESPONDENT
Really? In the shower?

NATURALLY 7 编曲暨第一男中音　罗杰・托马斯
我们倾向这么认为。

CNN 特派员　夏侬・库克
但是你们却没有乐器。

NATURALLY 7 编曲暨第一男中音　罗杰・托马斯
这么说也没错。

鼓、贝斯、吉他、喇叭、DJ 刮碟，所有我们会的东西……我们想得到的就会尝试用声音表达出来。

CNN 特派员　夏侬・库克
谁负责吉他，电吉他的声音？

NATURALLY 7 编曲暨第一男中音　罗杰・托马斯
嗯，华伦模拟的电吉他声音很棒……来一小段吧……

CNN 特派员　夏侬・库克
你是怎么找到这样的声音的？

NATURALLY 7 吉他手及鼓手　华伦・托马斯
哦，我只是……我想是有一天冲澡的时候。

CNN 特派员　夏侬・库克
真的吗？冲澡的时候？

Notes & Vocabulary

wrap one's mind around
清楚了解

wrap one's mind around sth. 在文中是指“只要脑袋想得到”，另一个意思是“对某事清楚了解”。

- Lance couldn't **wrap his mind around** some of the concepts in his advanced physics class.
  蓝斯无法完全了解高级物理课的教学内容。

名流轶事　非常体验　生活咀嚼　天地之间

7. vocal chord [ˋvokḷ] [kɔrd]
   声带

8. mean [min] *adj.* 出色的；很棒的
   Mandy makes a mean banana daiquiri.

ROGER THOMAS, ARRANGER AND FIRST BARITONE, NATURALLY 7

There is . . . a lot of sounds are in the shower!

WARREN THOMAS, GUITAR AND DRUMS, NATURALLY 7

A lot of sounds in the shower!

SHANNON COOK, CNN CORRESPONDENT

Who does the trumpet?

ROD ELDRIDGE, TRUMPET AND DJ, NATURALLY 7

I pinch[9] my lips together . . . (plays).

Some valves[10] were getting stuck.

SHANNON COOK, CNN CORRESPONDENT

Now you're actually pretending that you're playing a trumpet. Do you play the trumpet?

ROD ELDRIDGE, TRUMPET AND DJ, NATURALLY 7

I've touched a trumpet before, but no, no, I cannot play a trumpet. It's all a part of almost being able to produce the sound, I have to visualize[11] that I'm holding that instrument or whatever in my hand.

ROGER THOMAS, ARRANGER AND FIRST BARITONE, NATURALLY 7

While we were in France, one of the executives[12] there for the label was like, "If you could sing anywhere, would you go on the train in Paris tomorrow and just start singing during rush hour?" So we did, and uh . . .

NATURALLY 7 编曲暨第一男中音　罗杰・托马斯

很多声音都是冲澡的时候想到的！

NATURALLY 7 吉他手暨鼓手　华伦・托马斯

很多声音都是冲澡时创造出来的！

CNN 特派员　夏侬・库克

谁负责小号？

NATURALLY 7 小号手暨 DJ　罗德・艾德瑞奇

我把嘴唇抿住……（表演）。

有些阀门卡住了。

CNN 特派员　夏侬・库克

现在你真的是在假装吹小喇叭。你吹小喇叭吗？

NATURALLY 7 小号手暨 DJ　罗德・艾德瑞奇

我以前摸过小喇叭，但我不会吹小喇叭。其实就是尽量去发出那种声音，我必须假想自己手上正拿着那种乐器。

NATURALLY 7 编曲暨第一男中音　罗杰・托马斯

我们在法国的时候，有家唱片公司的一名主管说："如果你们能在任何地方演唱，你们愿不愿意明天乘坐巴黎的火车，然后就在高峰时间开唱？"于是我们就这么做了，然后……

Notes & Vocabulary

9. pinch [pɪntʃ] *v.* 捏；捏住；拧
Drew pinched the edge of the bag together to seal it.

10. valve [vælv] *n.*（管乐器的）活栓

11. visualize [ˋvɪʒuə͵laɪz]
v. 想象；使形象化
Jenny visualizes her success to help her achieve it.

12. executive [ɪgˋzɛkjutɪv]
n. 经理；业务主管

SHANNON COOK, CNN CORRESPONDENT

And it caught on[13] on YouTube.

ROGER THOMAS, ARRANGER AND FIRST BARITONE, NATURALLY 7

Yeah, it caught on a whole lot, so . . .

People are always imitating instruments. People are driving, they hear their favorite song, it gets to the guitar solo part, they don't stop singing. They actually start imitating, you know, the instrument they hear. We just decided to be crazy enough to, you know, bring it to the stage.

Naturally 7 人声乐团

成名经过

Naturally 7 在 1999 年由纽约的罗杰・托马斯与华伦・托马斯两兄弟与其他五位具有才华的歌手组成。多年表演后，他们逐渐受到注意，在一次纽约举办的无伴奏人声比赛中获得冠军，接着更获得全国比赛的胜利。

乐团成员职责及模仿的乐器

- 罗杰・托马斯（Roger Thomas）——
  音乐总监（musical director）、编曲、第一男中音（1st baritone）、饶舌
- 华伦・托马斯（Warren Thomas）——
  打击乐器（percussion）、单簧管（clarinet）、第三男高音（3rd tenor）
- 罗德・艾德瑞奇（Rod Eldridge）——
  刮碟（scratching）、小喇叭（trumpet）、第一男高音（1st tenor）
- 贾迈尔・瑞德（Jamal Reed）——
  电吉他（electric guitar）、第四男高音（4th tenor）
- 德怀特・斯图尔特（Dwight Stewart）——
  第二男中音（2nd baritone）
- 加菲尔・巴克利（Garfield Buckley）——
  口琴（harmonica）第二男高音（2nd tenor）
- 阿蒙德・修顿（Armand “Hops” Hutton）——
  低音乐器（bass）

图片提供 Musik i Väst

20-F.MP3 / 20-S.MP3 | *Naturally in Tune*

CNN 特派员　夏侬・库克
结果在 YouTube 上刮起旋风。

NATURALLY 7 编曲暨第一男中音　罗杰・托马斯
对，大受欢迎，所以……

人们总是在模仿乐器的声音。开车的时候，人们听到他们最喜欢的歌，歌曲播到吉他独奏的部分时，他们不会就停下来不唱，而是开始模仿听到的乐器声。我们只是决定要搞得彻底一点，把它弄到台上表演。

无伴奏人声乐团 a cappella

意大利文 a cappella [`akə`pəlɛ] 的英文解释为 in the style of chaple “以教堂方式唱歌”，是一种不靠乐器伴奏（accompaniment）、仅运用人声所创造出来的音乐，是从中世纪教堂音乐中发展出来的一种。教堂音乐自古就有无伴奏合唱，例如“格列高利圣咏”（Gregorian Chant），就是罗马天主教会正式礼拜仪式中所唱的圣歌。

图片提供：flickr/Lady P.P.

Notes & Vocabulary

13. catch on [kætʃ] [ɔn]
流行起来
The song caught on in the U.S. and soon became internationally popular.

生活咀嚼 ㉑ 来自破铜烂铁的绝妙音符

Junk Rock

South Korean Music Group Turns Trash into Musical Instruments

图片提供：noridan

PAULINE CHIOU, CNN ANCHOR

One man's trash could be another man's treasure, and it is possible to find music in the junkyard[1] as much as in the concert hall. Kristie Lu Stout meets up with[2] the group noridan as part of our Eye on South Korea.

KRISTIE LU STOUT, CNN ANCHOR AND CORRESPONDENT

Jamming[3] at the noridan workshop[4] in Seoul, these performers are clearly enjoying their work. One artist tells me about the origin of the troupe's[5] name.

"The first part, nori, means play, and dan means group," she says. "We believe everything in life is included in the word 'play.' You have relationships,

21-F.MP3
21-S.MP3

CNN 主播　邱波林
一个人的垃圾可能是另一个人的宝藏，而在垃圾场发现音乐的可能性就和在音乐厅一样大。克莉丝蒂•陆•史道在《放眼韩国》中要见见 noridan 这个团体。

CNN 主播兼特派员　克莉丝蒂•陆•史道
这些演奏者在首尔的 noridan 工作坊里即兴演奏，他们很明显地正陶醉在表演之中。一位表演者告诉我们这个团体名称的起源。

她说："前面的 nori 代表'玩乐'，而 dan 代表'团体'，我们认为生活中的每件事都涵

Notes & Vocabulary

One man's trash could be another man's treasure.
各有所好
字面意思是"一个人的垃圾可能是另一个人的宝藏"，表示每人喜好和需要不同，意思近似于"各有所好"。trash 可以用 junk 直接替换，而 one man 和 another man 也可用人名、称谓代入。

· Will collects and sells old items because he believes one man's trash could be another man's treasure.
威尔收集、售卖二手商品，因为他认为有人不要的可能正是别人想要的东西。

1. junkyard [ˋdʒʌnk͵jɑrd]
n.【美】废物堆积场
2. meet up with（依约）见面；会面
Ben often meets up with his friends after school to play soccer.
3. jam [dʒæm] *v.* 即兴演奏
The young band jammed in their basement.
4. workshop [ˋwɜk͵ʃɑp]
n. 工作坊
5. troupe [trup]
n.（演员、歌手等的）表演团

名流轶事　非常体验　生活咀嚼　天地之间

you have learning, you have dreams, you have achievements."

The performance group started about five years ago. There are 86 members in the troupe [that] not only perform, but they also manage[6] the business.

REN HONG, NORIDAN CO-FOUNDER

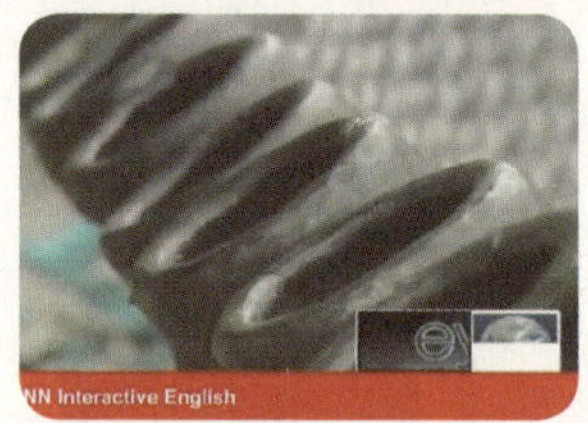

Noridan looks like just [a] normal performing group, but not only [a] performing group, but also we are [a] social enterprise in [South] Korea. So the reason that we make [made] noridan as a social enterprise is also [that] ~~the~~ self-employment[7] is [a] very important issue in [South] Korea.

KRISTIE LU STOUT, CNN ANCHOR AND CORRESPONDENT

Noridan's performers also spread an environmental message using only instruments made from recycled materials that they designed themselves.

So this is The Rickshaw[8] instrument, how does it work?

REN HONG, NORIDAN CO-FOUNDER

Well, um, playing . . . and moving.

KRISTIE LU STOUT, CNN ANCHOR AND CORRESPONDENT

But this is all made out of recycled, found materials.

REN HONG, NORIDAN CO-FOUNDER

Right, right, right.

KRISTIE LU STOUT, CNN ANCHOR AND CORRESPONDENT

So, where did you find this, and where did you find what's underneath?[9]

盖在‘玩乐’这个词中。你有友谊，你有知识，你有梦想，你有成就。”

这个表演团体成立于五年前，有 86 位成员，他们不仅参与演出，还负责经营管理。

noridan 共同创办人　洪仁

noridan 看起来就像是一般的表演团体，但我们不只是一个表演团体，我们在韩国还是一个社会企业。我们之所以将 noridan 变成社会企业，是因为自营自雇在韩国是一个非常重要的议题。

CNN 主播兼特派员　克莉丝蒂·陆·史道

noridan 的表演者也传达了环保的信息。他们只使用由再生材料制成的乐器，而这些乐器是他们自己设计的。

所以这是人力车乐器，这要如何演奏？

noridan 共同创办人　洪仁

嗯，敲奏，然后移动。

CNN 主播兼特派员　克莉丝蒂·陆·史道

但是这都是由回收和找到的材料制成的。

noridan 共同创办人　洪仁

是的，是的，是的。

CNN 主播兼特派员　克莉丝蒂·陆·史道

所以，你是在哪里发现这个的？你在哪里找到被掩埋起来的东西？

Notes & Vocabulary

6. manage [ˋmænɪdʒ]
   v. 管理；负责（公司、球队等）
   Jenny manages a small used bookstore in her neighborhood.
7. self-employment [ˏsɛlfɪmˋplɔɪmənt]
   n. 自营；自己开业
8. rickshaw [ˋrɪkˏʃɔ] *n.* 人力车
9. underneath [ˏʌndɚˋniθ]
   adv. 掩盖在下面

名流轶事 非常体验 生活咀嚼 天地之间

REN HONG, NORIDAN CO-FOUNDER

Well, in a construction yards and streets—everywhere.

KRISTIE LU STOUT, CNN ANCHOR AND CORRESPONDENT

So this is garbage, basically.

REN HONG, NORIDAN CO-FOUNDER

Right, so everything could be an instrument or the material for instruments.

KRISTIE LU STOUT, CNN ANCHOR AND CORRESPONDENT

The performance group runs music workshops for local students . . .

This is C.

REN HONG, NORIDAN CO-FOUNDER

Uh-huh.

KRISTIE LU STOUT, CNN ANCHOR AND CORRESPONDENT

. . . and also for visiting journalists.

REN HONG, NORIDAN CO-FOUNDER

F!

KRISTIE LU STOUT, CNN ANCHOR AND CORRESPONDENT

This is The Sprocket[10]—part man-powered vehicle, part musical playground.[11] It has delighted[12] noridan's audiences in [South] Korea, Australia and the UK. So, I thought I would give it a try . . . sticking to[13] some familiar musical territory.[14]

Can I take you home?

noridan 共同创办人　洪仁
嗯，在建筑工地和街道，任何地方。

CNN 主播兼特派员　克莉丝蒂 • 陆 • 史道
所以这基本上是垃圾。

noridan 共同创办人　洪仁
是的，所以所有东西都可以变成乐器，或是制成乐器的材料。

CNN 主播兼特派员　克莉丝蒂 • 陆 • 史道
这个演奏团体为当地学生举办音乐工作坊……

这是 C。

noridan 共同创办人　洪仁
嗯哼。

CNN 主播兼特派员　克莉丝蒂 • 陆 • 史道
也给造访的新闻记者。

noridan 共同创办人　洪仁
F!

CNN 主播兼特派员　克莉丝蒂 • 陆 • 史道
这是链轮，一部分是人力车，一部分是音乐游乐场。它娱乐了 noridan 在韩国、澳大利亚和英国的观众。所以，我认为我会试试，就坚守熟悉的音乐领域吧。

我可以把你带回家吗？

Notes & Vocabulary

10. sprocket [ˋsprɑkət] *n.* 链轮
11. playground [ˋpleˏgraʊnd]
    n.（集体聚会游乐的）活动场地
12. delight [dɪˋlaɪt]
    v. 使高兴；使愉快
    The magician delighted the children at the party.
13. stick to 忠于；信守
    Peter rarely sticks to projects he begins.
14. territory [ˋtɛrəˏtorɪ]
    n. 领域；地区

More about noridan

团名由来：

nori 代表“玩乐”，dan 代表“团体”，对 noridan 来说，“玩乐”这个词可以涵盖生活中的一切，通过玩乐，noridan 的团员认识彼此、培养想象力、享受成果及最终通过这一切所获得的成就感。

noridan 的性质：

不只是表演团体，还以工作坊形式为弱势群体（underprivileged class）提供艺术教育，并以“社区设计”（community design）概念努力营造以乐器为中心的公共空间（例如公园游乐场这类公共场所）。

noridan 的“自营”之道：

不同于一般对“自营”就是“个人独立开业、经营”的解释，noridan 的“自营”近似于社会企业中强调员工主动参与决策（decision making）、管理的“员工所有”经营类型。在 noridan 这个团体里，员工没有高低阶层之分，组织的领导人也只是团体中的一分子，而非掌控、管理团体者。团体由成员共同经营，收入也由所有成员共同均分。通过这样的自营精神，noridan 希望成为文艺领域的社会企业典范。另外，由于 noridan 在日本等其他国家也有分部，所以在各国 noridan 根据当地文化因地制宜，并与当地人交流的同时，各国 noridan 仍希望能将这种自营的精神传播给当地人，好让世界各地都能更了解其自营之道。

资料来源：noridan

生活咀嚼 ㉒ 猴子服务生　餐馆活招牌

Monkey Business

Tokyo Bar Patrons[1] Go Bananas for Hairy Little Waiters

图片提供：noridan

CNN ANCHOR

In a struggling economy people tend to eat out less often or to pass up[2] a night of drinking at the bar.

CNN ANCHOR

Yeah, it's a tough time for waiters, waitresses and bar tenders, and layoffs[3] are frequent.

CNN ANCHOR

Ah, but one tavern[4] in Tokyo is trying to build its clientele[5] and its staff['s] job security with a little monkeying around. Kyung Lah reports and explains.

22-F.MP3
22-S.MP3

CNN 主播
在经济困境中，大家都会倾向于减少外出就餐，或是减少到酒吧小酌一番。

CNN 主播
没错，目前这个时节对服务生和酒保实在相当辛苦，裁员的现象也很常见。

CNN 主播
不过，东京一家居酒屋却想借着要猴戏来营造顾客群，并且保住员工的工作机会。景兰带来以下报道，说明这是怎么一回事。

Notes & Vocabulary

标题扫描

go bananas

情绪激动

此短语原指猴子看到香蕉时高兴地又叫又跳，后来用来形容“情绪激动”，等于 go nuts、go crazy。此文章因为主角是会当服务生的猴子，所以标题也有双关语的意思。

· The crowd went bananas when the pop singer stepped onstage.
观众在那位流行歌手一站上舞台时全都疯狂了。

1. patron [ˋpetrən]
   n. 主顾；老顾客
2. pass up [pæs] [ʌp]
   【口】拒绝；放弃
   The basketball player passed up a scholarship to play professionally.
3. layoff [ˋleˏɔf] n. 裁员
4. tavern [ˋtævən] n. 小酒馆
5. clientele [ˏklaɪnˋtɛl]
   n.（总称）顾客

名流轶事 非常体验 生活咀嚼 天地之间

KYUNG LAH, CNN CORRESPONDENT

When you order a beer at Kayabuki Tavern, the waiter scampering[6] to your table is in a monkey suit, a real one. From the hot hand towels to the ashtrays to taking your money and delivering your change,[7] 5-year-old Fuku-chan and 12-year-old Yat-chan are working the tables, unlike thousands of food service employees who are expected to lose their jobs this year.

It's a tough time for Tokyo's 160,000 restaurants; 2008 will be a record-breaker for the number of restaurant bankruptcies[8] in Tokyo. Kayabuki says, sure, it's relying on a gimmick,[9] but that gimmick is keeping it open.

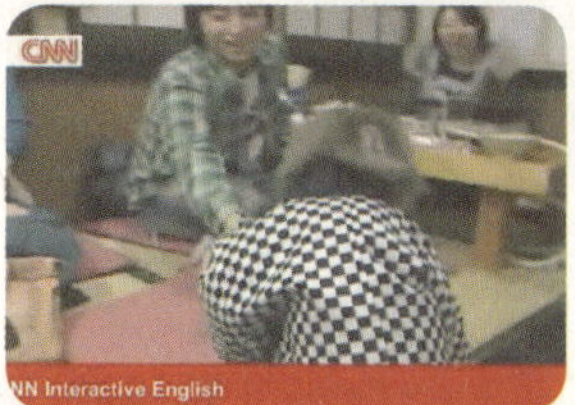

"Because of my monkeys, we get all kinds of customers," says the tavern's owner. "We're not affected by the economic downturn."[10]

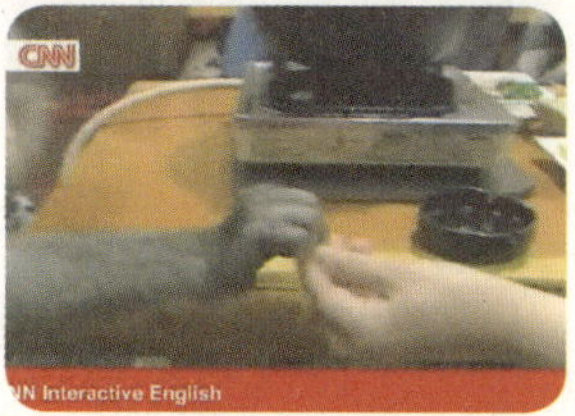

They're even bringing in tourists from around the globe.

KAYE FENNER, AMERICAN TOURIST

It's crazy.

KYUNG LAH, CNN CORRESPONDENT

The Fenners from St. Joseph, Michigan, saw the waiter monkeys on YouTube and just had to see it for themselves as part of their Tokyo vacation—not exactly something they'd see back home.

CNN 特派员 景兰

到茅葺居酒屋点一杯啤酒，跑向你桌子的服务生不但一副猴子的装束，而且真的就是猴子。不论是递送热手巾或烟灰缸还是收钱找钱，5 岁大的阿福和 12 岁大的阿谷在桌子之间忙来忙去，完全不像今年数以千计的饮食服务业员工那样面临失业危机。

对东京的 16 万家餐厅来说，目前正处于非常艰难的时光。2008 年将会是东京餐厅破产数量创新高的一年。茅葺表示，他们确实是在耍花招，但就是因为这个花招，他们才能继续经营下去。

“我的这两只猴子吸引各式各样的顾客，”这家居酒屋的老板说道：“我们没有遭到经济衰退的影响。”

他们甚至还吸引了全球各地的游客。

美国游客 凯依・费纳

真是太好玩了。

CNN 特派员 景兰

来自密歇根州圣约瑟夫的费纳夫妇，在 YouTube 网站上看到了这两只猴子服务生，于是决定到东京度假的时候一定要前来亲眼目睹——他们在家乡可看不到这样的景象。

Notes & Vocabulary

6. scamper [ˋskæmpɚ]
   v. 蹦蹦跳跳
   The students scampered out of the way of their school principal.
7. change [ˋtʃendʒ]
   n. 零钱（不可数）
8. bankruptcy [ˋbæŋkˏrəp(t)sɪ]
   n. 破产
9. gimmick [ˋgɪmɪk]
   n. 花招
10. downturn [ˋdaʊnˏtɜn]
    n. 经济衰退

GREG FENNER, AMERICAN TOURIST

I don't think they'd allow it. I mean, I see absolutely nothing wrong with it, but the animal rights people probably wouldn't allow it.

KYUNG LAH, CNN CORRESPONDENT

The owner gets around that by working his pet monkeys only two hours a day. Health department inspectors[11] gave this a green light, as long as the monkeys wear clothes, says Otska.

Now they're a nightly[12] fixture,[13] even helping to answer the phone. All they ask is a soybean or two from customers, who are eating up the monkey show and the tavern's daily dishes. And for one restaurant surviving a global economic slowdown, that's something to cheer about.

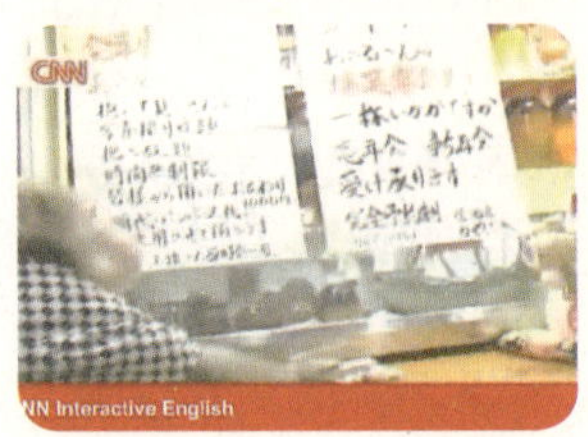

美国游客　格雷格·费纳

美国应该不会允许这种做法。我是说，我完全看不出这么做有什么问题，可是那些动物权益保护者大概不会允许这种行为。

CNN 特派员　景兰

老板只让他的宠物猴子每天工作两小时，因此得以规避侵犯动物权益的问题。卫生部门的检查员核准了这样的做法。大家说，只要这两只猴子穿上衣服就可以。

现在，他们每晚都会固定出现，甚至还会帮忙接电话。他们只会向顾客讨一两颗大豆。顾客因为着迷于这样的耍猴把戏，也就不惜到这里用餐。对于这家在全球经济衰退中挣扎求生的餐厅来说，这样的现象绝对值得拍手称庆。

Notes & Vocabulary

get around sth.

避开；规避

get around 就像是绕道而行，所以也就避掉了原本的冲突，通常是指“逃避掉了某些规定”的意思。

· Tammy got around the office online chat ban by using her smart phone.
谭米使用智能型手机规避办公室禁止在线聊天的规定。

give sth./sb. a green light

核准；许可

绿灯通常代表可以通行的意思，因此 give . . . a/the green light 也就是给予“核准；许可”。

· Gina's supervisor gave her the green light to start a new advertising project.
吉娜的主管同意她进行一个新的广告企划。

eat up

非常喜欢；着迷

词组 eat up 在这里是指 enjoy sth. completely，也就是“非常喜爱某事物”的意思。

· The children ate up the juggler's performance.
小朋友们非常着迷于小丑杂技的表演。

11. inspector [ɪnˋspɛktɚ] *n.* 检查员
12. nightly [ˋnaɪtlɪ] *adj.* 晚上的
The doctor told Jack to limit his nightly bowls of ice cream to once a week.
13. fixture [ˋfɪkstʃɚ]
n. 长期或固定参与某事的人

生活咀嚼 ㉓ 酒店房间放《圣经》的由来

Bedside Companion

The Gideons Celebrate 100 Years of Placing Bibles in Hotels Rooms

RICHARD QUEST, BUSINESS TRAVELER

There are few certainties[1] in life, but when it comes to hotels, there are three things of which I can be sure. They're called the three "Bs"—the bathroom, the bed and, of course, the Bible. Next year, the Gideons celebrate 100 years, a full century, of placing Bibles in hotel rooms. Why do they do it?

The styles may change, hotel rooms adapt,[2] but there's one accessory[3] that's been there unchanged for a century—the Bible, usually located in that bedside drawer. Often tan[4] in cover, stamped[5] with that insignia:[6] "Placed by the Gideons."

23-F.MP3
23-S.MP3

《商务旅行家》 理查德·奎斯特

人生无常，不过一谈到酒店，倒有三件事情是我敢确定的。这三件事称为“三 B”——浴室、床，当然还有《圣经》。明年基甸会的成员就要欢庆 100 周年了，他们在酒店房间里放置《圣经》的工作已经推行了整整一个世纪。他们为什么要这么做呢？

风格也许会变，酒店房间也会随着时代更新，可是有一项配置却百年来维持不变。这项配置就是《圣经》，通常放在床头边的抽屉里。酒店房间里的《圣经》封面通常是褐色的，而且印着这段文字：“基甸会致赠”。

Notes & Vocabulary

1. certainty [ˋsɜtn̩tɪ]
   n. 确定；必然
2. adapt [əˋdæpt]
   v. 改造（以适应）
   Engineers adapted the application for use on cell phones.
3. accessory [ækˋsɛsərɪ]
   n. 配件；附属品
4. tan [tæn] *adj.* 浅褐色的
   Rex wore his tan suit to his job interview.
5. stamp [stæmp]
   v. 压印；盖章；打上标签
   The immigration official stamped the visa in Trent's passport.
6. insignia [ɪnˋsɪgniə]
   n.（表示身份的）佩章；图徽

名流轶事 非常体验 生活咀嚼 天地之间

DR. EDWARD ADAMS, KING'S COLLEGE LONDON

Essentially, it goes back to the time of the Reformation where one of the big ideas of the movement was to make sure that everyone from the highest to the lowest in society would have a Bible in their own language in their own hands.

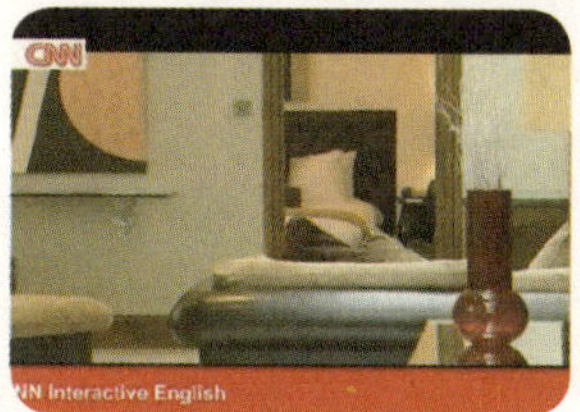

RICHARD QUEST, CNN BUSINESS TRAVELER

The Gideons have been giving away Bibles since 1909. Nearly one and a half billion Bibles have been distributed.[7]

With today's diversity[8] of beliefs, should hotels be so closely allied with one religion? Many hotel chains are now widening the beliefs.

伦敦国王学院　爱德华·亚当斯博士

基本上，这种做法可追溯至宗教改革运动时期。当时的一个主要想法，就是要让社会上所有的人都拥有一部自己语言的《圣经》。

《商务旅行家》 理查德·奎斯特

基甸会自从 1909 年开始发送《圣经》，至今已送出将近 15 亿本。

在当前这个信仰多元化的时代，酒店是否应该只和一种宗教保持这么密切的关系？许多连锁酒店都已开始注意到不同宗教信徒的需求。

Notes & Vocabulary

ally with 与……结盟；联合

ally 读做 [ə'laɪ] 或 ['æ'laɪ]，名词指“同盟国；联盟”，动词则是“结盟；联合；联姻”，常写成 ally oneself with/to 加上结盟的对象。be allied to 还有“类似；与……是同类”的意思。

- The manufacturer allied with one of its competitors to boost production.
  那家制造商和其中一个对手联合以提高生产量。

相似词

associate with 结合；合伙；结识

- The city official associated with known organized crime figures.
  那位市政府官员和知名的犯罪组织分子联手。

collaborate with 合作

- The school district collaborated with a large software manufacturer.
  该校区与一家软件大厂合作。

join forces with 与……通力合作

- The charity joined forces with several business leaders to provide holiday gifts to poor families.
  那个慈善机构与几位商界领袖合作，送过节礼物给贫穷家庭。

7. distribute [dɪˋstrɪbjut]
   v. 发配；配给
   The manager distributed the bonuses to the office staff.

8. diversity [dəˋvɜsətɪ]
   n. 多元性；多样性

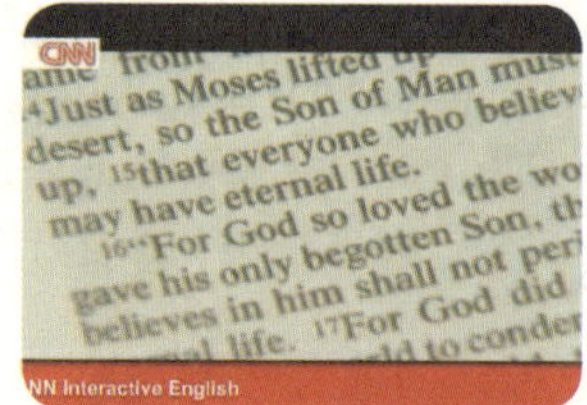

Marriot, which is owned by a Mormon[9] family, offers a Bible, plus a copy of the Book of Mormon. And the Hilton group leaves it up to their local managers to decide what's religiously proper in that society.

THOMAS LANGE, G.M., COURTHOUSE DOUBLETREE BY HILTON

Most travelers know that there is a Bible in the room so they . . . the bookers usually call us and inform us that the guest is non-Christian or is Muslim,[10] indeed, and then we will ask them, "Would you like us to mark the room against Mecca? Would you like us to provide [you] with a prayer rug and a Koran[11]?"

And then we will go, as a hotel, and get these things and prepare the rooms, and, matter of fact, especially in London, this is a very common amenity[12] that hotels provide.

DR. EDWARD ADAMS, KING'S COLLEGE LONDON

Sacred[13] texts from the major world religions should be available, but, again, there's a simple pragmatic[14] economic point insofar as it costs money to disseminate[15] these texts, and the Gideons, with the resources behind them, have taken that initiative.

由摩门教家族经营的万豪酒店，房间里除了《圣经》之外，还有一本《摩门经》。希尔顿集团则交由各地的经理自行决定什么宗教的经典比较适合当地社会。

希尔顿法院大楼双树旅馆总经理　托马斯•朗格

大多数旅客都知道房间有《圣经》，所以订房人员通常会打电话给我们，向我们告知入住的宾客是非基督徒或穆斯林。这时候，我们就会问对方：“您要不要我们在房里加上指出麦加方位的标志？要不要我们准备祈祷毯和《可兰经》？”

然后我们就会按照对方需求布置房间。实际上，这是酒店常见的服务，在伦敦尤其如此。

伦敦国王学院　爱德华•亚当斯博士

酒店应该备齐世界各大宗教的经典。但话说回来，只要准备这些经典需要花钱，酒店自然就会有经济上的考虑。所以，拥有资源的基甸会才会主动出击。

Notes & Vocabulary

up to 由……决定

up to 在口语中可表达的意思很多，本文中是“由……决定”，后面可接人或事物。

- It is up to Emily where we celebrate her birthday.
  由艾蜜丽决定我们去哪里帮她庆生。

insofar as 在某程度或范围内；由于

也写作 in so far as 或 in as far as，当作连接词词组，后面接从句，表示“到……的程度”或“在……的范围内”，也就是 to the extent/degree that 的意思。

take the initiative 采取主动

表示“采取主动”，有“率先采取行动；带头做”的意思，常用在解决问题、开展运动上。

9. Mormon [ˋmɔrmən]
   n. 摩门教（徒）
10. Muslim [ˋmʌsləm]
    n. 穆斯林；回教（徒）
11. Koran [kəˋræn] *n.* 可兰经
12. amenity [əˋmɛnətɪ]
    n. 福利设施；（环境等）舒适
13. sacred [ˋsekrəd] *adj.* 神圣的
    The city is home to several sacred sites.
14. pragmatic [prægˋmætɪk]
    adj. 实际的
    Nathan is always pragmatic in his business dealings.
15. disseminate [dɪˋsɛmə͵net]
    v. 散播；普及
    The wire service disseminates news to several media outlets.

RICHARD QUEST, CNN BUSINESS TRAVELER

The Gideons' policy of promotion[16] certainly seems to work. Each Bible placed in a hotel room has an estimated[17] six-year life span.[18] It's a potential readership[19] of 2,300 people per Bible.

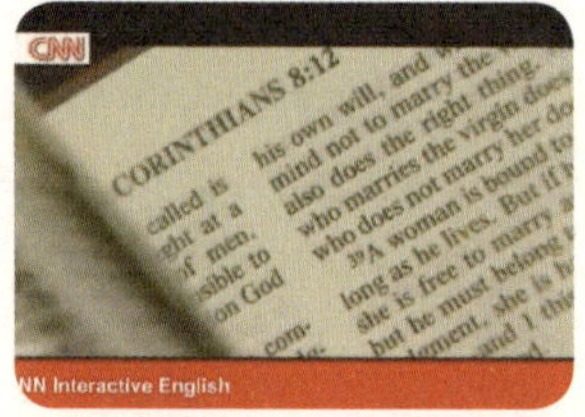

Some will read it in a moment of crisis, others will use it to give thanks, but everyone who needs it, will still find it right there.

The Gideons International 国际基甸会

由来

国际基甸会是一个国际性的福音传道基督教组织，1899 年成立于美国威斯康星州（Wisconsin）简斯维尔（Janesville）。“基甸” Gideon 一词出自《旧约全书》（Old Testament）〈士师记〉（“Book of Judges”），他是一名以色列审判官，被认为是一个完全相信并遵行上帝旨意的人，该会会员也称为 Gideon。

发放圣经的典故

基甸会的创始人与早期会员以旅行商人居多，1907 年一名理事（trustee）提议给每个酒店房间提供（furnish）一本《圣经》，1908 年此提议获得会员大会（convention）采纳并开始实施，至今已在全球 180 个国家发送 80 种语言的版本。

《商务旅行家》 理查·奎斯特

基甸会的推广策略看来确实有效。据估计，放在酒店里的《圣经》平均寿命为 6 年。因此，一本《圣经》的读者就可能多达 2300 人。

有些人会在人生面临危机的时候把《圣经》拿起来看，有些人则会用《圣经》向上天感恩。总之，有需要的人会随手可得。

Notes & Vocabulary

16. promotion [prəˋmoʃən]
n. 推广；宣传

17. estimate [ˋɛstəˏmet]
v. 估计
Sherman estimated the amount of capital he would need to launch his business.

18. life span [laɪf] [spæn]
寿命；生命期限

19. readership [ˋridəˏʃɪp]
n. 读者人数；读者身份

天地之间

天地之间 ㉔ 世界高楼比一比　哈利法塔到底有多高

A Towering[1] Achievement[2]

Imagining the Burj Khalifa in Your Hometown

图片提供：Poco a poco

PAULINE CHIOU, CNN ANCHOR

The world's tallest building is now officially open. Check out the spectacular[3] celebration in Dubai. The Burj Khalifa has 168 stories of offices and residential[4] units. Now, what if you picked up the building and dropped it into the heart of, say, another city like Tokyo, London or New York? Well, our CNN correspondents give you a look at the transformed skylines.[5]

KRISTIE LU STOUT, CNN INT'L. CORRESPONDENT

It stands over 800 meters tall, but can you picture[6] just how big the Burj Dubai really is? Using Google Earth and a 3-D model of the tower created by the Google user Quixote 3-D, we can put the Burj Dubai in some of the world's biggest cities.

24-F.MP3
24-S.MP3

CNN 主播　邱波林

世界最高的建筑已正式竣工迎客。看看迪拜壮观的庆祝活动。哈利法塔共有 168 层楼，其中包括办公室与住宅。假如把这座建筑摆在东京、伦敦或纽约的市中心，会怎么样呢？本台特派员将带您看看改变之后的天际线。

CNN 国际特派员　克莉丝蒂・陆・史道

这座建筑高度超过 800 米，可是你能想象迪拜塔究竟有多高大吗？利用 Google Earth 及谷歌使用者 Quixote 3-D 制作的迪拜塔立体模型，我们可以把迪拜塔放在全球名列前茅的几座大城市里。

Notes & Vocabulary

1. towering [ˋtaʊərɪŋ]
   adj. 高耸的；卓越的
   The towering building dominates the city's skyline.
2. achievement [əˋtʃivmənt]
   n. 成就；功绩
3. spectacular [spɛkˋtækjələ]
   adj. 壮观的；壮丽的
   The lookout point offers a spectacular view of the Grand Canyon.
4. residential [ˏrɛzəˋdɛnʃəl]
   adj. 住宅的；适合居住的
   The quiet residential neighborhood is the perfect place to raise a family.
5. skyline [ˋskaɪˏlaɪn]
   n. 天际线；地景的轮廓
6. picture [ˋpɪktʃə] *v.* 描述；想象
   Gerald pictured himself lying in a hammock on the beach when thinking of his upcoming vacation.

This is the famous Hong Kong skyline, and this is Google Earth's version of the skyline with one addition,[7] the Burj Dubai. As you can see, it is almost twice the height of Hong Kong's tallest skyscraper,[8] 2IFC, and it's taller than the mountains surrounding Hong Kong Harbor. Now, that is what it would look like here, and our correspondents around the world have been playing the same game.

KYUNG LAH, CNN INT'L. CORRESPONDENT

I'm Kyung Lah in Tokyo. This is Shabuya Crossing, made famous in the movie *Lost in Translation*. Not too many tall buildings here, and in Tokyo overall there aren't that many skyscrapers. You put the Burj in any Japanese neighborhood, it would dwarf[9] everything.

The reason there aren't that many skyscrapers: the number of earthquakes, strict city codes[10] and Japan has just gone through two decades of slow economic growth, so the skyline here, a glimpse[11] into the economy and geology[12] of Japan.

DON RIDDELL, CNN INT'L. CORRESPONDENT

I'm Don Riddell in London at one of our picture postcard sites, the Houses of Parliament and Big Ben. What would the Burj Dubai look like here? Well, to be quite honest, I can't imagine. It would dwarf the entire city. For a start, Big Ben really wouldn't be that big. The Burj would be eight-and-a-half times higher than the iconic clock face.

这是香港著名的天际线；这是 Google Earth 里加上了迪拜塔的天际线。各位可以看到，比起中国香港最高的摩天大楼 2IFC，迪拜塔是它的将近两倍高，也比维多利亚港周围的山都还要高。这是迪拜塔在这里看起来的模样，而我们派驻世界各地的特派员也都玩了相同的游戏。

CNN 国际特派员　景兰

我是景兰，这里是东京。这是涉谷交叉口，因为电影《爱情，不用翻译》而著名。这里没有太多的高楼大厦，整个东京其实也没有太多的摩天大楼。不论把迪拜塔放在日本的哪个地方，其他建筑都会显得非常娇小。

这里之所以没有太多摩天大楼，是因为日本地震多，都市法规相当严格，而且日本经济也才刚经历了 20 年的缓慢增长。所以，从这里的天际线，即可窥见日本的经济与地理状态。

CNN 国际特派员　唐 • 利德尔

我是唐 • 利德尔，在伦敦为您带来报道。这里是伦敦的著名景点：国会大厦与大本钟。如果把迪拜塔放在这里，看起来会是什么样？老实说，我实在无法想象。整座城市一定都会相形失色。别的不说，大本钟看起来就不会那么大了。迪拜塔的高度是这座著名钟塔的 8.5 倍高。

伦敦并非以摩天大楼闻名。不久之后，欧洲

Notes & Vocabulary

7. addition [əˋdɪʃən] *n.* 增加物
8. skyscraper [ˋskaɪˏskrepɚ] *n.* 摩天楼；摩天大厦
9. dwarf [dwɔrf] *v.* 使显得矮小
   The tall basketball star dwarfed the other players on the team.
10. code [kod] *n.* 法规；准则
11. glimpse [glɪmps] *n.* 一瞥；瞥见；略见
12. geology [dʒɪˋɑlədʒɪ] *n.* 地质；地质学

名流轶事　非常体验　生活咀嚼　天地之间

Well, London isn't really known for its skyscrapers. It will soon be home to the tallest building in Europe, but at 300 meters high, the Shard London Bridge will still only be less than half the height of the Burj Dubai.

SUSAN CANDIOTTI, CNN CORRESPONDENT

I'm Susan Candiotti on a freezing, blustery[13] winter day in New York, and this is Columbus Circle, the southern entrance to Central Park, the Big Apple's biggest green space among a cavern[14] of high-rises[15] and skyscrapers. It's pretty hard to picture, but if you plunked down the Burj Dubai in the middle of Central Park, well, it would tower over the Empire State Building. Measuring just over 440 meters, it's slightly over half as tall as the Burj Dubai. Imagine that.

KRISTIE LU STOUT, CNN INT'L. CORRESPONDENT

Now, the Burj will also reclaim[16] a title that used to be held by the Arab world. For thousands of years, the tallest structure in the world was this, the Great Pyramid of Giza. You can see just how far we've come since then.

最高的建筑将会坐落在这里。不过，伦敦桥沙德大楼虽然会高达 300 米，却还不及迪拜塔的一半。

CNN 特派员　苏珊·康迪欧提

我是苏珊·康迪欧提，在纽约这个冰冷风大的冬日为您报道。这里是哥伦布圆环，是中央公园的南入口。在大苹果四处林立的高楼大厦当中，中央公园是城里最大的一片绿地。虽然很难想象，但如果把迪拜塔摆在中央公园的中心，其高度将远高于帝国大厦。帝国大厦的高度只稍微超过 440 米，只有迪拜塔的一半再多一点。真是难以置信。

CNN 国际特派员　克莉丝蒂·陆·史道

现在，迪拜塔也将为阿拉伯世界夺回原有的头衔。过去数千年来，世界上最高的建筑物一直是吉萨金字塔。看看人类今天的进展已和当初距离了多远。

Notes & Vocabulary

plunk down

猛然放下

plunk 也拼作 plonk，原指“刮奏；快速弹拨”吉他或琴键，发出短促的声音，后来引申出“随意地放下”及“随便坐下；重重坐下”之意，常与 down 连用。

- After dinner, Silva plunked down Alex's birthday gift in the center of the table.
  晚餐过后，希薇雅把亚历山大的生日礼物随意地放在餐桌中央。

13. blustery [ˋblʌstərɪ] *adj.* 刮大风的
    Donald brought a jacket with him in case the weather turned blustery.
14. cavern [ˋkævərn]
    n. 大山洞；岩洞
15. high-rise [ˋhaɪˋraɪz] *n.* 高楼
16. reclaim [rɪˋklem]
    v. 拿回；取回；索回
    The team reclaimed their place at the top of league standings.

Burj Khalifa 哈利法塔

高度：828 米

占地：464 511 平方千米

兴建：2004 年 9 月 21 日至 2009 年 10 月 1 日

开业：2010 年 1 月 4 日

设计：芝加哥 SOM 建筑事务所 Adrian Smith

造价：15 亿美元

楼层：200 层

楼层使用：

60 F 以上	大楼设备
156F-159F	通信广播
125F-155F	企业办公室及大楼设备
124F	At the Top 观景台（世界最高）
123F	Sky Lobby 空中楼阁及游泳池（世界最高）
122F	At.mosphere 餐厅
111F-121F	企业办公室
77F-110F	住家及大楼设备
76F	Sky Lobby 空中楼阁
44F-75F	住家及大楼设备
43F	Sky Lobby 空中楼阁
38F-42F	Armani 精品酒店套房及大楼设备
9F-37F	Armani 住宅及大楼设备
GF-8F	Armani 精品酒店
大厅	Armani 精品酒店
B1-B2	停车场及大楼设备

世界高楼比一比

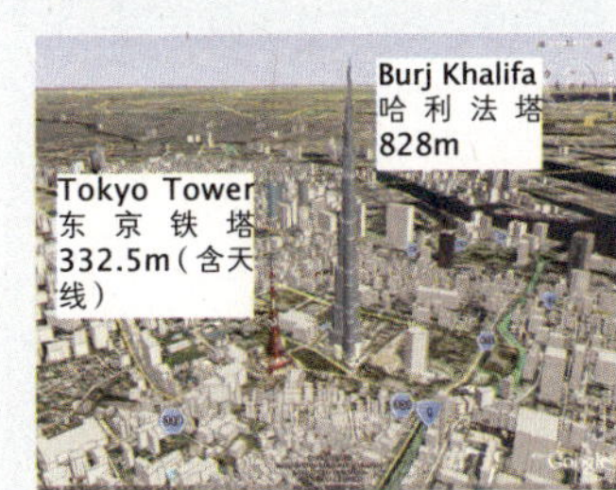

如果哈利法塔在东京……

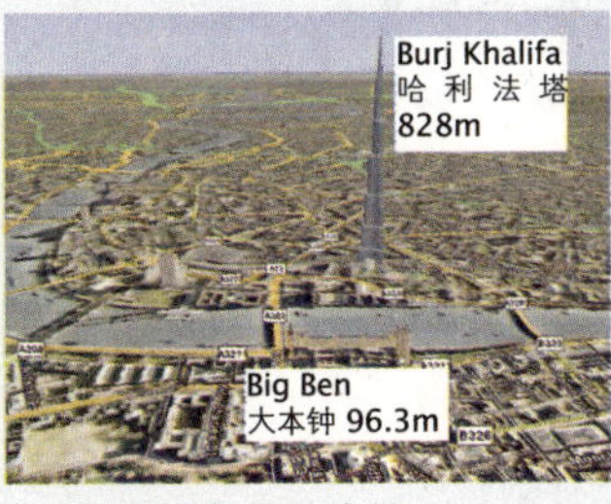

如果哈利法塔在伦敦……

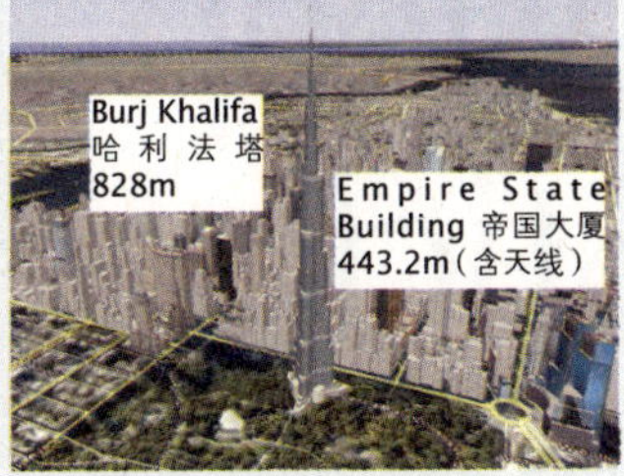

如果哈利法塔在纽约……

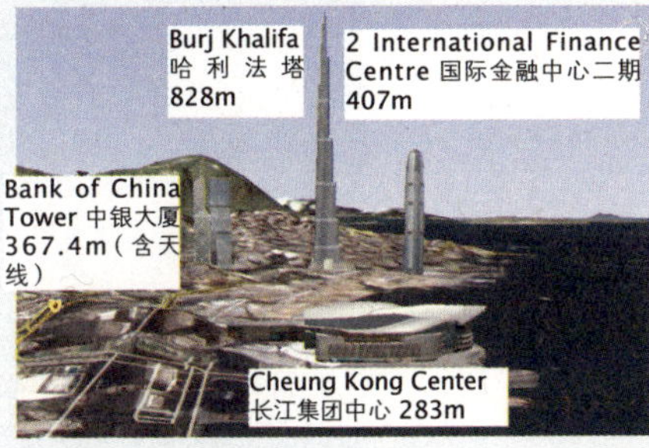

如果哈利法塔在香港……

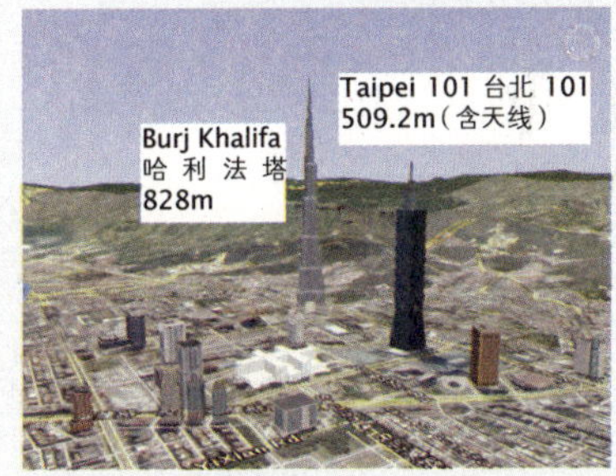

如果哈利法塔在台北……

天地之间 ㉕ 降低飞行安全风险的对策——让机长小睡片刻

Asleep at the Stick[1]

Tired Pilots May Soon Catch Their 40 Winks on the Wing

ANNA COREN, CNN ANCHOR

Well, we've all been known to catch 40 winks on a plane, assured the pilot is wide[2] awake. Well, think again. As CNN's Allan Chernoff found out, cockpit[3] napping is about to be endorsed.[4]

ALLAN CHERNOFF, CNN SENIOR CORRESPONDENT

NASA studied the idea of pilot naps here at its Silicon Valley research center 20 years ago and found naps to be effective and safe in reducing[5] pilot fatigue.[6]

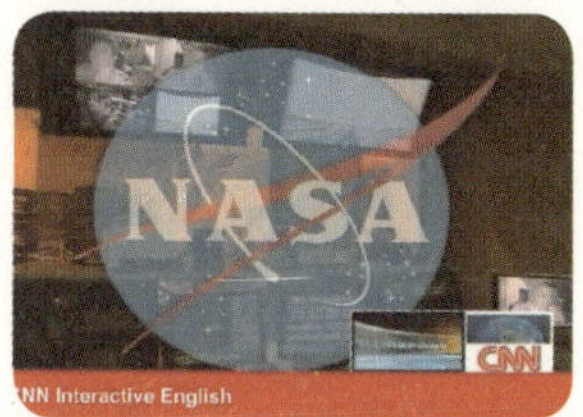

25-F.MP3
25-S.MP3

CNN 主播　安娜·可伦

我们乘坐飞机都不免会小睡一下，并且相信飞行员一定会保持清醒。这个嘛，你最好再想想。本台的艾伦·切诺夫采访发现，在驾驶舱里打盹的行为即将获得认可。

CNN 资深特派员　艾伦·切诺夫

二十年前，美国国家航空航天局就在硅谷研究中心研究过允许飞行员小睡一段时间的构想，结果发现这么做对于降低飞行员的疲劳非常有效，而且也相当安全。

Notes & Vocabulary

catch 40 winks

小睡片刻

wink 可指“很短的（睡眠）时间；眯一下”，而“40”这个数字在《圣经》中则有“相当大量；相当长时间”的含义，如诺亚方舟故事中就形容淹没世界的大雨下了 40 个昼夜（And the rain was upon the earth forty days and forty nights.）。所以 catch/get 40 winks 便以“多眯了好几下”比喻“小睡片刻”，意同 take a nap。

- I'll just catch 40 winks before I get to work.
  我在上班前要小睡一下。

1. stick [stɪk] *n.* 飞机的操纵杆
2. wide [waɪd] *adv.* 充分地
3. cockpit [ˋkɑkˏpɪt]
   n.（飞机或赛车的）驾驶舱
4. endorse [ɪnˋdɔrs]
   v.（公开）赞成；认可
   The President is unlikely to endorse this policy.
5. reduce [rɪˋdus]
   v. 减少；减低
   The newly issued law should reduce drunk driving accidents.
6. fatigue [fəˋtig] *n.* 疲累

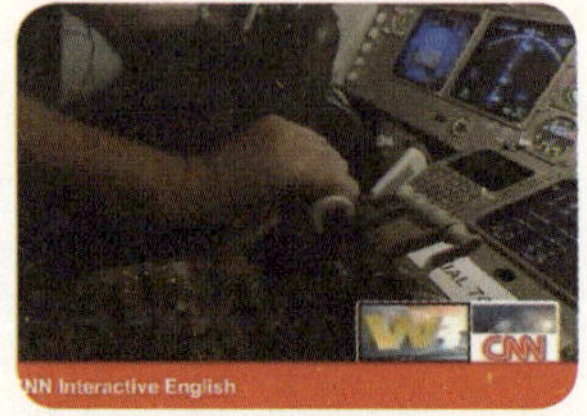

CURT GRAEBER, FORMER NASA SCIENTIST

The FAA paid for that research, and we've shown very clearly that the nap really improved[7] performance and alertness[8] of the flight crews.[9]

ALLAN CHERNOFF, CNN SENIOR CORRESPONDENT

Now an airline industry advisory[10] committee has told the Federal Aviation Administration, "We recommend that the FAA endorse controlled cockpit napping."

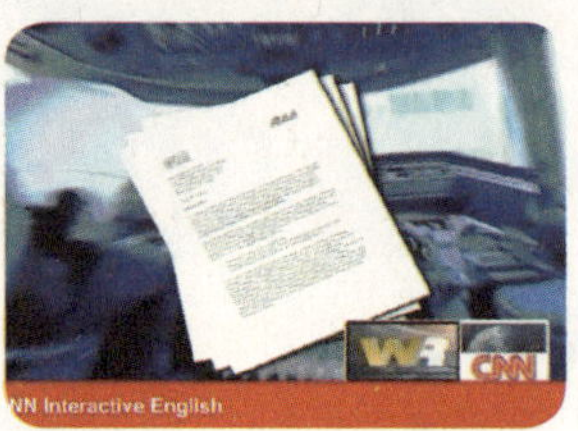

MELISSA MALLIS, FLIGHT RESEARCH ASSOCIATES

Power napping, which we often refer to it as, can help increase physiological[11] alertness and [decrease] sleepiness. And so it is a strategy that can be used to help mitigate[12] and manage[13] fatigue during any 24/7 environment.

ALLAN CHERNOFF, CNN SENIOR CORRESPONDENT

Foreign carriers,[14] including British Airways and Air Canada, for years have permitted naps on longer flights, allowing one pilot to rest in the cockpit while the other pilot mans[15] the controls.[16] Aviation[17]

前美国国家航空航天局科学家　科特·格瑞柏

那项研究是由美国联邦航空管理局资助进行的。我们确切证明小睡一会儿的确改善了机组人员的表现与警觉性。

CNN 资深特派员　艾伦·切诺夫

现在，一个航空顾问委员会向美国联邦航空管理局指出："我们建议美国联邦航空管理局认可适度的驾驶舱睡眠行为。"

飞行研究事务所　梅莉莎·马利斯

我们通常称之为强效小睡。这能提高生理警觉性，降低睡意。所以，在任何 24 小时无休的环境里，这种策略都有助于缓和及控制疲劳程度。

CNN 资深特派员　艾伦·切诺夫

多年来，包括英国航空与加拿大航空在内的外国航空公司都允许飞行员在长途飞行途中小睡一会儿。驾驶舱里可以有一人休息，由另一人操控飞机。航空科学家指出，这么做

Notes & Vocabulary

7. improve [ɪm`pruv] *v.* 改善
The teacher changed his instructional practices, hoping to improve student achievement.

8. alertness [ə`lɜtnɪs] *n.* 警觉性

9. crew [kru]
n.（飞机上的）全体工作人员

10. advisory [əd`vaɪzərɪ]
adj. 咨询的；顾问的
The advisory council works as an independent expert body that advises the government on food security issues.

11. physiological [ˌfɪzɪə`lɑdʒɪkḷ]
adj. 生理上的；生理学的
Physiological needs are those required for human survival.

12. mitigate [`mɪtəˌget]
v. 减缓；减轻
Measures need to be taken to mitigate the effects of global warming.

13. manage [`mænɪdʒ] *v.* 对付；控制
There are many software packages on the market for parents to manage their children's computer use.

14. carrier [`kærɪɚ]
n. 从事运输业的公司

15. man [mæn] *v.* 操纵机器
A team of operators is manning the equipment.

16. control [kən`trol]
n.（机器或车辆的）操纵装置；按钮

17. aviation [ˌevɪ`eʃən]
n. 航空；飞行

scientists say that helps ensure both pilots are fresh[18] for their biggest challenge: approach[19] and landing.

CURT GRAEBER, FORMER NASA SCIENTIST

We want crews to be well-rested and alert on the approach and landing. The idea of a controlled rest in the flight deck[20] helps that happen. It's a safeguard.[21]

ALLAN CHERNOFF, CNN SENIOR CORRESPONDENT

But some pilots fear their managers could force them to work even harder if naps were permitted.

CAPT. JAMES RAY, AIRLINE PILOTS ASSOC.

I believe that airline management would certainly push pilots if napping were allowed in the cockpit. They would tell pilots, you know, I don't care if you're fatigued or not, just go ahead and jump in a cockpit and go fly. And you know what? Now you can take a nap, so you'll be fine.

ALLAN CHERNOFF, CNN SENIOR CORRESPONDENT

In fact, the Airline Advisory Committee is recommending the FAA allow pilots to fly more consecutive[22] hours during daytime to increase the current eight-hour limit. In return, airlines would reduce the hours pilots have to be on duty[23] so they can get a good night's sleep. The National

可确保两名飞行员都能够以饱满的精神面对他们最大的挑战：进场与着陆。

前美国国家航空航天局科学家　科特•格瑞柏

飞行人员在进场与着陆的时候必须休息充分，并且保持高度警觉。在驾驶舱里适度休息有助于达成这个目标。这是一种防护措施。

CNN 资深特派员　艾伦•切诺夫

不过，有些飞行员担心小睡行为一旦获得准许，主管可能会加重他们的工作。

民航飞行员协会　詹姆斯•雷

一旦允许在驾驶舱里小睡，我相信航空公司的管理阶层一定会逼迫飞行员接受更繁重的工作。他们会对飞行员说，我才不管你是不是觉得疲劳，你给我进驾驶舱开飞机就对了。反正现在你可以小睡一下，所以不会有问题的。

CNN 资深特派员　艾伦•切诺夫

实际上，航空顾问委员会就建议美国联邦航空管理局允许延长飞行员的日间连续飞行时数，放宽现行的 8 小时上限。另一方面，航空公司则必须减少飞行员的值勤时数，让他们晚上能够好好睡一觉。美国国家运输安全委员会表示，飞行员疲劳已导致了许多意外

Notes & Vocabulary

18. fresh [frɛʃ] *adj.* 精力充沛的
    The classroom was filled with fresh, eager faces on the first day of school.
19. approach [əˋprotʃ]
    n. 进场（即飞机开始准备着陆到到达跑道上空 15 米高度间的航行阶段）
20. flight deck [flaɪt] [dɛk]
    （飞机的）驾驶舱
21. safeguard [ˋsef͵gɑrd]
    n. 安全措施
22. consecutive [kənˋsɛkjətɪv]
    adj. 连续不断的
    It has snowed for five consecutive days.
23. on duty 值班；值勤；上班
    Some police officers work as security guards when not on duty.

Transportation Safety Board says pilot fatigue has caused numerous accidents and mishaps.[24] For 19 years, fatigue has been on the safety board's most-wanted list of urgent safety issues that need to be addressed.[25]

DEBORAH HERSMAN, NTSB CHAIRMAN

It is beyond overdue.[26] It is needed right now. We can't wait another year.

ALLAN CHERNOFF, CNN SENIOR CORRESPONDENT

Indeed, FAA regulations on pilot flight and duty time are decades old and do not consider the scientific studies on napping that were done 20 years ago. FAA's new administrator, Randy Babbitt, a former pilot, has put the issue of pilot fatigue on the fast track. He and his staff are evaluating the advisory committee recommendations.[27] He says he plans to issue[28] new proposed[29] rules by the end of the year.

与事故。19 年来，在该委员会认为最迫切需要解决的安全议题当中，疲劳问题一直名列其中。

美国国家运输安全委员会主席　德博拉·赫斯曼

这个解决方案已经拖太久了，现在必须马上实施。我们不能再等一年了。

CNN 资深特派员　艾伦·切诺夫

的确，美国联邦航空管理局的飞行员飞行与值勤时数规定已是数十年前的产物，并未把 20 年前针对飞行员小睡进行的科学研究纳入考虑。曾任飞行员的美国联邦航空管理局新局长兰迪·巴比特决定要尽快处理飞行员疲劳的问题。他和他手下的人员正在评估顾问委员会的建议。他说他计划在年底前发布新的建议规范。

Notes & Vocabulary

fast track

快速成功之路

fast track 是指“快速成功的途径或方法”，以达到特定目标或取得重大进展，例如取得同意、引起重视、平步青云。另外也可用动词 fast-track 表示“加快进程、作业以达到目标”。

· Many saw job-hopping as the fast track to higher pay.
许多人将跳槽视为加薪的快速之道。

24. mishap [ˋmɪsˏhæp] *n.* 意外事故

25. address [æˋdrɛs]
v. 设法解决；处理
Our products are designed to address the needs of real users.

26. overdue [ˏovɚˋdu]
adj. 早该完成的
We welcome this change and think it's long overdue.

27. recommendation
[ˏrɛkəmənˋdeʃən] *n.* 正式建议

28. issue [ˋɪʃu] *v.* 宣布；公布
The politician issued a statement acknowledging his illegitimate child.

29. propose [prəˋpoz]
v. 提议；提出
The budget cut was proposed by the majority of the lawmakers.

天地之间 ㉖ 当现代地铁遇上古文明 土耳其海底隧道挖出千年古迹

Tunnel[1] to the Past

Modern and Ancient Worlds Collide[2] in Project Linking Europe to Asia

图片提供：Reuters 达志

PAULINE CHIOU, CNN ANCHOR

Ambitious[3] plans are underway in Istanbul, Turkey to help the city cope with rapid growth and a growing population. A massive[4] tunnel is being constructed that will literally connect Asia with Europe, but as the city takes steps to ensure its future, discoveries are being made linking it to its past. Ivan Watson explains.

IVAN WATSON, CNN CORRESPONDENT

It's a common sight in Istanbul's traffic-choked streets—angry drivers; most residents quick to tell you and each other the city's transport system is overwhelmed.[5]

26-F.MP3
26-S.MP3

CNN 主播　邱波林

土耳其伊斯坦布尔正在进行着规模宏大的计划，帮助应付该城市的快速发展及逐渐增加的人口。一条真的能连接亚洲与欧洲的巨大隧道正在兴建中，但就在伊斯坦布尔逐步确立城市的未来之时，有些发现却将它与过去联系起来。伊凡·沃森带来详细报道。

CNN 特派员　伊凡·沃森

这是伊斯坦布尔交通堵塞的街道上常见的场景——火冒三丈的驾驶员；大部分的居民连忙向你和他人诉说该城市的交通系统已经不堪重负了。

Notes & Vocabulary

1. tunnel [ˋtʌnḷ] *n.* 隧道；地道
2. collide [kəˋlaɪd]
   v. 碰撞；相撞；冲突
   Plans to build a new factory collided with strict environmental regulations.
3. ambitious [æmˋbɪʃəs]
   adj. 耗资（时、力）的；有雄心的；野心勃勃的
   The city began an ambitious project for a new international airport.
4. massive [ˋmæsɪv]
   adj. 巨大的；大规模的
   The government made massive cuts to military spending.
5. overwhelm [ˏovɚˋhwɛlm]
   v. 击败；压垮；难以承受
   The workload in law school overwhelms many students.

ZEYNEP BUKET, ENGINEER, MARMARAY PROJECT

Istanbul is a dynamically changing city, every year increasing population. So, therefore, we are in need of radical[6] systems.

IVAN WATSON, CNN CORRESPONDENT

The radical solution[7]—build a new subway tunnel beneath the Bosporus Strait, the spectacular body[8] of water that cuts this city in two.

UNIDENTIFIED ENGINEER

We will connect two continents,[9] Asia and Europe.

IVAN WATSON, CNN CORRESPONDENT

First, engineers dredged[10] a trench.[11] They then submerged[12] and buried 11 massive tunnel segments,[13] each longer than a football field. Workers now toil[14] in the gloom of this 1.4-kilometer-long tube on the bottom of the sea. Since Istanbul is located in an active earthquake zone, engineers have had to prepare for the worst, building an emergency bunker[15] beneath the sea.

UNIDENTIFIED ENGINEER

If the sea comes in, and the water level comes to that level, everybody gets inside, close the sealed door and . . .

IVAN WATSON, CNN CORRESPONDENT

. . . survives in here.

UNIDENTIFIED ENGINEER

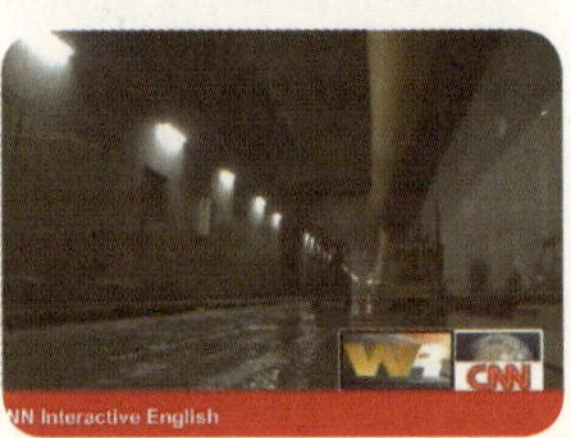

Yes.

马尔马雷计划工程师　札内普·布克特

伊斯坦布尔是个不断变化、充满活力的城市，人口每年都在增加，所以我们需要彻底更新系统。

CNN 特派员　伊凡·沃森

彻底的解决之道——在博斯普鲁斯海峡这个将城市一分为二的壮观水体底下，兴建一条新的海底隧道。

不知名工程师

我们会连接亚洲和欧洲两块大陆。

CNN 特派员　伊凡·沃森

首先，工程师挖掘一条沟渠，然后埋入 11 条长度比足球场还长的巨大隧道。工人们现在在海底这个 1.4 千米长的阴暗管道里辛苦工作。由于伊斯坦布尔位于活跃的地震带上，工程师必须做好最坏的打算，在海底建造一个逃生洞。

不知名工程师

如果海水灌进来，水位到达那里，大家就到里面把密闭门关上，然后……

CNN 特派员　伊凡·沃森

……在这里避难。

不知名工程师

对。

Notes & Vocabulary

6. radical [ˋrædɪkl̩]
   adj. 彻底的；根本的；极端的
   The president promised radical changes to the healthcare system.
7. solution [səˋluʃən]
   n. 解决办法、手段；解答
8. body [ˋbadɪ]
   n.（物质）一大团、块、堆
9. continent [ˋkantənənt]
   n. 大陆；洲
10. dredge [drɛdʒ]
    v. 清淤；疏浚；挖掘
    Engineers dredged the harbor to make it safe for large ships to anchor there.
11. trench [trɛntʃ] *n.* 沟；渠；壕
12. submerge [səbˋmɜdʒ]
    v. 沉入水中；浸没；淹没
    The hippo submerged itself in the river.
13. segment [ˋsɛgmənt]
    n. 部分；分段；段
14. toil [tɔɪl]
    v.（长时间）苦干；辛苦劳动
    The workers toiled from dawn to dusk to complete the construction on time.
15. bunker [ˋbʌŋkɚ]
    n. 掩体；地下碉堡；防空

IVAN WATSON, CNN CORRESPONDENT

When this tunnel is completed, subway trains are expected to carry more than a million people a day between Europe and Asia. But, in their rush to modernize Istanbul, city planners ran into an unforeseen[16] obstacle—the lost fourth-century Byzantine port of Theodosius, discovered right where one of the subway stations is to be built.

PROF. YUCEL YILMAZ, GEOLOGIST

I think it's one of the unique project[s], not for us but for the world.

IVAN WATSON, CNN CORRESPONDENT

Here, hundreds of meters from the sea, an army of workers and archaeologists[17] have uncovered a fleet[18] of 34 thousand-year-old boats.

This is the biggest ship that's been discovered at this archaeological site, a 40-meter-long cargo ship that archaeologists have nicknamed the Titanic. They believed it carried wheat from Egypt to Constantinople.

And look—next to the ancient timbers[19] that are being preserved[20] as they're uncovered here with water, you can see remains of when this was a port—an old sheep bone, old ceramics[21] that we can see here from more than a thousand years ago, and even oyster and clamshells from when this was a natural harbor.

CNN 特派员 伊凡・沃森

等隧道完工，预计地铁每天会运载超过 100 万人往返欧亚之间。然而，正当都市计划人员急着让伊斯坦布尔现代化时，却碰到了出乎预料的难题——就在其中一个车站的预定地，发现了消失的 4 世纪拜占庭帝国（注）的狄奥多西港。

地理学家 于榭尔・耶尔玛兹教授

我想这是个独一无二的计划，不只对我们而言如此，对全世界亦然。

CNN 特派员 伊凡・沃森

这里在海平面数百米之下，有一群工人和考古学家已经挖掘出了 34 艘已有千年历史的船队。

这是在这个考古遗址发现的最大的一艘船，一艘长达 40 米的货船，考古学家们昵称其为泰坦尼克号。他们相信这艘船把小麦从埃及运到君士坦丁堡。

再看这个——这些保存下来的老旧船骨用水清洗后露出了原貌，你可以看到旁边有此地仍是港口时的遗迹——古老的绵羊骨，我们可以看到这里有超过千年的陶瓷器，甚至还有此地还是天然港口时的牡蛎与蚌壳。

注：拜占庭帝国（Byzantine Empire）又称为东罗马帝国（Eastern Roman Empire），领土曾扩及亚洲西部和非洲北部。拜占庭帝国通常被认为开始自公元 395 年直至 1453 年。

Notes & Vocabulary

in one's rush to V.

某人匆忙地做某事

rush 作名词有“匆忙；仓促”的意思，in one's rush 指“某人匆忙行事”，后面加 to V. 表示急忙去做的事。

- In Gerald's rush to make it to the airport on time, he forgot one of his bags.
  贾里德赶着准时到机场，结果有一个旅行袋忘了拿。

16. **unforeseen** [ˌʌnfɔrˋsin]
    adj. 没想到的；始料未及的
    As long as we don't encounter any unforeseen complications, the project should proceed on schedule.
17. **archaeologist** [ˌɑrkɪˋɑlədʒɪst]
    n. 考古学家
18. **fleet** [flit] *n.* 船队；舰队；车队
19. **timber** [ˋtɪmbɚ] *n.*（造船的）船骨；肋材；（建筑的）梁木；木料
20. **preserve** [prɪˋzɝv]
    v. 保存；维护
    Workers preserved the antique furniture with painstaking care.
21. **ceramic** [səˋræmɪk]
    n. 陶瓷制品

Excavating[22] this treasure trove[23] of history has delayed construction of the tunnel by at least four years and added untold[24] millions of dollars to the new transport project. In the rush to move forward, an accidental discovery of this city's ancient past.

Marmaray Tunnel 马尔马雷隧道

施　　工：2004 年 5 月开工，预计 2012 年竣工。

起　　讫：伊斯坦布尔位于亚洲的盖布泽（Gabze）到位于欧洲的哈卡立（Halkal）

长　　度：约 13.7 千米，穿过博斯普鲁斯海峡的部分约 1.4 千米，位于海平面下 60 米处，将是世界最深的海底隧道。

运　　输：预计能把伊斯坦布尔的火车运载使用率从 3.6% 提高到 27.7%，市区铁路线配合整修及加装铁轨，每小时载客量（capacity）可达 75 000 人次。

古迹挖掘：2005 年在耶尼卡帕车站预定地挖掘到君士坦丁大帝时期的古城墙遗迹（remains）及数艘沉船残骸，证实是 4 世纪拜占庭帝国狄奥多西港的遗迹，其后又挖出 34 艘 7 ~ 11 世纪的船只。

此外，考古学家也在该地发现 4 座史前时代的墓穴，骸骨有 8000 年之久，可见伊斯坦布尔在石器时代（Stone Age）就有人类定居。

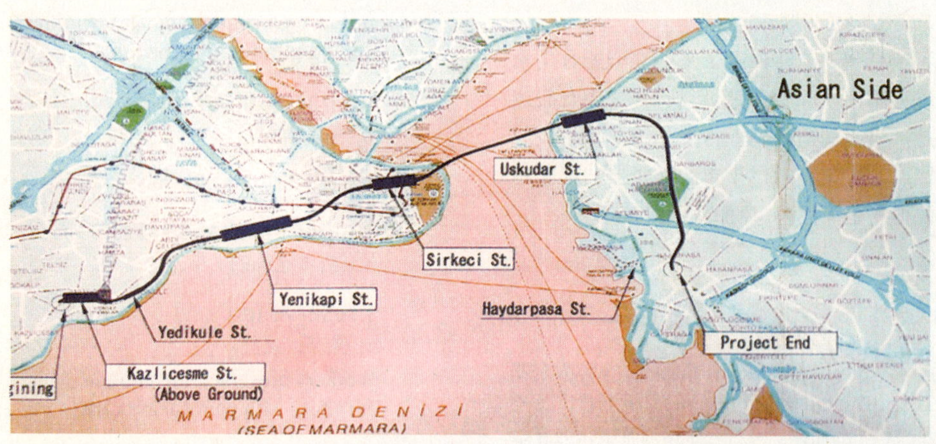

挖掘这个地下的历史宝藏耽误了隧道兴建进度至少四年的时间，而且给这个新的运输计划增加了数百万美元的费用。在急起迎向未来的时候，却意外发现了这个城市的古老过去。

Istanbul 伊斯坦布尔

旧称有 Byzantium "拜占庭"、Constantinople "君士坦丁堡"、Stamboul "斯坦布尔" 等，为当今土耳其共和国最大城市及文化、金融重镇，人口超过 1000 万。伊斯坦布尔横跨欧洲和亚洲，是世界上唯一横跨两个大陆的都市，中间的博斯普鲁斯海峡（Bosporus Strait）控制了船只在黑海的进出，自古就是兵家必争之地。

Notes & Vocabulary

22. excavate [ˋɛkskə͵vet]
v. 挖掘（古物等）；开凿
The archeologists excavated the site of the ancient settlement.

23. treasure trove [ˋtrɛʒɚ] [trov]
埋藏地下的宝藏；无主的财宝

24. untold [͵ʌnˋtold]
adj. 算不清的；难以形容的（大、坏等）
Past flu pandemics resulted in untold numbers of deaths.

名流轶事 非常体验 生活咀嚼 天地之间

天地之间 ㉗ 不明飞行物真的存在？美国官员的真实体验

UFO Files Reopened

Conference Urges[1] a Second Look at Unexplained Encounters[2]

CNN ANCHOR

Unidentified flying objects—the phrase makes you smile, doesn't it? Well, to some people they are real travelers from the great beyond. To others, they're just a joke. Now, a panel[3] of former pilots[4] and government officials is calling on the U.S. to investigate[5] the possibilities. Gary Tuchman has a look.

GARY TUCHMAN, CNN NATIONAL CORRESPONDENT

If you flew on Air France from Nice to London on January 28, 1994, your captain says he saw a UFO 1,000 feet long just outside your window.

27-F.MP3
27-S.MP3

CNN 主播

不明飞行物——这个名词会让你觉得想笑，不是吗？对某些人而言，不明飞行物是真正存在于宇宙中的旅行家。对其他人而言，不明飞行物不过是个笑话罢了。如今，有一群前飞行员和政府官员组成的专案小组呼吁美国针对这件事的可能性进行调查。盖瑞・图奇曼带来报道。

CNN 国内特派员　盖瑞・图奇曼

如果你在 1994 年 1 月 28 日乘坐法国航空公司的班机由尼斯飞往伦敦，那么你的机长会说他看到你的窗外有一架长 1000 英尺的不明飞行物。

Notes & Vocabulary

the great beyond 遥远之处

beyond 在这里作名词，意为“远处”，the great beyond 则表示“非常遥远的地方”，文中是指“遥远的太空”。

其他“外太空；宇宙”的单词

- the outer world
- outerspace
- universe
- cosmos

call on sb. 号召；请求

call on 是指为了某事找人来帮忙，即“号召；召集”的意思，或要求对方做某事。call on 另外还有“拜访”的意思。

- The governor called on the public to use less water during this dry weather.
  州长请求民众在天旱期间减少用水。

call 的常用词组

call for sth. 要求

- The animal rights group called for an end to medical tests on animals.
  保护动物团体要求停止用动物进行药物测试。

call the shots 指挥；掌控

- David called the shots around the office while his boss was gone.
  大卫的老板不在时，办公室由他坐镇指挥。

1. urge [ɜdʒ] *v.* 力劝；极力主张
   Todd's financial advisor urged him to pay off his debts.
2. encounter [ɪnˋkaʊntɚ] *n.* 遭遇；遇见
3. panel [ˋpænḷ] *n.* 专门小组；专题讨论小组
4. pilot [ˋpaɪlət] *n.* 飞行员
5. investigate [ɪnˋvɛstəˏget] *v.* 调查；研究
   Police detectives investigated a string of mysterious deaths.

名流轶事　非常体验　生活咀嚼　天地之间

JEAN-CHARLES DUBOC, RETIRED AIR FRANCE CAPTAIN

It seemed to be a huge flying disk.

GARY TUCHMAN, CNN CORRESPONDENT

The now retired pilot is one of 14 men, mainly former government and military officials from seven different countries, talking about their UFO experiences.

This conference[6] took place in Washington, and the cast[7] of characters was almost strangely, well, conventional.[8] One of the believers—former Governor of Arizona Fife Symington.

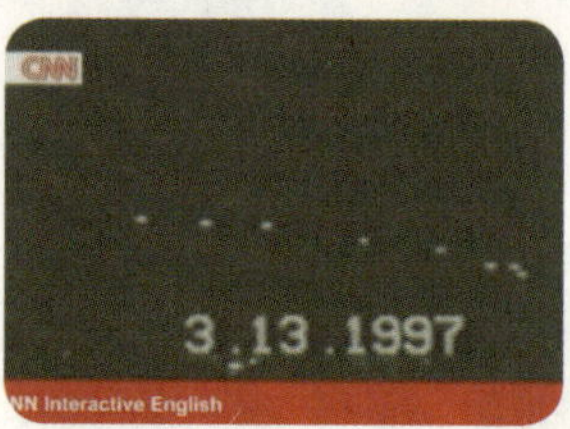

The so-called Phoenix lights were seen by many people in 1997. Skeptics[9] say they were military aircraft or flares,[10] but not the former governor.

FIFE SYMINGTON, FORMER ARIZONA GOVERNOR

It was probably some form of an alien[11] spacecraft.

GARY TUCHMAN, CNN CORRESPONDENT

Lots of agreement on this panel. This retired Iranian air force pilot said he saw a UFO while flying.

General Parviz Jafari says he tried to fire a missile,[12] but much of his plane became inoperative.[13]

GENERAL PARVIZ JAFARI, FORMER IRANIAN AIR FORCE PILOT

All the instrument[s][14] were fluctuating.[15] The radio had garbled.[16] Even, I couldn't have communication with my pilot in my back seat, who was operating the radar.

退休法航机长　让查尔斯·杜波克
看起来像是一架巨型的飞碟。

CNN国内特派员　盖瑞·图奇曼
这位已退休的机长是14名谈论他们个人的不明飞行物经历的其中一人，这些人多半是来自7个国家的前政府和军方官员。

这场会议在华盛顿举行，奇怪的是，与会的人物几乎清一色是一般人，其中一位是前亚利桑那州州长费佛·塞明顿。

许多人在1997年目睹了所谓的凤凰城光点。对此持怀疑态度的人说，那些是军用飞机或闪光信号，但这位前州长却不这么认为。

前亚利桑那州州长　费佛·塞明顿
那可能是某种形式的外星飞船。

CNN国内特派员　盖瑞·图奇曼
这个专案小组的看法相当一致。这位退休的伊朗空军飞行员说，他在飞行途中目睹了一架不明飞行物。

帕尔韦兹·贾法瑞将军说，他试图发射一枚飞弹，但是他的座机大部分都已经失灵。

前伊朗空军飞行员　帕尔韦兹·贾法瑞将军
所有仪器都在跳动。无线电一片噪声，我无法和后座负责操作雷达的驾驶员通话。

Notes & Vocabulary

6. conference [ˋkɑnferens]
n. 研讨会；正式会议
7. cast [kæst] n. 阵容
8. conventional [kənˋvɛʃənḷ]
adj. 传统的
Conventional wisdom suggests that the Chinese stock market has peaked.
9. skeptic [ˋskɛptɪk] n. 怀疑论者
10. flare [flɛr] n. 闪光信号；照明弹
11. alien [ˋeliən] adj. 外星人的
Maxine swears she saw an alien spacecraft.
12. missile [ˋmɪsḷ] n. 飞弹
13. inoperative [ɪnˋɑpərətɪv]
adj. 无法运作的
Without fuel, the generator was inoperative.
14. instrument [ˋɪnstrəmənt]
n. 仪器；器具
15. fluctuate [ˋflʌktʃəˏet]
v. 波动；动摇
The price of oil fluctuated throughout the year.
16. garble [ˋgɑrbḷ]
v. 曲解；篡改
Jenny purposely garbled her phone message.

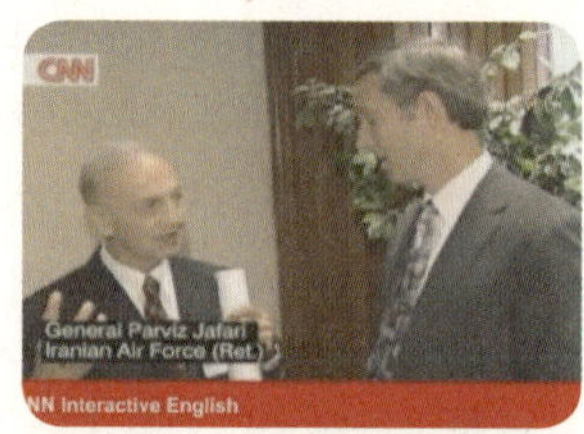

GARY TUCHMAN, CNN CORRESPONDENT

So, your . . . so, none of your equipment[17] worked. Your missiles didn't work. Do you think it's because this was an alien from another world?

GENERAL PARVIZ JAFARI, FORMER IRANIAN AIR FORCE PILOT

Oh, yes. Yeah.

GARY TUCHMAN, CNN CORRESPONDENT

You're sure of that?

GENERAL PARVIZ JAFARI, FORMER IRANIAN AIR FORCE PILOT

Yeah, I'm sure.

GARY TUCHMAN, CNN CORRESPONDENT

This retired U.S. Air Force sergeant[18] stationed[19] in England said he walked up to a UFO that landed in a forest.

UNIDENTIFIED RETIRED AIR FORCE SERGEANT

It maneuvered[20] through the trees and shot off at an unbelievable rate of speed.

GARY TUCHMAN, CNN CORRESPONDENT

A man running for president just said he saw a UFO.

REP. DENNIS KUCINICH (D-OH), PRESIDENTIAL CANDIDATE

I did. And the rest of the account[21]—it was [an] unidentified flying object.

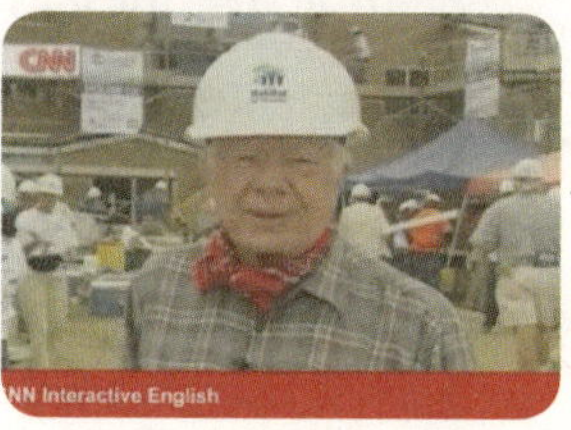

CNN 国内特派员　盖瑞・图奇曼
所以你……你的设备都失灵了。你的飞弹失灵了。你认为这是一个外星球来的物体造成的？

前伊朗空军飞行员　帕尔韦兹・贾法瑞将军
是的。

CNN 国内特派员　盖瑞・图奇曼
你确定吗？

前伊朗空军飞行员　帕尔韦兹・贾法瑞将军
对，我确定。

CNN 国内特派员　盖瑞・图奇曼
这名曾驻扎在英格兰、现已退休的美国空军中士表示，他曾经走上一架降落在森林里的飞碟。

不具名退休空军中士
它巧妙地在树林间穿梭，然后以难以置信的速度飞快离去。

CNN 国内特派员　盖瑞・图奇曼
有位正在竞选总统的人才刚说他看见过不明飞行物。

民主党总统候选人　众议员丹尼斯・库新尼奇
我看到过不明飞行物，终归一句，那是一架不明飞行物。

Notes & Vocabulary

17. equipment [ɪ`kwɪpmənt]
n. 配备；装备

18. sergeant [`sɑrdʒənt] *n.* 中士

19. station [`steʃən] *v.* 驻扎；部署
The Army stationed Mike in Okinawa for his first tour of duty.

20. maneuver [mə`nuvɚ]
v. 敏捷地行动；巧妙地操纵
Chad maneuvered his car through the obstacle course.

21. account [ə`kaunt]
n. 理由；解释

GARY TUCHMAN, CNN CORRESPONDENT

And so did a man who was president.

JIMMY CARTER, FORMER PRESIDENT OF THE UNITED STATES

I and about 25 others saw something in the air that changed colors and was round . . .

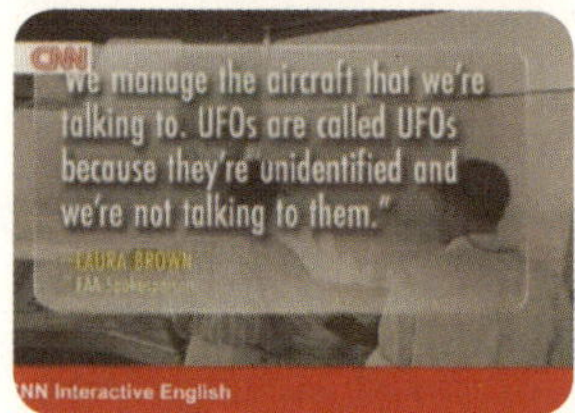

GARY TUCHMAN, CNN CORRESPONDENT

Although Jimmy Carter says he doesn't think it was from another planet, most of these people differ on that point and want the FAA to investigate all these claims.

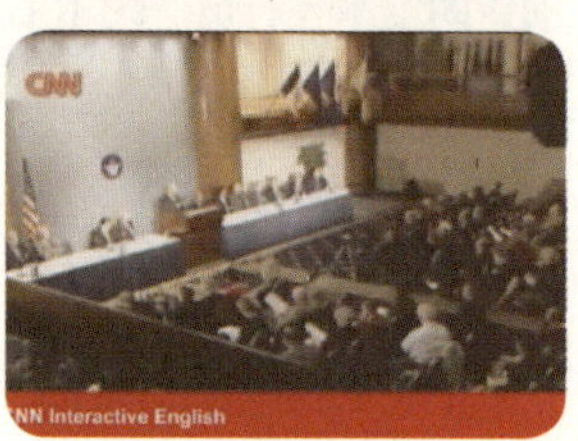

But the FAA says that's not its job. "We manage the aircraft that we're talking to. UFOs are called UFOs because they're unidentified and we're not talking to them."

And it's precisely[22] because no one's talking that everybody here is trying harder to make them believe.

UFO 的语源故事

美国最早报道的目睹（sighting）不明飞行物的事件发生在 1947 年，当时以 flying saucer "飞碟" 指称圆盘状的神秘飞行物；1950 年美国政府创造了较正式的名称 unidentified flying object "不明飞行物"；1953 年出现缩写（acronym）UFO；1959 年有了有关不明飞行物研究的 ufology "不明飞行物学" 和 ufologist "不明飞行物学家"。

关于不明飞行物的传闻始于第二次世界大战结束时。大战期间，美国率先制造出原子弹（atom bomb），开启人类对科技的神秘想象。当时在美国西南部的沙漠地区有许多秘密军事设施（military installation），因此也有人怀疑不明飞行物只是美军研发的极秘飞行器（aircraft）。美国空军在 1948 年聘请了西北大学天文学（astronomy）教授 Joseph Allen Hynek 针对不明飞行物进行调查，成为日后不明飞行物研究的基础。

CNN 国内特派员　盖瑞 • 图奇曼

还有一位曾经当过总统的人也这么说。

美国前总统　吉米 • 卡特

我和其他大约 25 个人看到天空中有个东西，它会改变颜色，外形是圆的。

CNN 国内特派员　盖瑞 • 图奇曼

虽然卡特说他不认为那东西是从另一个星球而来，但这些人大多不同意，并要求美国联邦航空管理局（注）调查这些说法。

但是美国联邦航空管理局表示，这并非其职责所在。“我们管理的是可以沟通的飞行器，不明飞行物之所以被称为不明飞行物，就是因为它们的身份不明，而我们不会跟它们沟通。”

正是因为没人在负责与不明飞行物沟通，所以在座的每一个人才会更努力地要让他们相信。

注：全名为 Federal Aviation Agency，是负责全美所有飞行安全与管制的机构。

Notes & Vocabulary

22. precisely [prɪˋsaɪslɪ]
adv. 确切地；精确地

㉘ 哥伦比亚毒贩太嚣张　土制潜艇也出笼

Deep Running[1]

Drug Traffickers[2] Turn to Submarines to Smuggle[3] Illicit[4] Cargo

图片提供：AP 达志、U.S. DEA

SUZANNE MALVEAUX, CNN ANCHOR

Ecuadorian authorities are reporting the seizure[5] of a makeshift[6] submarine designed for transporting large amounts of cocaine. U.S. Drug Enforcement agents say it's the first time a fully operational drug-smuggling sub has been seized.

But the practice is not entirely new. Smugglers have increasingly been using the subs to avoid detection on the high seas.[7] Our CNN's Karl Penhaul has been following the story and he filed this report.

28-F.MP3
28-S.MP3

CNN 主播 苏珊娜·玛尔维斯

厄瓜多尔当局正在报道查获用作运输大量可卡因的临时潜艇。美国毒品管制局表示这是第一次查获毒品走私专用的潜艇。

然而这样的案件并非前所未闻。走私者渐渐使用潜艇来逃避公海上的侦察。本台特派员卡尔·潘霍追踪了整起事件并整理了以下报道。

Notes & Vocabulary

1. run [rʌn]
   v.【俚】走私；偷运；非法携带
   Jeremy's grandfather was a fisherman who also ran rum during Prohibition.
2. trafficker [ˋtræfɪkɚ]
   n. 非法买卖者
3. smuggle [ˋsmʌgl̩] *v.* 走私；偷运
   A freight truck smuggled stolen goods across the border.
4. illicit [ɪˋlɪsət] *adj.* 非法的；违法的
   A local merchant was arrested for selling illicit drugs out of his business.
5. seizure [ˋsiʒɚ]
   v. 破获；充公；没收
6. makeshift [ˋmek͵ʃɪft]
   adj. 勉为替代的；权宜的
   Mandy set up a makeshift food stand at the weekend outdoor market.
7. high sea [haɪ] [si] 公海

KARL PENHAUL, CNN CORRESPONDENT

A spotter plane tracks something plowing through[8] the choppy[9] seas. The Colombian Navy and U.S. Coast Guards are on the tail of[10] a hand-built submarine.

The cargo—eight tons of pure cocaine, according to Colombian authorities. That's almost half a billion dollars' worth on the streets of Europe or America.

The traffickers scuttle[11] the sub, sending the cargo to the bottom of the Pacific. The Coast Guard says it's a tactic[12] to destroy evidence of the crime.

Watch this crew bail out[13] during a different chase. Minutes later, another six tons of cocaine sink.

Pursuits on the high seas like these are rare. That's because the subs are almost impossible to detect, even though few are designed to dive fully underwater.

MARIO RODRIGUEZ, COLOMBIAN NAVY

The semisubmersible[14] is more difficult to detect because it has a low profile[15] in the sea. Criminals paint them a certain color to camouflage[16] them and avoid detection from the air.

KARL PENHAUL, CNN CORRESPONDENT

The Navy believes the cartels[17] may now be smuggling out almost half their cocaine in fleets[18] of narco[19] subs using Colombia's Caribbean and Pacific coasts.

CNN 特派员　卡尔·潘霍

一架侦察机追踪费力穿越波涛汹涌海面的物体。哥伦比亚海军和美国海岸警卫队正紧追一艘手工制造的潜艇。

哥伦比亚当局表示，潜艇上的货物是 8 吨重的纯可卡因，在欧洲和美洲市值将近 5 亿美元。

这些走私者凿沉了这艘潜艇，让这些货物沉至太平洋海底。海岸警卫队表示这是毁灭犯罪证据的手段。

在另一个缉查行动中，看看这些船员正在把水舀出去。几分钟之后，又有 6 吨重的可卡因沉没至海底。

在公海上这样的追捕行动是很少见的，因为潜艇几乎侦察不到，即使几乎没有潜艇是设计成能够完全潜入海中的。

哥伦比亚海军　马里欧·罗德里格斯

这种半潜式的潜艇更难侦察到，因为它的船身轮廓低平，在海中很不显眼。犯罪者将潜艇漆成特定颜色来加以伪装，并且躲避空中的侦察。

CNN 特派员　卡尔·潘霍

海军表示犯罪同党可能已在哥伦比亚的加勒比海和太平洋海岸间利用运毒潜艇船队运走了将近一半的可卡因。

Notes & Vocabulary

8. plow through
奋力通过；努力穿过
The skier plowed through the snow drifts.

9. choppy [ˋtʃɑpɪ]
adj. 波涛汹涌的；不平静的
The choppy seas made sailing into the narrow harbor entrance difficult.

10. on the tail of 紧追；尾随
The police are on the tail of a burglar.

11. scuttle [ˋskʌtl̩]
v. 凿沉（船）；故意破坏
The navy scuttled an aging warship to create an artificial reef.

12. tactic [ˋtæktɪk]
n. 手段；招数；策略

13. bail (out) [bel] *v.* 舀水（倒掉）
Mike bailed out the canoe to keep it from sinking.

14. semisubmersible [ˏsɛmɪsəbˋmɝsəbl̩]
n. 半潜式平底船；半潜式潜水艇

15. have a low profile 保持低调
The sports car has a low profile that makes it more streamlined.

16. camouflage [ˋkæməˏflɑʒ]
v.（军事）伪装；（用保护色）隐蔽
The soldiers camouflaged their campsite to avoid detection.

17. cartel [kɑrˋtɛl] *n.* 同业联盟

18. fleet [flit] *n.* 舰队；船队；机队

19. narco [ˋnɑrko]
n. 迷幻药；致幻毒品（= narcotics）

At a Pacific coast base, Second Mate[20] Juan Carlos Noguera shows me around some of the subs that have been confiscated.[21] Fiberglass on a wooden frame, twin diesel engines, the price tag,[22] around $1 million. Most of that's not for materials, but to buy the silence of the boat builders.

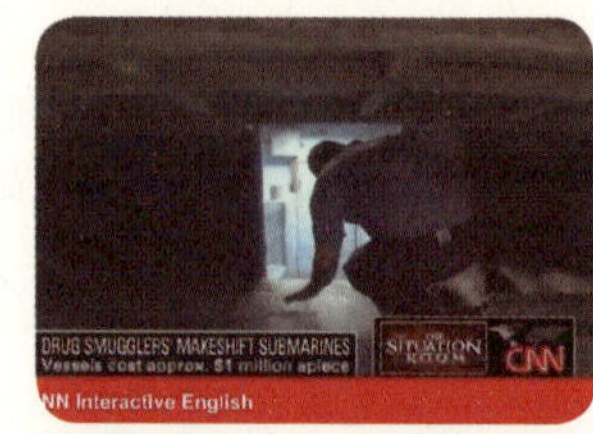

Under the hatch,[23] it feels like a floating coffin.

It's hot down here now, and once this is in the open waters with the sun beating down on it, the temperature could soar,[24] and there are only a few breathing tubes throughout here.

The semi-submersibles travel three main smuggling routes,[25] according to the Navy. Direct to Mexico or Central America takes around six days. The longest route through the Galapagos Islands takes more than two weeks.

Along the northern reaches[26] of Colombia's Pacific coast, speedboats remain the number-one enemy. They dash[27] into Panama or Costa Rica in as little as six hours.

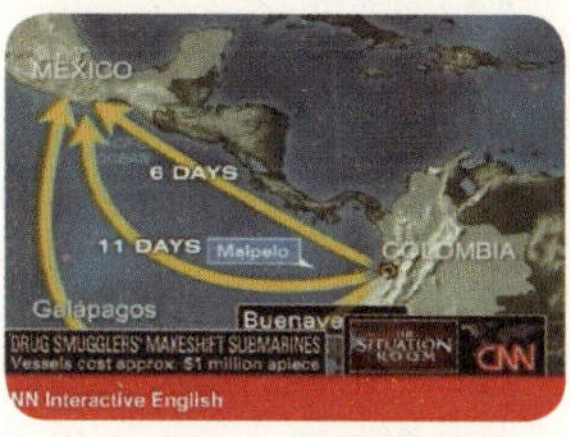

I join a Coast Guard team on a speedboat they call Midnight Express. Buenaventura's Colombia's biggest seaport, handling thousands of containers every day, all potential stowaway[28] sites for drugs.

There's a huge tuna fishing fleet, too. Ships' captains may be tempted[29] by easy money, but are wary of[30] the consequences.

在太平洋海岸基地，二副胡安·卡洛斯·诺格拉带我看了一些被查扣的潜艇。木框上有玻璃纤维、双柴油引擎，标价大约是 100 万美元。那些钱大部分并非用来购买材料，而是用来堵住造船者的嘴。

在舱口下，感觉像是一具漂浮的棺木。

现在下面这里就已经相当热了，而一旦在开放水域，阳光强烈照射这架潜艇时，温度将会暴增，而且整艘潜艇只有几根呼吸管。

根据哥伦比亚海军的资料，这些半潜水式的潜艇有三条主要的走私路线。直达墨西哥或中美洲要花上约 6 天的时间。穿越加拉帕戈斯群岛的最长路线则要花上超过两周的时间。

沿着哥伦比亚太平洋沿岸的北缘地区，快艇仍旧是最棘手的侦察对象。他们在短短六小时之内便可直奔巴拿马或哥斯达黎加。

我登上被称作“午夜快车”的海岸警卫队快艇。布埃纳文图拉是哥伦比亚最大的海港，每天要处理数千个货柜，它们都有可能藏匿毒品。

也有大型的鲔鱼船队。船长也许很容易被不义之财收买，但是他们对后果也是提心吊胆的。

Notes & Vocabulary

20. second mate [ˋsɛkənd] [met]
【海】二副

21. confiscate [ˋkɑnfəˏsket]
v. 没收；充公
Transit authorities confiscated Mary's hand lotion before she boarded the plane.

22. price tag [praɪs] [tæg]
标价；定价

23. hatch [hætʃ]
n.（船甲板或机舱底）舱口；舱门

24. soar [sor] v. 急增；猛升
The temperature soared by midday.

25. route [rut] n. 路线；途径

26. reaches [ˋritʃɪz]
n. 边缘地带；外缘地区（复数）

27. dash [dæʃ] v. 猛冲；急奔
Simon dashed to the supermarket to pick up a bottle of wine before his guests arrived.

28. stowaway [ˋstoəˏwe]
n. 偷渡者

29. tempt [tɛmpt]
v. 诱惑；利诱；怂恿
The offer of a new job tempted Greg, but he turned it down in the end.

30. be wary of 谨慎；提防；留神
Most nutritionists are wary of fad diets.

CAPTAIN EDWARD PICON, COLOMBIAN NAVY

They say they risk losing their families and they know if the drugs get lost, their families will be killed.

KARL PENHAUL, CNN CORRESPONDENT

Night falls and a Navy patrol boat heads out on a fresh mission to board rust-bucket[31] cargo ships and hunt for cocaine. A captain radio's word, he's only transporting cattle, gasoline and food.

Nothing's found. One of the cargo ship's crew seems to resent[32] the search.

UNIDENTIFIED MALE

The economy is real difficult right now. There's more unemployment than jobs. That's one of the biggest things fuelling crime.

KARL PENHAUL, CNN CORRESPONDENT

For the Colombian Navy it's a war of stealth,[33] trying to stem[34] the tide of cocaine on and under the waters—a war in which traffickers are using homemade technology to sink to new depths.

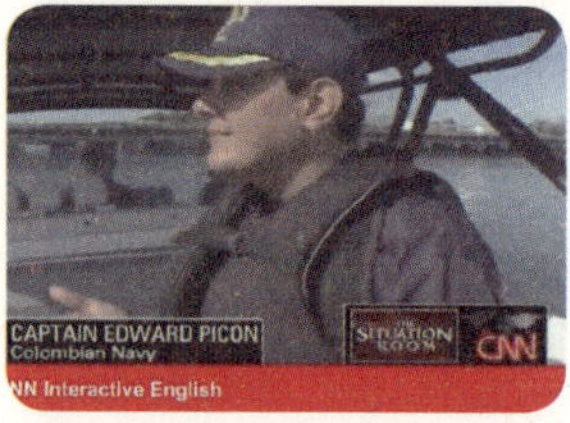

28-F.MP3 / 28-S.MP3 | *Deep Running*

哥伦比亚海军　爱德华·派肯上校
他们表示自己是冒着失去家人的风险，而且他们知道如果毒品不见的话，家人将会遭到杀害。

CNN 特派员　卡尔·潘霍
夜晚降临，一艘海军巡逻艇出航执行一项新的任务，登上一艘生锈破旧的货船缉查可卡因。一位船长通过无线电表示，他只是运送牛只、汽油和食物。

一无所获。其中一位货船船员似乎非常讨厌这样的搜捕行动。

不知名男子
现在经济状况实在很困难。失业人口比职位空缺还要多。那是助长犯罪的最大原因之一。

CNN 特派员　卡尔·潘霍
对于哥伦比亚海军而言，这是一场秘密战役，试着遏止海面上和海面下的可卡因走私，在这场战役中，走私者利用土制技术的道行更高一筹了。

Notes & Vocabulary

31. rust bucket [rʌst] [ˋbʌkət]
【俚】破旧生锈的船（或车）

32. resent [rɪˋzɛnt] *v.* 憎恶；憎恨
Tina resented her sister's success.

33. stealth [stɛlθ]
n. 秘密行动；偷偷摸摸

34. stem [stɛm]
v. 遏止；阻止；封堵
New customs regulations stemmed the flow of pirated goods out of China.

天地之间 ㉙ 飞机里的空气安全吗

Shared Air

Information to Help You Breathe Easy about Healthy Flying

图片提供：photos.com

Richard Quest, Business Traveller

When it comes to travel, the one part of the experience when we really feel out of control is when we're cooped up in the tin can better known as the plane. Think about it—hundreds of other people breathing, sneezing, coughing the same air. How dangerous is it? What can we catch? Luckily for us, Ayesha Durgahee has been sifting[1] the myths from reality.

AYESHA DURGAHEE, CNN CORRESPONDENT

Shoulder to shoulder, strangers confined[2] in one space in a stale[3] and stuffy[4] cabin. We no longer have to inhale[5] other people's cigarette smoke; instead there's the perception[6] of inhaling other people's germs.

29-F.MP3
29-S.MP3

《商务旅行家》 理查德·奎斯特

一旦谈到旅行，我们真正觉得无能为力的部分，就是关在飞机这个铁罐里的时候。想想看，除了你之外，还有数以百计的人在同一团空气中呼吸、打喷嚏、咳嗽。这种情形有多危险？我们可能会感染什么样的疾病？所幸，阿叶莎·杜尔加希帮我们区辨了迷思与真相。

CNN 特派员 阿叶莎·杜尔加希

肩并肩，陌生人共同关在一个污浊拥挤的座舱里。这时再也不必吸到别人的二手烟，却可能吸进别人身上的细菌。

Notes & Vocabulary

(be) coop(ed) up

把……关在狭小的空间

coop 作为名词时意为“禽舍；鸡笼”，而动词词组 coop up 常用被动式，表示“把……关在狭小的空间”。

- Kids get upset **when cooped up** inside during the typhoon.
  小孩子讨厌在台风天的时候被关在家里。

1. **sift** [sɪft] *v.* 过滤；详查
   The manager sifted through the client’s file to find their address.
2. **confine** [kənˋfaɪn] *v.* 禁闭；幽禁
   Police confined the thief until he confessed to his crime.
3. **stale** [stel] *adj.* 不新鲜的；污浊的
   Kim opened her window to replace the room’s stale air with fresh air.
4. **stuffy** [ˋstʌfɪ]
   adj. 通风不良的；闷热的
   Marianne said she could not breathe in the stuffy upstairs room.
5. **inhale** [ɪnˋhel] *v.* 吸入
   The fireman hurt his lungs by inhaling too much smoke from the house fire.
6. **perception** [pɚˋsɛpʃən]
   n. 感知；知觉

JOE BIDEN, U.S. VICE PRESIDENT

But you're in a confined aircraft. When one person sneezes, it goes all the way through the aircraft.

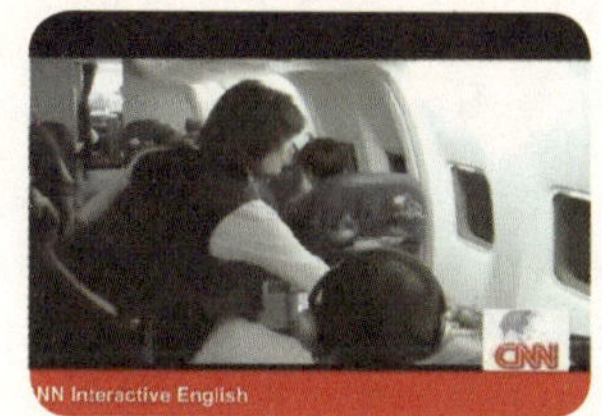

AYESHA DURGAHEE, CNN CORRESPONDENT

Air in the cabin doesn't actually move backwards or forwards. It enters from the top of the cabin and is drawn vertically[7] to floor level, taking any germs lurking[8] in the air with it. By the time the air reenters[9] the cabin, it has been filtered[10] using high-efficiency particulate[11] air—or HEPA—filters that reduces the risk of transmitting[12] airborne[13] diseases.

HEPA filters are the same ones used in hospital operating theaters. They're 99.9 percent efficient at removing bacteria[14] and viruses, so the air that we breathe on board is actually cleaner than the air in your office. HEPA filters may do a good job at providing us with cleaner, fresher air, but what happens if you hear someone cough or sneeze?

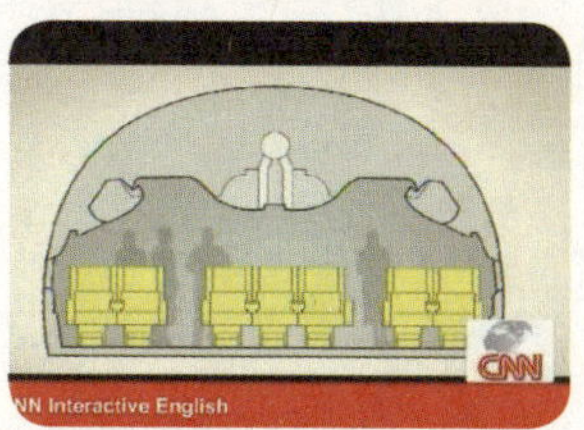

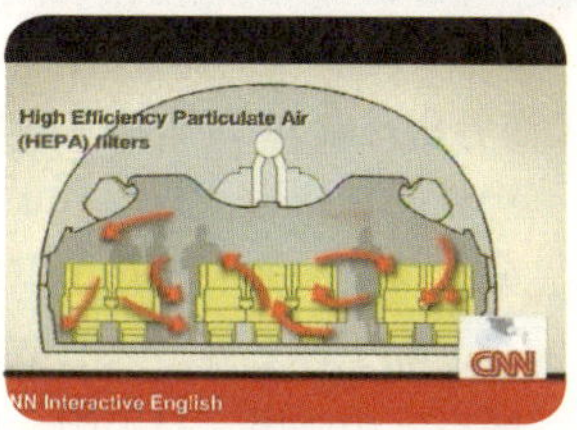

美国副总统　乔 • 拜登
可是你身在封闭的飞机里。只要一个人打喷嚏，细菌就会在整架飞机里散播。

CNN 特派员　阿叶莎 • 杜尔加希
机舱里的空气其实不会前后流动，而是从顶端送入，然后垂直由地板吸出，连同空气中潜伏的病菌一起吸走。同样的空气再次送入机舱的时候，早已通过高效率空气微粒滤芯（简称 HEPA）的过滤，降低了向空气中散播传染病的风险。

HEPA 滤芯跟在医院手术室用的相同，它们过滤细菌与病毒的有效率高达 99.9%，因此我们在飞机上呼吸的空气比在你办公室里的还要干净。HEPA 滤芯虽可为我们带来洁净清新的空气，但你如果听到别人咳嗽或打喷嚏，又会如何呢？

Notes & Vocabulary

7. vertically [`vɜtɪkəlɪ]
adv. 垂直地；直立地

8. lurk [lɜk] *v.* 潜伏；偷偷地行动
The scared kitten lurked in the shadows waiting to be given food to eat.

9. reenter [ri`ɛntɚ] *v.* 再进入；重返
The theme park allows visitors to exit and reenter anytime during the day.

10. filter [`fɪltɚ] *v.* 过滤；滤除
The air conditioner filters dust and dirt from the air.

11. particulate [pɑr`tɪkjəˏlet]
adj. 微粒的
Breathing particulate air means you might breathe invisible gases or particles.

12. transmit [træns`mɪt]
v. 传播；传染
Pink eye is transmitted by eye-to-hand contact.

13. airborne [`ɛrˏborn]
adj. 空中传播的；空降的
People wear masks to block airborne germs.

14. bacteria [bæk`tɪriə]
n. 细菌（bacterium 的复数）

DR. RICHARD DAWOOD, FLEET STREET CLINIC

If a person sneezed two rows behind you, you might be at risk from direct inhalation of some of those droplets,[15] but you what you wouldn't be at risk from is the idea that those droplets would be taken into the ventilation[16] system and then would be blown out at you in the fresh air supply. Filtration of air within the aircraft cabin is highly efficient, and you can expect probably a full change of air within the cabin every three minutes or so.

AYESHA DURGAHEE, CNN CORRESPONDENT

Airlines aren't required to make public their cabin air data, and there are no rules for humidity,[17] temperature or bacteria levels. There's very little information available. In fact, the last key findings were in 2001, where in the U.S. an aircraft using only recirculated[18] air was compared with an aircraft using outside air. The study showed that 20 percent of passengers on both aircraft contracted[19] a cold within a week of stepping off the plane, suggesting that we are more susceptible to[20] illness when we fly.

弗利特街诊所　理查德·达伍德医师

如果坐在你身后两排的乘客打喷嚏，你就有可能直接吸入他的分泌物，但这些分泌物不会进入空气循环系统继而跟着新鲜空气一起吹到你脸上。机舱里的空气过滤效率很高，大约每三分钟就会把机舱里的空气全部换新。

CNN 特派员　阿叶莎·杜尔加希

航空公司不需要公开机舱空气资料，机舱的湿度、温度或细菌数量也没有任何规定。我们能够获取的信息非常少。实际上，最近一次的关键研究是在 2001 年，以美国一架只使用循环空气的飞机和一架引进外部空气的飞机进行比较。研究结果显示两架飞机的乘客都有 20% 在下机后一周内感冒，可见我们搭飞机的时候比较容易感染疾病。

Notes & Vocabulary

be at risk 处于危险中

risk 是“危险；风险”的意思，而 be at risk 也类似于 be in danger，都是用来描述“身处危险之中”的意思。

- Vivian's mother had heart disease and she knew she was at risk, too.
  薇薇安的母亲曾患有心脏病，所以她知道她也有风险。

15. droplet [ˋdrɑplət] *n.* 小滴
16. ventilation [ˏvɛntəˋleʃən] *n.* 通风
17. humidity [hjuˋmɪdətɪ] *n.* 湿气；湿度
18. recirculate [rɪˋsɜkjəˏlet] *v.* 循环
    The heart helps to recirculate blood through the body.
19. contract [kənˋtrækt] *v.* 得（病）；负（债）
    You cannot contract AIDS by sitting next to someone who has it.
20. susceptible to [səˋsɛptəbl̩] [tu] 易受……影响的
    People with light skin are more susceptible to sunburns.

名流轶事　非常体验　生活咀嚼　天地之间

DR. RICHARD DAWOOD, FLEET STREET CLINIC

We certainly know that there's an increased rate of respiratory[21] infection[22] in people who travel. There are certainly factors in the aircraft that could make it more likely. One of these is the general dryness of the cabin air. It's pumped in from the outside, and that removes the an important layer of protection—the moisture film[23] that lines the mouth, the nose, the throat, the respiratory passages.[24] That acts as an important barrier.[25] When that's gone, it is certainly possible that bacteria and viruses can break through.

AYESHA DURGAHEE, CNN CORRESPONDENT

It's not just about the quality of the air we breathe on board that leaves our immune systems weakened.[26] It's the combination of time zone changes, jet lag and the stress of the airport—all part and parcel of the travel process.

弗利特街诊所　理查德•达伍德医师

我们确实知道人在旅行的时候，呼吸道感染的比率会上升。机舱里的确有些因素会提高呼吸道疾病的感染率。其中一个因素就是机舱空气的湿度较低。机舱的空气是从外面送进来的，这么一来就会除去一道重要的保护层——也就是嘴巴、鼻子、喉咙、呼吸道上的黏膜。这层黏膜是一道重要的屏障。一旦没有了这道屏障，细菌和病毒就有可能侵入我们体内。

CNN 特派员　阿叶莎•杜尔加希

不只是我们在飞机上呼吸的空气的品质会削弱我们的免疫系统。时区的改变、生理时差，还有机场的压力，都是旅行过程中不可避免的因素。

Notes & Vocabulary

part and parcel (of)

不可或缺的部分

parcel 可以指“邮包；包裹”，但是在这个惯用语中 parcel 是指“整体中不可或缺的东西”，所以 part and parcel 就是“不可或缺的部分”。

- Wearing a helmet is part and parcel of riding a bike in the city.
  在都市里骑自行车戴安全帽是非常重要的。

21. respiratory [rɪˋspaɪrəˏtorɪ] *adj.* 呼吸的
    Jimmy's respiratory infection meant he had trouble breathing.
22. infection [ɪnˋfɛkʃən] *n.* 传染病
23. film [fɪlm] *n.* 薄膜；薄皮
24. passage [ˋpæsɪdʒ] *n.* 通道；通路
25. barrier [ˋbærir] *n.* 障碍物；路障
26. weaken [ˋwikən] *v.* 削弱；减弱
    Grandma's stroke weakened the right side of her body.

天地之间 30 导盲，马也行

Riding Blind

Officials Struggle[1] to Define[2] the Role of Service Animals for the Disabled[3]

图片提供：AP

CNN ANCHOR

When you think of a service animal, a dog may come to ~~your~~ mind, but what about a horse? Well, [for] one woman in Texas who's legally blind, that's the animal she uses to get around. David Schechter has her story.

TABITHA DARLING, BLIND HORSE TRAINER

You've gotta go quiet, otherwise you'll freak them out even more.

DAVID SCHECHTER, WFAA-TV REPORTER

If horses could talk, they'd surely say nice things about Tabitha Darling.

30-F.MP3
30-S.MP3

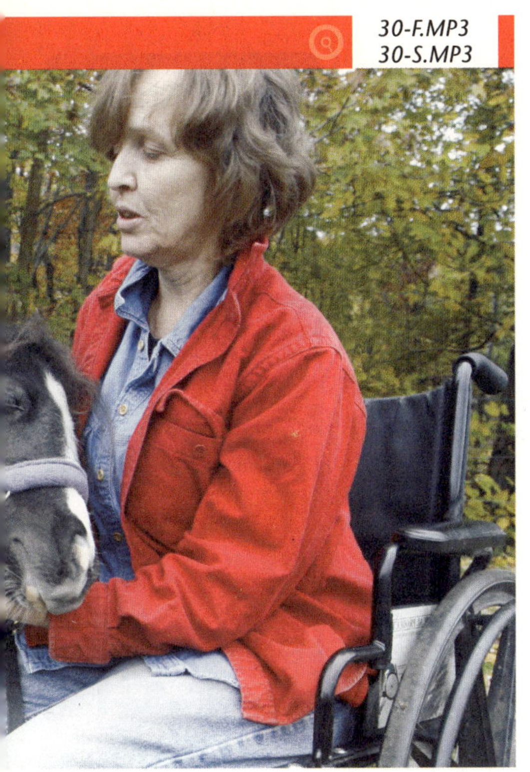

CNN 主播

只要提到服务性动物，一般人首先想到的可能就是狗儿。不过，如果是马儿呢？得克萨斯州有一位法定盲人妇女，就是利用马带路。戴维·谢赫特带来以下报道。

盲人驯马师　泰贝莎·达玲

你要保持安静，否则你会更把它们吓着了。

WFAA 电视台记者　大卫·谢赫特

马儿如果会说话，一定会说泰贝莎·达玲的好话。

Notes & Vocabulary

get around

应付；克服

get around 原本指"绕过某物行进"，比喻"避开困难或障碍"，如文中是"顺利应付；克服"的意思，另外也常表示"规避、躲避（法律、限制等）"。

- Daniel got around missing her deadline by outsourcing some of her work.
  丹妮尔把她的一些工作外发，总算没有拖过截止期限。
- The hacker got around the company's network security.
  那个黑客躲过了那家公司的网络安全防护。

1. struggle [`strʌgḷ] *v.* 挣扎；费劲
   Paul struggles every year to prepare his taxes on time.
2. define [dɪ`faɪn] *v.* 下定义；界定
   Being a doctor defines who Jeff is.
3. disabled [dɪs`ebḷd]
   adj. 残障的；有缺陷的
   The school is now more accessible to disabled students.

名流轶事　非常体验　生活咀嚼　天地之间

TABITHA DARLING, BLIND HORSE TRAINER

Good boy. Good Boy.

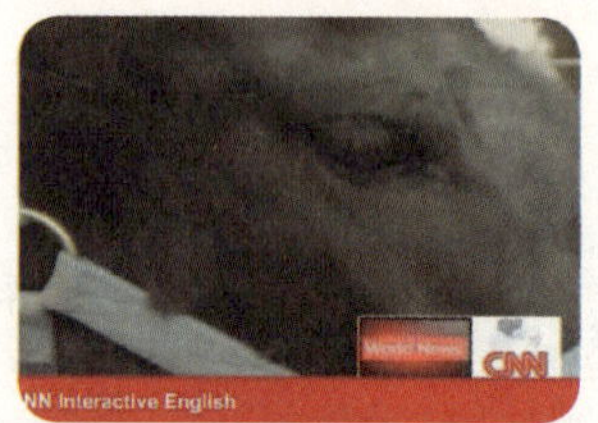

DAVID SCHECHTER, WFAA-TV REPORTER

She's training this one after years with an abusive[4] owner.

TABITHA DARLING, BLIND HORSE TRAINER

The whole idea is to get them not scared of it. It's kinda like raising a kid; you gotta teach 'em the very basics, and the . . . on their level.

DAVID SCHECHTER, WFAA-TV REPORTER

Once, she even trained a horse to work with the disabled.

TABITHA DARLING, BLIND HORSE TRAINER

I do think that there should be an allowance[5] for comfort and therapy[6] animals, simply because—who are we to judge when somebody needs something?

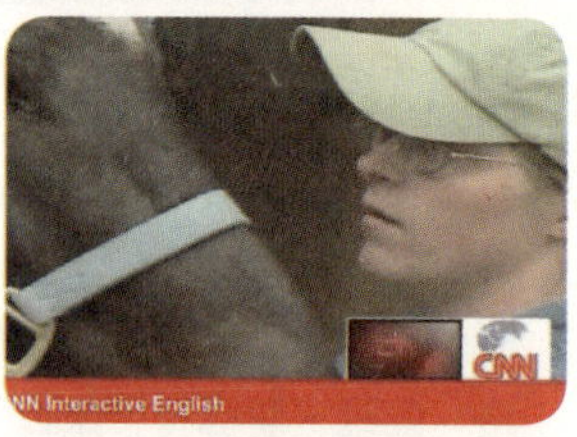

DAVID SCHECHTER, WFAA-TV REPORTER

Carolyn Finefrock relies heavily on her dog, Ellie. Carolyn is concerned that an expanding list of service animals—from snakes to ferrets[7]—are used by people who may not really need them.

CAROLYN FINEFROCK, GUIDE DOG OWNER

Are they disabled enough to have the right? Are they disabled at all? Are they faking?

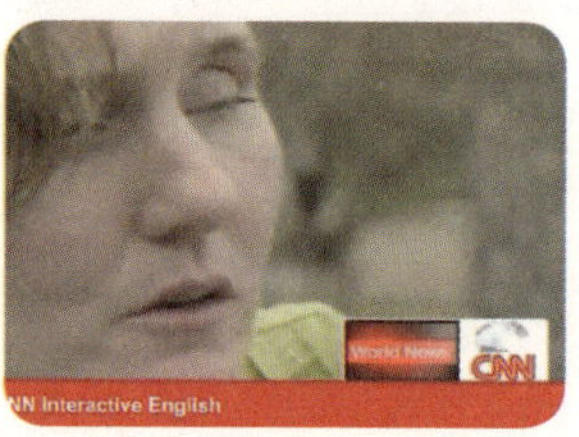

盲人驯马师　泰贝莎 • 达玲
乖孩子，乖孩子。

WFAA 电视台记者　大卫 • 谢赫特
她现在训练的这匹马，曾经遭主人虐待多年。

盲人驯马师　泰贝莎 • 达玲
重点就是让它们不要害怕。这有点像养小孩一样，你一定要教它们最基本的东西，而且……要合乎它们能够吸收的程度。

WFAA 电视台记者　大卫 • 谢赫特
她以前还训练过一匹马帮助残障人士。

盲人驯马师　泰贝莎 • 达玲
我认为应该允许抚慰性及治疗性动物的存在，原因很简单——我们凭什么判定别人需要什么东西呢？

WFAA 电视台记者　大卫 • 谢赫特
卡罗琳 • 范弗拉克非常依赖她的狗儿艾莉。卡罗琳担心，一旦把服务性动物的种类范围扩大——包括蛇类乃至雪貂——可能会被不是真正有需要的人士利用。

导盲犬饲主　卡罗琳 • 范弗拉克
那些人的残障程度达到了拥有服务性动物的资格了吗？他们真的残疾了吗？还是只是假装而已？

Notes & Vocabulary

4. abusive [əˋbjusɪv]
   adj. 虐待的；恶待的
   Brandi was in an abusive relationship before she met Thomas.

5. allowance [əˋlauəns]
   n. 容许；认可

6. therapy [ˋθɛrəpɪ]
   n. 治疗

7. ferret [ˋfɛrət] *n.* 雪貂；白鼬

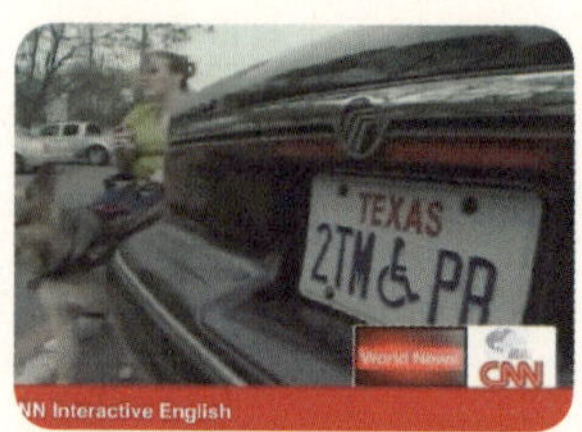

DAVID SCHECHTER, WFAA-TV REPORTER

But Tabitha is not just a horse trainer; she is also legally blind. Though her vision is better than Carolyn's, Tabitha relies on the service and friendship of her pony. Trixie's leading Tabitha six miles to downtown Fort Worth. The horse has the route[8] memorized, . . .

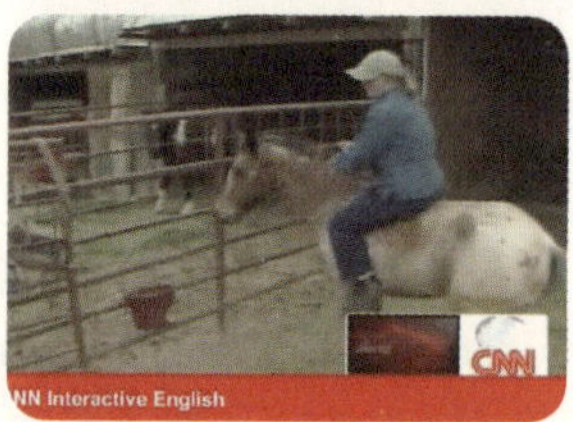

TABITHA DARLING, BLIND HORSE TRAINER

We've been together for about eight years now.

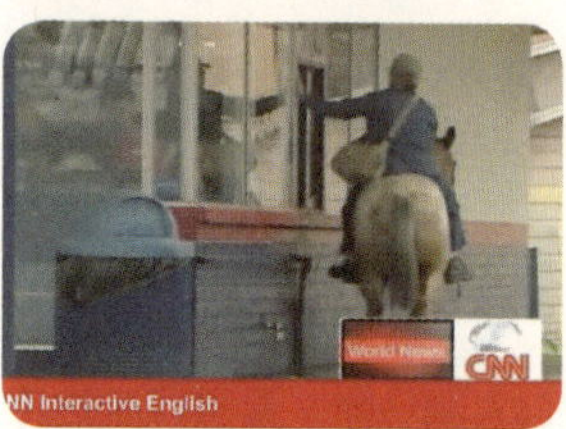

DAVID SCHECHTER, WFAA-TV REPORTER

. . . including the drive-through.[9]

TABITHA DARLING, BLIND HORSE TRAINER

I'm hungry. [She] gives me the independence in getting out there that I need, too. Because of that, my life is happier.

CAROLYN FINEFROCK, GUIDE DOG OWNER

But the problem is where does the line get drawn.

DAVID SCHECHTER, WFAA-TV REPORTER

The use of service animals in public is protected under the law. But as the variety[10] of service animals has expanded, the federal government is considering limiting use to dogs only, as originally intended.

Charlotte Steward is an advocate[11] for the rights of the disabled. She is opposed to[12] any changes.

WFAA 电视台记者　大卫・谢赫特
不过，泰贝莎不只是驯马师，还是法定盲人。她的视力虽然比卡罗琳好，但仍然必须依赖她的小马的协助和友谊。特里克茜引导着泰贝莎前往 6 英里外的沃斯堡市中心。这匹马已经记住了路线……

盲人驯马师　泰贝莎・达玲
我们已经相处了差不多 8 年。

WFAA 电视台记者　大卫・谢赫特
……包括得来速。

盲人驯马师　泰贝莎・达玲
我饿了。她让我能够独立前往我需要去的地方。我的生活因此而快乐得多了。

导盲犬饲主　卡罗琳・范弗拉克
问题是界线该划在哪里。

WFAA 电视台记者　大卫・谢赫特
在公共场所使用服务性动物是受到法律保护的。不过，服务性动物的种类已然扩增，联邦政府正考虑按照原本的规划，把范围限缩至以狗儿为限。

夏洛特・史都华德是残障人权拥护者。她反对改变现状。

Notes & Vocabulary

draw the/a line 区分；设限
字面意思是“画线”，比喻“区分混淆的事物”时后面的介词用 between。另外也可表示“对某事物设限”，介词用 at。

- The charity draws a line between giving people the tools to improve their lives and just giving out money.
  那个慈善机构给人们工具改善生活，和只送给他们钱不同。
- Bobby enjoys thrilling experiences, but he draws the line at skydiving and bungee jumping.
  巴比喜爱体验刺激，但是仅止于跳伞和高空弹跳。

8. route [rut/raʊt] *n.* 路线
9. drive-through [ˋdraɪv͵θru] *n.* 得来速；免下车服务（窗口）
10. variety [vəˋraɪətɪ] *n.* 种类
11. advocate [ˋædvəkət] *n.* 提倡者；拥护者
12. be opposed to 反对
    The organization is opposed to testing products on animals.

名流轶事　非常体验　生活咀嚼　天地之间

CHARLOTTE STEWARD, DISABLED RIGHTS ADVOCATE

If you need that in order to feel comfortable or secure,[13] why shouldn't you be able to? Again, it's just like using a walker or a cane, in my opinion.

DAVID SCHECHTER, WFAA-TV REPORTER

It's one thing to debate what should and should not be a service animal while it's working outside. But what happens when a disabled person brings an animal inside, and it's not a dog?

Under the law, stores must welcome all service animals or possibly face a discrimination[14] lawsuit.[15] The government says limiting use to only dogs means more predictability[16] for stores and continued acceptance for those who need animals the most, like Carolyn Finefrock.

CAROLYN FINEFROCK, GUIDE DOG OWNER

It would be better than letting people abuse it and put it at risk for everyone else who's got real, legitimate[17] disabilities.

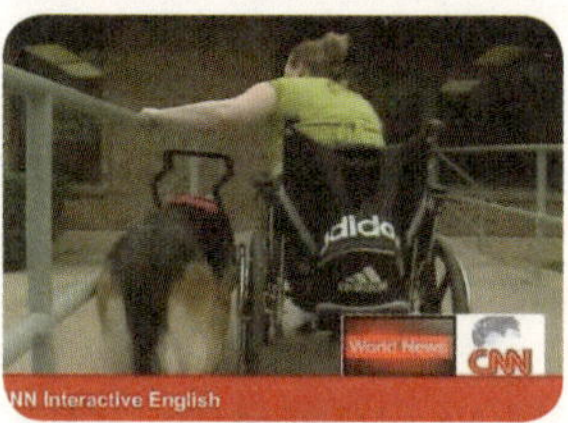

DAVID SCHECHTER, WFAA-TV REPORTER

The trouble is, is there anyone who can say the way Trixie opens up Tabitha's world is not legitimate?

TABITHA DARLING, BLIND HORSE TRAINER

She's kind of, pretty much, my life.

残障人权拥护者　夏洛特 • 史都华德
你如果需要这样的动物才能获得舒适或者安全感，为什么不可以呢？在我看来，这就像使用助行器或拐杖一样。

WFAA 电视台记者　大卫 • 谢赫特
争论哪些动物才能担任外出的服务工作是一回事，但残障人士如果把不是狗儿的动物带进室内呢？

按照法律规定，商家必须接纳服务性动物，否则就可能吃上歧视罪名的官司。政府表示，把服务性动物的种类限缩至只有狗儿，表示商家较能预测可能碰到的状况，而最需要动物协助的人也能持续被接受，例如卡罗琳 • 范弗拉克。

导盲犬饲主　卡罗琳 • 范弗拉克
有限制总好过任人滥用权利，导致有真正合理残疾的人士权益受损。

WFAA 电视台记者　大卫 • 谢赫特
问题是，有谁能说特里克茜为泰贝莎拓展人生的方式是不合理的？

盲人驯马师　泰贝莎 • 达玲
她可以说是我的生命。

Notes & Vocabulary

13. **secure** [sɪˋkjʊr]
adj. 安心的；无忧虑的
Trisha felt secure living in a gated community.

14. **discrimination** [dɪsˏkrɪməˋneʃən]
n. 歧视；不公平对待

15. **lawsuit** [ˋlɔˏsut]
n. 诉讼（尤指非刑事案件）

16. **predictability** [prɪˏdɪktəˋbɪlətɪ]
n. 可预测性

17. **legitimate** [lɪˋdʒɪtəmət]
adj. 合法的；正当的
Few of the calls the help desk received were for legitimate problems.

名流轶事　非常体验　生活咀嚼　天地之间

Service Animals 服务性动物

图片提供：superkas83

定义

指受过训练来协助（assist）做各种工作的动物，主要用于医疗协助（medical assistance）、执法（law enforcement）和搜救（search-and-rescue）。

医疗协助动物的类型

1. 导盲动物（guide animal）——引导视障者
2. 助听动物（hearing animal）——指示听障者
3. 服务动物（service animal）——其他协助

图片提供：DanDee Shots、Frans de Waal、Karin Langner-Bahmann

常用动物

根据美国残障者法案（Americans with Disabilities Act, ADA），医疗协助动物包括导盲犬（guide dog）、导听犬（signal dog）及其他"为了残障人士之福利（benefit）训练来做各种任务的动物"。除了狗之外，常见的还有：

- 猫——提示（signal）声音、预测疾病发作
- 卷尾猴（capuchin monkey）——拿东西、转门把、翻书等
- 迷你马（miniature horse）——导盲、拉轮椅、协助帕金森病患者